Bulletin of the German Historical Institute

Supplement 11 (2015)

Staging a Dream: Untold Stories and Transatlantic Legacies of the March on Washington

Introduction and Prologue

INTRODUCTION
UNTOLD STORIES: THE MARCH ON WASHINGTON – NEW PERSPECTIVES AND TRANSATLANTIC LEGACIES

Marcia Chatelain and Britta Waldschmidt-Nelson

If you were to peruse a volume on the most famous, easily recognized, or frequently cited speeches of the twentieth century, you would likely find Dr. Martin Luther King Jr.'s 1963 March on Washington for Jobs and Freedom address, commonly known as the "I Have a Dream" speech. In less than twenty minutes, King framed the root causes and consequences of the nation's racial and economic injustice in the "five score years" between the Emancipation Proclamation and August 28, 1963. Although King's speech included a pointed critique of police brutality, race-based economic malfeasance, and the limits of black social mobility, most references to King's speech focus on the latter section in which the evocative preacher shared the vision of his dream and exclaimed, "let freedom ring."[1] Repeated references to only the most optimistic parts of King's speech, delivered before hundreds of thousands of marchers and television viewers, have skewed perceptions of what happened that day and led to a distancing between King's rhetoric of dreams and freedom and the historical realities of that day, King's leadership, and the freedom struggle. Among the myriad annual remembrances and recitations of King's vision of a world where the content of one's character would supplant the importance of the color of one's skin, there are critical absences. Often, the celebration of these very specific elements of King's speech obscures the richness and intricacies of the event that brought King to Washington, DC — the actual March on Washington.

Instead of rehearsing popular notions about King's dreams, this volume seeks to ask questions that are often forgotten in one-dimensional approaches to celebrating the march. The essays that follow use the sharp tools of historical analysis to ask better questions about why King's speech happened as it did, and why it had such a tremendous impact at that particular moment. This process generates highly useful and intriguing inquiries: How did organizers pay for all the elements of the march, from its placards and sound equipment to the travel expenses of guests from across the country? Despite a program with 18 distinct segments with their own speakers or performers, why do we commemorate so few of the others who approached the podium facing the Lincoln Memorial that day? By focusing on the others who addressed the crowd, what can we

1 Martin Luther King Jr., "Address at the March for Jobs and Freedom, August 28, 1963," in *I Have a Dream: Writings and Speeches That Changed the World*, ed. James M. Washington, 102-106 (Glenview, 2003).

understand about the position of the civil rights movement in 1963? Considering the integral role music played in movement organizing, what kind of music did the marchers listen to as they stood shoulder-to-shoulder on the National Mall? What do we make of the near absence of women among the speakers and featured guests? Which African Americans supported the march, which disapproved, and why? How was news of the march reported elsewhere in the world, and how did U.S. allies and enemies understand what was happening? *Untold Stories* attempts to answer these questions and to add a transnational perspective by bringing together an array of fresh scholarly reflections on the March on Washington. By delving more deeply into the events of that seemingly understood and widely known occasion, this volume's contributors — scholars from the U.S., the United Kingdom, and Germany — assess the traditional narratives about the march while adding new and exciting stories, expanding upon the existing literature on the civil rights movement.

As the traditional markers of the civil rights movement — organized marches, grassroots activism, and legislative battles — slowly wound down in the late 1970s and 1980s, scholars crafted a narrative of movement building, which in many cases focused rather narrowly on great men and great organizations, while paying limited attention to the role of female leadership. One of the most significant contributions of this first generation of scholarly and cinematic work came in the form of a documentary series: Henry Hampton's highly regarded public television series *Eyes on the Prize: America's Civil Rights Struggle*. Its companion guide of edited documents from the movement provided some of the best oral histories as well as footage of the movement from those who were at the forefront, including Jo Ann Gibson Robinson, Myrlie Evers, and Bob Moses.[2] Taylor Branch's multivolume series on King and the civil rights movement introduced a popular audience to the many figures and turning points of "America in the King Years."[3] Organizational histories such as Clayborne Carson's *In Struggle: SNCC and the Black Awakening of the 1960s* provided context for understanding the vital and exhaustive work of organizing on many fronts in order to achieve gains in civil rights while absorbing the fallout from conflict and shifts in institutional dynamics and membership.[4] And, of course, there is an ever increasing number of King biographies as well as studies of his leadership style, his religious and philosophical development, his rhetoric, his death, and other topics.[5]

Gradually, scholars of the movement — shaped by the rise of women's and gender history, critical race theory, and the challenge of

2 The citations that follow are by no means a thorough accounting of the scholarship on the civil rights movement. Rather, they highlight the evolution of the ways the scholarship has shifted over the past thirty years. Henry Hampton, "Eyes on the Prize," Blackside Inc. (1987, 1990); and Juan Williams, ed., *Eyes on the Prize: America's Civil Rights Years, 1954-1965*, 2nd ed. (New York, 2013).

3 See Taylor Branch, *Parting the Waters: America in the King Years, 1954-1963* (New York, 1988); idem, *Pillar of Fire: America in the King Years, 1963-1965* (New York, 1998); and idem, *At Canaan's Edge: America in the King Years, 1965-1968* (New York, 2006). See also David J. Garrow, ed., *We Shall Overcome: The Civil Rights Movement in the United States in the 1950s and 1960s*, 3 vols. (New York, 1989).

4 Clayborne Carson, *In Struggle: SNCC and the Black Awakening of the 1960s* (Cambridge, MA, 1981).

5 See, e.g., David J. Garrow, *Bearing the Cross: Martin Luther King, Jr., and the Southern Christian Leadership Conference* (New York, 1986 and 1999); Peter Ling, *Martin Luther King, Jr.* (New York, 2004); Harvard Sitkoff, *King: Pilgrimage to the Mountaintop* (New York, 2008); and Shermann E. Pyatt, *Martin Luther King, Jr.: An Annotated Bibliography* (New York, Westport, London, 1986).

gearing scholarship to examine historical intersections — began to ask new questions about civil rights. Moving away from a singular focus on male leaders and powerful groups, John Dittmer, Jo Ann Robinson, Vicki Crawford, Angela Davis, Barbara Ransby, Kay Mills, and other scholars considered the roles of class, region, and gender to broaden the received notions of 1960s leadership and strategy.[6] Further, heeding Jacquelyn Dowd Hall's call to rethink periodization in the history of civil rights, scholars such as Danielle McGuire created a new timeline for the movement, viewing its origins in black women's activism against sexual assault.[7] Moreover, an increasing number of studies focusing on the relationship among international human rights, anticolonialism, the Cold War, and African American civil rights advocacy, also revise the timeline, extending it significantly further back than the classic "1954-1968" period.[8] Recently, cultural historians have also focused scholarly attention on the art, literature, photography, fashion, and music of the movement, deepening our appreciation of the many avenues for expression during this tumultuous yet creative era.[9]

As U.S.-based scholars have shaped and shifted the conversations about the civil rights movement, their colleagues across the Atlantic have also embarked on dynamic approaches to this voluminous history.[10] British and German historians have used the U.S. civil rights

6 John Dittmer, *Local People: The Struggle for Civil Rights in Mississippi* (Urbana, 1995); Jo Ann Robinson, *The Montgomery Bus Boycott and the Women Who Started It* (Knoxville, 1987); Vicki Crawford et al., eds., *Women in the Civil Rights Movement Trailblazers and Torchbearers, 1941-1965* (New York, 1990); Angela Y. Davis, *Women, Race, and Class* (New York, 1981); Barbara Ransby, *Ella Baker and the Black Freedom Movement: A Radical Democratic Vision* (Chapel Hill, 2003); and Kay Mills, *This Little Light of Mine: The Life of Fannie Lou Hamer* (New York, 1993).

7 Jacquelyn Dowd Hall, "The Long Civil Rights Movement and the Political Use of the Past," *Journal of American History* 91,

no. 4 (March 2005): 1233-63; Danielle L. McGuire, *At the Dark End of the Street: Black Women, Rape and Resistance — a New History of the Civil Rights Movement from Rosa Parks to the Rise of Black Power* (New York, 2011).

8 See, e.g., Carol Anderson, *Eyes off the Prize: The United Nations and the African American Struggle for Human Rights, 1944-1955* (Cambridge, UK, 2003); and idem, *Bourgeois Radicals: The NAACP and the Struggle for Colonial Liberation, 1941-1960* (Cambridge, UK, 2014); as well as Thomas Borstelmann, *The Cold War and the Color Line: American Race Relations in the Global Arena* (Cambridge, MA, 2001).

9 See, e.g., Brian Ward, *Just My Soul Responding: Rhythm and Blues, Black*

Consciousness, and Race Relations (Berkeley, 1998); Leigh Raiford, *Imprisoned in a Luminous Glare: Photography and the African American Freedom Struggle* (Chapel Hill, 2013); Tanisha C. Ford, "SNCC Women, Denim, and the Politics of Dress," *Journal of Southern History* 79, no. 3 (2013): 625-58; Ruth Feldstein, *How It Feels to Be Free: Black Women Entertainers and the Civil Rights Movement* (Oxford, 2013); Shana L. Redmond, *Anthem: Social Movements and the Sound of Solidarity in the African Diaspora* (New York, 2013); Sharon Monteith, *SNCC's Stories: Narrative Culture and the Southern Freedom Struggle of the 1960s* (Athens, 2015); and Emily Raymond, *Stars for Freedom: Hollywood, Black Celebrities, and the Civil Rights Movement* (Seattle, 2015).

10 The earliest examples of such scholarship include Immanuel Geiss, *Die Afro-Amerikaner* (Frankfurt, 1969); and Heinrich Grosse, *Die Macht der Armen: Martin Luther King und der Kampf für soziale Gerechtigkeit* (Hamburg, 1971). Some other examples of groundbreaking British and German studies of the civil rights movement are Richard H. King, *Civil Rights and the Idea of Freedom* (Oxford, 1992); Brian Ward, *Media, Culture, and the Modern African American Freedom Struggle* (Gainesville, 2003); Sharon Monteith and Peter Ling, *Gender in the Civil Rights Movement* (New Brunswick, 2004); Manfred Berg, *The Ticket to Freedom: The NAACP and the Struggle for Black Political Integration* (Gainesville, 2005); and Iwan Morgan and Philip Davies, eds., *From Sit-Ins to SNCC: The Student Civil Rights Movement in the 1960s* (Gainesville, 2012). See also Britta Waldschmidt-Nelson, *From Protest to Politics: Schwarze Frauen in der Bürgerrechtsbewegung und im Kongreß der Vereinigten Staaten* (Frankfurt, New York, 1998); idem, *Dreams and Nightmares: Martin Luther King Jr., Malcolm X and the Struggle for Black Equality in America* (Gainesville, 2012); and Simon Wend, *The Spirit and the Shotgun: Armed Resistance and the Struggle for Civil Rights* (Gainesville, 2006). Of course, much excellent scholarship exists on the civil rights movement in other European countries, but it is beyond the scope of this volume to include it here.

movement as a sounding board for comparing and contrasting racial and ethnic tensions among European populations of color. Post-1945 Europe witnessed significant growth in the population of blacks due to romantic relationships and marriages between African American soldiers and European women against a complex backdrop of rising immigration from former colonies. The visibility and activism of these communities naturally led to comparisons to the black civil rights movement in the U.S. Additionally, the movement's idealism and commitment to democracy also prompted young Europeans to consider the future of their respective nation's commitment to these principles, as well as the role Europe should play in securing global peace in the decades of post-World War II reconstruction.[11]

African American artists, scholars, and soldiers fueled the notion that France, Britain, and postwar Germany were racial havens for blacks seeking refuge from Jim Crow, and historians sometimes uncritically reproduced these characterizations. But European scholars have also provided a sound corrective to this truncated perception by highlighting the way icons of the U.S. civil rights movement helped European communities of color coalesce around issues of race and class discrimination. Relatedly, transatlantic communication about what civil rights means in each national context helps scholars appreciate the specificity of place, as well as the intricacies of confluences and collaborations. In his new study on Malcolm X's visit to Britain in 1964, volume contributor Stephen Tuck captures British understandings of the Black Power movement in the last moments of Malcolm X's life and examines how American racial politics informed a burgeoning racial consciousness among British people of color.[12] Transatlantic connections are also important to Maria Höhn and Martin Klimke's examination of black soldiers in occupied Germany after the fall of Nazism because they credit exchanges between these soldiers and West Germans with broadening awareness of U.S. civil rights and fortifying the hopes of those dedicated to establishing a truly democratic Germany.[13]

With a strong foundation of scholarship on both sides of the Atlantic, a conference at the German Historical Institute in Washington, DC, held in September 2013, served as the inspiration of this volume. Initiated by three movement scholars — from Germany (Britta Waldschmidt-Nelson), the United Kingdom (Sharon Monteith), and the United States (Marcia Chatelain) — this meeting of historians and civil rights activists from the United States and Europe convened to commemorate the

11 See, e.g., Norbert Finzsch and Dietmar Schirmer, *Identity and Intolerance: Nationalism, Racism, and Xenophobia in Germany and the United States* (Cambridge, New York, 1998); Günter H. Lenz and Peter J. Ling, eds., *Multiculturalism, National Identity, and the Uses of the Past* (Amsterdam, 2000); and Robin D. G. Kelley and Stephen Tuck, eds., *The Other Special Relationship: Race, Rights, and Riots in Britain and the United States* (New York, 2015).

12 Stephen Tuck, *The Night Malcolm X Spoke at the Oxford Union: The Transatlantic Story of Antiracist Protest* (Berkeley, 2014).

13 Maria Höhn and Martin Klimke, *A Breath of Freedom: The Civil Rights Struggle, African American GIs, and Germany* (New York, 2010). Photography scholar Tina Campt takes up the issue of Afro-European identity in *Image Matters: Archive, Photography, and the African Diaspora in Europe* (Durham, 2012). See also Britta Waldschmidt-Nelson, "We Shall Overcome": The Impact of the American Occupation and the Black Civil Rights Movement on Race Relations and Social Protest in Germany," in *The Transatlantic Sixties: Europe and the United States in the Counterculture Decade*, ed. Clara Juncker, Gregorz Kosc, Sharon Monteith, and Britta Waldschmidt-Nelson, 66-97 (Bielefeld, 2013).

Introduction and
Prologue / Music and
the March / Transatlantic
Legacies / Different Views
and Voices / Visual Histories and
Cultural Memories

fiftieth anniversary of the march. Determined to tell the march's untold stories and to assess the immediate as well as long-term legacy of this seminal event, the new research contained in this *GHI Bulletin* aims to capture the multiplicity of perspectives and conditions that made and sustained that moment in 1963 on both sides of the Atlantic.

This volume begins with a prologue by movement alumnus, scholar, and editor of Martin Luther King Jr.'s papers, Clayborne Carson, who challenges the reader to reconsider the periodization of King's life as a political and intellectual radical. Resisting the narrative of King's slow crawl toward an anti-capitalist position, Carson argues in favor of a long view of King's appreciation of socialism, his embrace of economic and structural analyses of racism, and the high stakes involved in keeping King's ideological commitments quiet. He presents King as a scholar, activist, and pragmatist who may have only been able to fully share his views with his spouse, Coretta Scott King, and encourages scholars — junior and senior — to use not only King's public proclamations but also his private papers, especially his letters to Coretta, to develop a more complete picture of the famous leader.

Despite the contemporary focus on the "I Have a Dream" speech, the actual March on Washington program was filled with presentations that warrant serious, scholarly attention. The first section, "Music and the March," thus highlights one type of presentation — the musical performances — to consider the relationship between the movement and popular music. In his piece, Brian Ward analyzes how the interracial lineup of musical acts — from Peter, Paul, and Mary to Joan Baez and the SNCC Freedom Singers — reflected the way that folk music and reworded Negro spirituals became freedom music. While protest songs helped to organize and inspire those involved in the mass movement, popular musical acts were slow to enter the public fray of civil rights. Ward seeks to answer why, despite the clear interest of rhythm-and-blues artists in the civil rights movement, so few of them were publicly visible in its activities, including the March on Washington. Using oral histories and biographies, Ward looks at how black popular musicians in jazz and rhythm and blues negotiated their politics and their popularity. Ward's essay reminds us of the importance of the sounds of freedom present at the march and throughout the African American freedom struggle.

The second section, "Transatlantic Legacies," then moves away from the march itself to reflect on the ways that the march, the civil rights movement more generally, and Martin Luther King Jr. were perceived in Germany and England. Given King's position as an ordained Baptist minister, it may come as a surprise that so few people in former West Germany thought of King as a theologian. In his contribution, Michael Haspel considers why this was so and contrasts this West German view, which remains dominant even today, with the East German context in which King's spiritual significance was widely recognized. By examining the impact of King's life and legacy on Germany before unification in 1990, Haspel traces the origins and demonstrates the limits of the West German view of King as primarily a social activist. By exploring King's theological texts, homiletics, and "his understanding of the *imago Dei*," he makes a compelling case for understanding King as a leader of both social and spiritual significance.

Activist and religious leader Heinrich Grosse, who traveled to Mississippi in the 1960s, writes a tribute to King's impact on German social movements after the 1963 march and beyond his death five years later. Grosse emphasizes the transnational nature of the movement and contends that many Germans "remembered the disturbing pictures of the brutal attacks on peaceful demonstrators in Birmingham, Alabama, only a few months [before the march]," and that these memories profoundly shaped their reactions to this historical event. Grosse's essay is a beautiful meditation on King and an introduction to the German context for understanding U.S. civil rights, with a brief history of the social movements that challenged the divided nation. From protests against the *Notstandsgesetze* (German Emergency Acts) in 1968 and the anti-nuclear proliferation movement to the rise in environmental activism, the March on Washington was present at the inception and growth of all efforts to organize Germans to resist state power and abuse. Grosse also pays particular attention to the immediate and long-term effects of King's visit to both West and East Berlin in 1964 and illustrates the centrality of the movement and its legacy for the demonstrations in East Germany that eventually brought down the Berlin Wall and the communist regime in 1989.

This section concludes with British scholar Stephen Tuck's piece on the ways the March on Washington was interpreted and understood around the world, and particularly among communities of color in the United Kingdom. After noting that "there were demonstrations in support of the March on Washington outside the American embassies in Egypt, Jamaica, Paris, Ghana, Israel, and Norway," Tuck shifts his attention to London, where 750 people marched from the Ladbroke Grove subway station to the American embassy three days after the march. Although Tuck cautions against making false equivalencies between the U.S. and the U.K., calling the British movement "asymmetrical" to King's movement, his essay reveals how Jamaican immigrants sought their own remedies for racial exclusion. By examining the "James Crow, Esquire" system of racism in the U.K. in a transatlantic context, Tuck's research advances a movement history steeped in diasporic, transnational conceptions of the world.

The third section, "Different Views and Voices," sheds light on features of the march and people's responses to it that have heretofore been rather hidden from view. Stephen Whitfield highlights Rabbi Joachim Prinz, the barely remembered president of the American Jewish Congress who spoke at the march. Whitfield's examination of Prinz and his influence on the lives of American Jews emphasizes the interreligious and interfaith aspects of both the march and the larger movement. Having fled the growing persecution of Jews in Germany in the 1930s, Prinz found Southern racism in the United States as intolerable as Nazism — a racism of which Jews were also sometimes guilty. Writing of Prinz's reaction to a racial incident that involved a black friend in Atlanta in 1937, Whitfield explains how Prinz "told his hosts how appalled he was that Jews, who were 'the classic victims of racial persecution,' could be racist." Prinz also compared the fate of Southern blacks to the experiences of the Jewish people in Europe during the Nazi era. Whitfield elaborates on the comparison via a textual analysis of Harper Lee's 1960 novel *To Kill a Mockingbird*, which portrays racism in a Southern town during the Great Depression. As Whitfield shows, Prinz's presence of mind and his commitment to justice placed him in an important genealogy of progressive Jews who supported civil rights.

The other often hidden voices were those of conservative blacks who were highly critical of the March on Washington, which Angela Dillard studies in her contribution. While the historical footage and photographs of the more than 250,000 marchers on the National Mall indicates widespread support for the freedom struggle, it does not mean there was a univocal idea of freedom and civil rights. Dillard's treatment of James Meredith — the Air

Force veteran who integrated the University of Mississippi in 1962 — and Reverend J. H. Jackson — president of the National Baptist Convention and head of the prominent Olivet Baptist Church in Chicago — is a refreshing break from expected statements about conflicts between King and the supposedly more radical, black nationalist Malcolm X. Incorporating Meredith's and Jackson's conservative critiques of King, the march, as well as the goals of the mainstream civil rights organizations into her analysis, Dillard challenges scholars to engage more deeply with intra-racial dissent. She also cautions against letting present feelings about the march stand in for historical analysis and shows how divisive the March on Washington was among contemporary Americans in general as well as within American African communities. By exposing neglected but principled stances against the march, Dillard's essay provides a new lens through which to look at these political, social, and ideological fissures.

The final section, "Visual Histories and Cultural Memories," turns to media presentations relating to the march and to Martin Luther King Jr.'s assassination five years later, highlighting the media's role in generating the contemporary importance, as well as the cultural memories, of these events. Allison Graham elucidates the context of the march's media presentation within 1960s news programming, documentary filmmaking, and American celebrity culture, bringing connections together with an examination of the broadcast of a public affairs show entitled *Hollywood Roundtable* that aired immediately after the march. The roundtable featured writer James Baldwin, actors Harry Belafonte, Marlon Brando, Sidney Poitier, and Charlton Heston, and director-screenwriter Joseph Mankiewicz. As Graham's analysis shows, these men successfully turned "attention from the cause of the march to the fact of the march" by discussing the paradox of a democracy that allowed for such a public demonstration even as it needed such a call for equal rights.

Lastly, David Chappell's essay tackles common misconceptions about the aftermath of King's 1968 murder in Memphis, namely, the belief that the announcement of his assassination on April 4 led to widespread violence on America's city streets. Chappell illustrates that many textbooks and retrospective media accounts of King's assassination to this day recall a "national upheaval, a great orgy of violence and destruction" that is actually quite misleading. By looking at the facts of the days after King's death rather than fears about the effects people expected King's death to have, Chappell not only corrects the myth of a violent uprising but also alerts scholars to King's legacy beyond the "I Have a Dream" speech. He places special emphasis on the important political gains of the civil rights movement after King's death, including the passage of the Civil Rights Act of 1968 (which focused on King's goal of eliminating discrimination in housing), the renewal and extension of the 1965 Voting Rights Act in 1982, the adoption of the King Holiday in 1986, and King-inspired activism surrounding sanctions applied to apartheid South Africa. By drawing a direct line from 1963 and 1968 to the present, Chappell points to both dreams that have been realized and those yet to be fulfilled.

The editors of this volume would like to thank the German Historical Institute (Washington, DC), the University of Nottingham, and Georgetown University very much for their generous financial and organizational support of our collaborative effort. We are especially grateful to the GHI and its director, Hartmut Berghoff, for the opportunity to publish this work as a supplement to the *Bulletin of the GHI*. Moreover, we would like to thank all of our contributors for their willingness to share the fruits of their research with us, for providing such wonderful papers, and for remaining patient and committed to this publication throughout the revision stages. We would also like to thank Bryan Hart, who produced the cover for this volume, as well as other colleagues at the GHI who provided support during the production phases of this work. Above all, we are deeply obliged to Patricia Casey Sutcliffe for her thoughtful and meticulous copyediting, as well as for her diligence, her creative suggestions, and overall cheerfulness.

We know some of the names — Martin Luther King Jr., Ralph Abernathy, Rosa Parks, and Ella Baker — but these are not the only ones that represent the magnitude and importance of the struggle; we know some of the places — Montgomery, Oxford, Greensboro, Selma — but we still need to expand our ideas about the geographical boundaries of the movement; we know some of the legacies — the passage of civil rights legislation, the end of apartheid, and the election of President Barack Obama — yet we know that we are always building upon the past. Given the state of race relations in America today, it is clear that many of the movement goals have yet to be fulfilled. This volume is dedicated to all the individuals whose courage and selfless commitment to the struggle for justice still inspire us. Their visions of freedom were expressed in the many marches and movements whose stories we are still challenged to discover, research, teach, and tell.

About the Editors

Britta Waldschmidt-Nelson is Deputy Director of the German Historical Institute in Washington, DC, and Professor of American History at the University of Munich. Her main research interests are Transatlantic History, African American Studies, Gender, and American Religious History. Her recent publications include *Dreams and Nightmares: Martin Luther King, Jr., Malcolm X and the Struggle for Black Equality in America* (2012); *The Transatlantic Sixties: Europe and the United States in the Countercultural Decade* (2013); and *Malcolm X: Der schwarze Revolutionär* (2015).

Marcia Chatelain is Assistant Professor of History and African American Studies at Georgetown University in Washington, DC. Her book *South Side Girls: Growing Up in the Great Migration* was recently published by Duke University Press. She is currently researching a book about the relationship among civil rights, fast food, and black capitalism.

Sharon Monteith is Professor of American Studies at the University of Nottingham and Co-Director (with Zoe Trodd) of the Centre for Research in Race and Rights located there. She works across literature, history, film, media, and cultural studies, usually in interdisciplinary studies of the civil rights movement and the American South. She has written and (co-)edited several books, including *The Cambridge Companion to Southern Literature* (2013) and is currently completing *SNCC's Stories: Narrative Culture and the Southern Freedom Struggle of the 1960s* for the University of Georgia Press and *The Civil Rights Movement: A Literary History* for Cambridge University Press.

PROLOGUE
MARTIN'S DREAM: THE GLOBAL LEGACY OF
MARTIN LUTHER KING JR.

Clayborne Carson

During the months before the fiftieth anniversary of the 1963 March on Washington for Jobs and Freedom, I had numerous opportunities to speak about the meaning of the event. I enjoyed the sugar high of media attention, followed swiftly by the depressing realization that, as suddenly as our scholarly opinions become newsworthy, they become old news. But, for a brief moment, it was possible for some of us scholars at this conference to display the wisdom that inevitably comes from years of research on topics that most people do not think much about. It's not difficult to impress reporters, who are amazed to learn that the march was indeed "for Jobs *and* Freedom," that John Lewis of the Student Nonviolent Coordinating Committee (SNCC) was forced to change his prepared speech when some march leaders thought it too militant, that no female civil rights leader gave a speech that day, and that Martin Luther King Jr. delivered his concluding "I Have a Dream" refrain extemporaneously.

Historians, of course, know that a vast amount of ignorance about the past could be corrected simply by visiting an archive and discovering the amazing facts waiting to be found in largely neglected documents. But we also know that these facts might as well be secrets because only a small minority of people ever visit an archive. Those of us who are academic historians also know that many amazing but little-known historical facts are secreted away in scholarly articles or in books published by struggling university presses.

For several decades now, my colleagues and I at Stanford's Martin Luther King, Jr., Research and Education Institute have been stashing "secrets" inside the published volumes of *The Papers of Martin Luther King, Jr.* and in articles based on King's papers. After participating in and observing the commemorations, I can report that, despite the considerable publicity about King and his dream, many of our secrets-in-plain-view remain so. This is certainly not because of a lack of accessible information about King, the most highly publicized and extensively studied African American of the twentieth century. Instead, I think it is because of a widespread tendency, especially in the United States, to view King narrowly as a black civil rights leader, a description that is accurate but hardly sufficient, because he was also a visionary leader with a unique awareness of the historical and global context of the modern African American freedom struggle. Just as it would be misleading to view Mohandas Gandhi simply as a leader of the Indian independence movement, we fail to recognize the essential identities of King and Gandhi when we ignore the abundant evidence that the two leaders played global as well as national leadership roles.

Another little-known, hidden-in-plain-sight fact to be found in King's papers is that he saw himself mainly as a social gospel minister rather than as a civil rights leader. Moreover, although he has often been described as having become increasingly radical during his final years, his writings from the period prior to the Montgomery bus boycott in 1955-1956 indicate that the Poor People's Campaign of 1968 marked a return to the social gospel convictions of his early ministry. In one of his earliest seminary papers, written in 1948 when he was nineteen — seven years before the start of the Montgomery boycott — he confidently defined his pastoral mission in a way that foreshadowed the 1968 Poor People's Campaign: "I must be concerned about unemployment, slumms [sic], and economic insecurity. I am a profound advocator of the social gospel."[1] King's "Autobiography of Religious Development," the fourteen-page, handwritten paper that he prepared the following year, noted his "anti-capitalist feelings," spurred by the sight of "numerous people standing in bread lines."[2] In one of the love letters he wrote during the summer of 1952 while courting former Progressive Party supporter Coretta Scott, he announced, "I imagine you already know that I am much more socialistic in my economic theory than capitalistic." He went on to say, "I would certainly welcome the day to come when there will be a nationalization of industry. Let us continue to hope, work, and pray that in the future we will live to see a warless world, a better distribution of wealth, and a brotherhood that transcends race or color."[3]

King was not quite as candid in his sermons as he was in his letters to Scott, but the sermons he delivered while assisting his father at the Ebenezer Baptist Church during the summer of 1953 (soon after his marriage in June) addressed racial segregation and discrimination in the context of the global struggle for peace with social justice. Several of these sermons criticized the "false Gods" of science, nationalism, and materialism. Sharply denouncing American chauvinism and anticommunism, King advised, "One cannot worship this false god of

1   "Preaching Ministry," ca. 1948, in *The Papers of Martin Luther King, Jr.*, Vol. 6: *Advocate of the Social Gospel, September 1948-March 1963*, 72.

2   *"An Autobiography of Religious Development,"* ca. 1950, in *The Papers of Martin Luther King, Jr.*, Vol. 1: *Called to Serve, January 1959-June 1951*, 359.

3   King to Coretta Scott, 18 July 1952, *Papers*, 6:123, 125, 126.

nationalism and the God of Christianity at the same time."[4] In another sermon he prepared that summer, he insisted that international peace was the "cry that is ringing in the ears of the peoples of the world," but that such peace could be achieved only when Christians "place righteousness first. So long as we place our selfish economic gains first we will never have peace … Indeed the deep rumbling of discontent in our world today on the part of the masses is [actually] a revolt against imperialism, economic exploitation, and colonialism that has been perpetuated by western civilization for all these many years."[5]

King's expansive Christian worldview was perhaps most evident in his sermon "Communism's Challenge to Christianity," in which he rejected communism as secularistic and materialistic but nonetheless insisted that it was "Christianity's most formidable competitor and only serious rival." Marxist ideas, he argued, should challenge Christians to express their own "passionate concern for social justice. The Christian ought always to begin with a bias in favor of a movement which protests against the unfair treatment of the poor, for surely Christianity is itself such a protest."[6]

In 1954, when he accepted the pastorate of Montgomery's Dexter Avenue Baptist Church, King did not mention civil rights reform but did assert that he came to Dexter "at a most crucial hour of our world's history; at a time when the flame of war might arise at any time to redden the skies of a dark and dreary world; at a time when men know all too well that without the proper guidance the whole of civilization can be plunged across the abyss of destruction."[7] Less than a year after King delivered his sermon on communism, he began pushing gently yet consistently against the complacency of a mostly middle-class congregation at Dexter that had resisted the activism of his predecessor, the Reverend Vernon Johns. He used his acceptance address as an occasion to assert his spiritual authority and to suggest the immensity of the task ahead. He cited the same social gospel credo (Luke 4:18–19) that his father had used in 1940 to describe the "true mission of the church": "The spirit of the Lord is upon me, because he hath anointed me to preach the Gospel to the poor; he hath sent me to heal the broken-hearted, to preach deliverance to the captives, and the recovering of sight to the blind, to set at liberty them that are bruised."[8]

In December 1955, Rosa Parks transformed the twenty-six-year-old social gospel advocate into a civil rights leader. King did not initiate

4 "The False God of Nationalism," 12 July 1953, *Papers*, 6:133.

5 "First Things First," 2 August 1953, in *Papers*, 6:144, 145.

6 "Communism's Challenge to Christianity," 9 August 1953, in *Papers*, 6:147.

7 King to Dexter Avenue Baptist Church, 14 April 1954, in *Papers*, 2:260.

8 "Acceptance Address at Dexter Avenue Baptist Church," 2 May 1954, in *Papers*, 6:166.

the Montgomery bus boycott movement, but, when he was unexpectedly asked in December 1955 to serve as head of the Montgomery Improvement Association (MIA), he quickly transformed a movement for better treatment on segregated buses into a struggle for transcendent goals rooted in prophetic religious ideals and American democratic traditions. In his first speech to a mass meeting, he used a phrase that would later reappear in his "I Have a Dream" speech: "We are determined here in Montgomery to work and fight until justice runs down like water and righteousness like a mighty stream." He audaciously assured black residents, "when the history books are written in the future, somebody will have to say, 'There lived a race of people, a black people ... who had the moral courage to stand up for their rights and thereby they injected a new meaning into the veins of history and of civilization.'"[9]

As the 381-day boycott approached its successful conclusion, King characteristically recognized the global significance of what had been accomplished in Montgomery. "Little did we know that we were starting a movement that would rise to international proportions," he said as the MIA hosted a gathering of southern activists in December 1956. The Montgomery movement, King proclaimed, "would ring in the ears of people of every nation ... would stagger and astound the imagination of the oppressor, while leaving a glittering star of hope etched in the midnight skies of the oppressed."[10] Within a few months of the end of the Montgomery boycott, King would take part in the independence ceremony marking the birth of the new nation of Ghana, where he was exhilarated by crowds shouting "Freedom!" He recalled, "I could hear that old Negro spiritual once more crying out: 'Free at last, free at last, Great God Almighty, I'm free at last.'"[11] Two years later, he would undertake his "pilgrimage ... to the Land of Gandhi," where he called upon India to "take the lead and call for universal disarmament."[12] Thus, King's global perspective was evident long before he became a Nobel Peace Prize laureate or a vocal critic of American military intervention in Vietnam.

Because King's decade-long detour from social gospel preaching to civil rights leadership has largely defined his historical significance for many Americans, his great oration at the March on Washington is typically seen as a seminal moment in the struggle for civil rights reform. Most of us who attended the march saw it, at least in part, as an effort to prod Congress to enact President Kennedy's pending civil rights proposals, but it is notable that King's speech made no

9 "MIA Mass Meeting at Holt Street Baptist Church," 5 December 1955, in *The Papers of Martin Luther King, Jr.*, Vol. 3: *Birth of a New Age, December 1955-December 1956*, 74.

10 "Facing the Challenge of a New Age." Address delivered at the First Institute on Nonviolence and Social Change, 3 December 1956, in *Papers*, 3:452.

11 Clayborne Carson, *The Autobiography of Martin Luther King, Jr.* (New York, 1998), 112-13.

12 *Autobiography*, 129.

Introduction and
Prologue

Music and
the March

Transatlantic
Legacies

Different Views
and Voices

Visual Histories and
Cultural Memories

mention of this legislation. Instead, King emphasized the American democratic and egalitarian ideals evoked in the Declaration of Independence. His reference to the "promissory note" signed by "the architects of our republic" drew inspiration from a long African American tradition of exposing the hypocrisy of white American leaders who had justified their revolution by affirming universal rights even while giving black Americans what King labeled "a bad check, a check which has come back marked 'insufficient funds.'"[13]

King's stunning oration at Mason Temple in Memphis on the eve of his assassination in April 1968 reaffirmed his self-identity as a leader expressing a global vision of liberation. After surveying previous great eras of history, he assured thousands of striking Memphis sanitation workers that he would choose to live during the time of their travail, even though, he acknowledged, the world was "messed up" and the nation was "sick": "Strangely enough, I would turn to the Almighty and say, 'If you allow me to live just a few years in the second half of the twentieth century, I will be happy.'"[14] Perhaps sensing that his life was near its end, he reaffirmed the prophetic global vision that had always guided his ministry:

> The masses of people are rising up. And wherever they are assembled today, whether they are in Johannesburg, South Africa; Nairobi, Kenya; Accra, Ghana; New York City; Atlanta, Georgia; Jackson, Mississippi; or Memphis, Tennessee, the cry is always the same: "We want to be free." And another reason that I'm happy to live in this period is that we have been forced to a point where we are going to have to grapple with the problems that men have been trying to grapple with through history. ... And also in the human rights revolution, if something isn't done and done in a hurry, to bring the colored peoples of the world out of their long years of poverty, their long years of hurt and neglect, the whole world is doomed. Now I'm just happy that God has allowed me to live in this period, to see what is unfolding.[15]

Many people see SNCC and King as quite different in many respects, but, after spending the first two decades of my adulthood in the thrall of SNCC and the next quarter century studying King, I have come to see them as moving along different routes toward similar conclusions. King, like SNCC's organizers, did not see the passage of civil rights legislation as the end of the struggle. King and most SNCC

13 Ibid.

14 Ibid., 359.

15 Ibid., 360.

workers did not retire from activism after the passage of the 1965 Voting Rights Act but instead increased the intensity and radicalism of their efforts. They insisted that it was necessary to look beyond the limited civil rights gains of the 1960s toward truly global liberation. King's radical vision encompassed "the barefoot and shirtless people" of the world, while SNCC workers identified most passionately with the disenfranchised black peasants of the Deep South.

The visionaries of the civil rights movement and of the anticolonial struggles recognized that the acquisition of citizenship rights was a historical achievement that would affect the majority of humanity. At the beginning of the twentieth century, most people were still peasants — poor, mostly illiterate, landless agricultural laborers without the basic rights of citizenship, unable to vote and participate in the political life of the country in which they lived. A small minority of these peasants would join revolutionary movements to overcome colonialism and systematic racial subordination, but more often they sought greater freedom and opportunity by leaving the American South to migrate to urban areas, as my mother and father did. A sizeable minority of peasants, including my ancestors, would benefit from the relative freedom of urban life as they struggled to build better lives for themselves and their children. King and other visionaries of the mid-twentieth century understood that these discontented black peasants and urban workers were potential recruits for the successful movements during the decades following World War II to overcome colonialism and the Jim Crow system. But these visionaries also saw that history's greatest freedom struggle did not end with the overthrow of systems of racial oppression.

The long struggle of peasants and their still-struggling urbanized descendants to improve their lives and to become full citizens was the most inspiring story of the twentieth century. The historical significance of King as well as SNCC is that they identified with those at the bottom of the American social structure and sought to remind those of us who are a few generations removed from peasantry that we have a responsibility to use our skills and resources to assist those who are poor, insufficiently educated, and politically powerless. When SNCC organizer Bob Moses traveled to the Mississippi Delta in 1960 and met with black voting rights activist Amzie Moore, a historic connection was made between a visionary black urban intellectual and a courageous rural grassroots leader. SNCC workers did not initiate the southern freedom struggle, but SNCC's projects in the Deep South enabled skilled and dedicated young organizers to connect with the local leaders who were already there. Similarly, when King traveled to Memphis in March 1968 to assist a strike of sanitation workers, another historical connection was made between a visionary black intellectual and black urban labor leaders one or two generations removed from peasantry. SNCC and King spearheaded history's greatest freedom struggle as it achieved a decisive victory over the American Jim Crow system. Similar historical connections elsewhere in the world overcame colonialism and the South African apartheid regime.

The Voter Education Project, once headed by former SNCC worker John Lewis, used the slogan "The Hands that Once Picked Cotton Now Can Pick a President." Indeed, one of the great achievements of the twentieth century has been the worldwide transformation of peasants into citizens capable of having a voice in determining the destiny of nations. I imagine that my late mother, who escaped peasantry in the American South, would have been amazed by the victories of the past century and pleased that her descendants have done so well. I wonder whether, in her most hopeful moments, she and others of her generation would have been so audacious or perhaps so sufficient in their faith to imagine that their children would someday participate in a movement to destroy the system of white supremacy that had oppressed them, or would someday incorporate the story of peasants becoming citizens into the narrative of American history, or would witness the inauguration of the son of an African freedom fighter as president of the United States.

The revolution envisioned by King in his last speech in Memphis has not been completed, but it offers a way of thinking about the topic that brought us together in 2013 for the conference that inspired this volume of essays. King's valiant life and SNCC's courageous challenge to white supremacy in the Deep South remind us of the large debt we owe to the ongoing liberation struggles of the world's peasants and to the urbanized descendants of those peasants.

Clayborne Carson is Martin Luther King Jr. Centennial Professor of History at Stanford University and the founding director of the Martin Luther King, Jr., Research and Education Institute. Since 1985 he has directed the King Papers Project, which has produced seven volumes of a definitive, comprehensive edition of King's speeches, sermons, correspondence, publications, and unpublished writings. Dr. Carson has also edited numerous other books based on King's papers and the movements King inspired, and recently he published a memoir, *Martin's Dream: My Journey and the Legacy of Martin Luther King, Jr.* (2013).

Music and the March

SOUNDS AND SILENCES: MUSIC AND THE MARCH ON WASHINGTON

Brian Ward

Introduction: Dream Songs

"We must remember that music tames the wildest beast," explained Carlton Reese, leader of the choir of the Alabama Christian Movement for Human Rights and composer-arranger of many popular freedom songs in the early 1960s. According to Reese, the importance of music in the movement lay in its power to unite people, both within the African American community and across racial lines. In particular, Reese noted how "We Shall Overcome" had emerged as "the theme song" of the movement, his analysis riffing, almost to the point of paraphrase, on the final section of Martin Luther King Jr.'s "I Have a Dream" speech at the March on Washington: "One day we're going to sit down and worship together and walk the streets together. Little white girls and little black boys will be able to pray together, sing together, and go to school together." Echoing the visionary appeal for interracial harmony with which King ended his speech, Reese concluded that "We Shall Overcome" was "a national song — a song of peace, understanding, and hope that one day we will overcome things that keep us from being together."[1]

The soaring rhetoric of King's "Dream" has become so ubiquitous in popular memory that it is hardly surprising that Reese would borrow its phrasing even as he echoed its sentiments. However, his comments also suggest deeper connections between the March on Washington and "We Shall Overcome" — a song of complex, biracial provenance whose title provided the optimistic tag line on the official program for the event and which the assembled masses sang several times during the day.[2] As Reese appreciated, the song was emblematic of how music permeated the march and the broader movement, helping to define their spirit, goals, and meanings at literal and symbolic levels.

Most accounts of the March on Washington dutifully note that there was a lot of singing on August 28, 1963, much of it impromptu, led by the marchers themselves as they made their way to, along, and from the National Mall. Some accounts list the most prominent singers who appeared; several repeat the beguiling story that it

1 Carlton Reese, "Freedom Songs," in *Foot Soldiers for Democracy: The Men, Women, and Children of the Birmingham Civil Rights Movement*, ed. Horace Huntley and John W. McKerley (Urbana and Chicago, 2009), 100-101.

2 For "We Shall Overcome," see Stuart Stotts, *We Shall Overcome: A Song that Changed the World* (New York, 2010); Allan M. Winkler, *"To Everything There Is a Season": Pete Seeger and the Power of Song* (New York, 2011), 98-100.

was only at the urging of gospel singer Mahalia Jackson that King abandoned his scripted remarks to revisit the "Dream" that he had revealed in several earlier speeches.[3] Nevertheless, accounts of the day's music and music-makers tend to be brief and are riddled with errors about who sang what, where, and to what end. Few writers, for example, differentiate between morning performances from a stage located halfway along the mall, others from the steps of the Lincoln Memorial during the hour immediately before the official program began, and those performances that were part of the official program.[4] In short, there has been little sustained attention to the role of music on the day or to the deeper significances of who appeared and who did not.

In seeking to address this oversight, the first section of this essay focuses primarily on the singers who did perform on the mall. Although Mahalia Jackson, soprano Marian Anderson, and the Eva Jessye Choir were the only artists listed on the official program, there was additional music at the morning and afternoon sessions, dominated by the sounds of folk artists such as Joan Baez, Bob Dylan, Peter, Paul and Mary, Odetta, and the SNCC Freedom Singers. Explaining why folk music — especially as purveyed by white artists — was so prominent at the march is a key concern of this essay. So, too, is a desire to understand the critiques of the strong white folk presence at the march, not least from Bob Dylan, which form the main topic in the second section of the essay.

For historians, silences are often as revealing as sounds, and the final section of the essay considers the kinds of artists who were conspicuously absent from the day's musical events. There was no place for jazz, blues, or rhythm and blues on the Mall. Technical considerations may have had a role to play here: getting the James Brown Revue onto the cramped podium in front of the Lincoln Memorial may have been one logistical challenge too many for hard-pressed organizers. Yet at various points during the day, technicians did manage to accommodate a piano, an organ, a smattering of brass, as well as acoustic guitars, so such problems were not insurmountable. Rather, these absences reveal the priorities of the mainstream civil rights movement as it courted middle-American white support through a politics of respectability, emphasizing the pursuit of core citizenship rights by a combination of legal challenges and nonviolent direct action protests that most Americans considered responsible and morally acceptable.[5] The absences also illuminate the dance of

3   Speechwriter and King aide Clarence B. Jones is the most cited source for the claim that Jackson's exhortations encouraged King to abandon his planned speech. See Clarence B. Jones, quoted in Kate Pickert, "One March," *Time*, August 26-September 2, 2013 ("I Have A Dream" Anniversary Double Issue), 54. See also, William P. Jones, *The March on Washington: Jobs, Freedom, and the Forgotten History of Civil Rights* (New York, 2013), 196-97; Gary Younge, *The Speech: The Story Behind Martin Luther King's Speech* (London, 2013), 119-20.

4   One of the most useful, if understandably fleeting, treatments of music in the march is Charles Euchner's *Somebody Turn Me Around: A People's History of the 1963 March on Washington* (Boston, 2010), especially 105-10, 184-88. See also Taylor Branch, *Parting the Waters: America in the King Years* (New York, 1988), 878, 881; Bernice Johnson Reagon, "Songs of the Civil Rights Movement," PhD dissertation (Howard University, 1975), 165-67.

5   For more on the politics of respectability in the civil rights movement, see Marisa Chappell, Jenny Hutchinson and Brian Ward, "'Dress Modestly, Neatly...As If You Were Going To Church': Respectability, Class and Gender in the Montgomery Bus Boycott and the Early Civil Rights Movement," in *Gender in the Civil Rights Movement*, ed. Peter Ling and Sharon Monteith (New Brunswick, 2004), 69-100.

engagement and avoidance that took place between the movement and some of the most popular and revered black musicians of the day.

Live on the Mall

The politics of respectability were evident in the decision of the march's main organizers, headed by Bayard Rustin, to include only classical and sacred music on the official program.[6] One of the movement's most important strategists, Rustin was instrumental in deciding which artists appeared and, of equal importance to the success of the event, secured a $20,000 grant from the Garment and Auto Workers unions to pay for the powerful sound system that carried the day's speeches, prayers, and songs down the Mall.[7] Celebrated soprano Marian Anderson was chosen to open formal proceedings at 2 p.m. with the national anthem. This publically proclaimed the patriotic intent of the demonstration and of the freedom struggle, which, in the midst of the Cold War, was often couched in terms of securing basic civil and voting rights for African Americans in order to close the credibility gap between America's democratic ideals and its discriminatory practices.[8]

Anderson's presence also carried additional symbolic resonance. In 1939 she had sung from the steps of the Lincoln Memorial after the Daughters of the American Revolution barred her from performing in Constitution Hall.[9] Two years later, when A. Phillip Randolph called for mass protest in Washington to demand equal opportunities in federal defense industries, he acknowledged the uplifting and cohesive power of music by proposing to conclude the event with a concert at the Lincoln Memorial, headlined by Anderson, fellow soprano Dorothy Maynor, and tenor Roland Hayes.[10] Although that wartime march never took place, the mere threat helped to secure Executive Order 8802, which banned discrimination in federally funded war industries. Twenty-two years later, as Randolph and Rustin planned another effort to secure federal support for black rights and economic aspirations through mass mobilization in the capital, Anderson was an obvious choice to open the official program.

Unfortunately, however, Anderson got caught in the crowds and arrived on the Mall too late to sing the national anthem as planned. Later she performed an unscheduled version of "He's Got the Whole World in his Hands" accompanied by her pianist.[11] With Anderson delayed, Virginia-born soprano Camilla Williams stepped in and opened the formal program with the "Star-Spangled Banner." An

6   William Jones notes that, despite an ever-expanding Administrative Committee chaired by Cleveland Robinson that included representatives of many civil rights and labor organizations, Rustin always "retained primary control over planning and preparation of the protest." Jones, *March on Washington*, 173. See also, John D'Emilio, *Lost Prophet: The Life and Times of Bayard Rustin* (Chicago, 2003), 327-31, 335-57.

7   Jones, *March on Washington*, 181.

8   For the Cold War context, see Mary Dudziak, *Cold War Civil Rights: Race and the Image of American Democracy* (Princeton, 2000).

9   See Raymond Arsenault, *The Sound of Freedom: Marian Anderson, the Lincoln Memorial and the Concert That Awakened America* (New York, 2010).

10   "100,000 in March to Capital," *Amsterdam News*, May 31, 1941.

11   Anderson's performance is available at Educational Radio Network, "The March Begins," August 28, 1963, WGBH Media Library and Archives, http://openvault.wgbh.org/catalog/march-592217-the-march-begins (accessed January 5, 2014).

internationally acclaimed performer in her own right, in 1946 Williams became the first African American to secure a contract with a major US opera company when she debuted in the New York City Opera's production of *Madame Butterfly*. In 1951, she played Bess in the first complete recording of George Gershwin's *Porgy and Bess*. Earlier in the afternoon of August 28, 1963, Williams had performed "Oh What a Beautiful City" from the steps of the Lincoln Memorial as part of the informal program that featured mostly folk music interspersed with short speeches by activists Fred Shuttlesworth and Ralph Abernathy, diplomat Ralph Bunche, and celebrities Burt Lancaster, Dick Gregory, Josephine Baker, and Harry Belafonte, who coordinated the star-studded Hollywood lineup.[12]

By 4 p.m., many in the crowd were wilting. Some had traveled overnight to Washington; some had been marching or waiting on the Mall since the early morning; two hours into the official program, the fierce August heat was taking its toll. Then Mahalia Jackson appeared on the podium. According to many eyewitnesses King's favorite singer revitalized the crowd with a rousing rendition of "I've Been 'Buked and I've Been Scorned" which, in the words of Charles Euchner, "expressed the deepest suffering of the black race, reaching back to the slave ships and centuries of bondage and broken hopes and dreams — but also painting the brightest picture of the Exodus and a better world." So enthusiastic was the crowd's response that Jackson performed an encore, a blistering version of "How I Got Over" that powerfully evoked the dignity and resolve of the African American community.[13]

Also prominent on the official program was the Eva Jessye Choir, the New York-based brainchild of a pioneering African American educator-choral leader who had served as George Gershwin's musical director for *Porgy and Bess*. The choir performed a medley of concertized spirituals culminating in "Freedom is Worth Shouting About" and, at the conclusion of the formal events, returned to the podium to lead one of the day's many renditions of "We Shall Overcome."[14]

Beyond the classical and gospel artists on the official program, a variety of other musical entertainment could be heard. The music coming from the side stage in the morning, like that heard during the informal program from the steps of the memorial in the early afternoon, was dominated by folk singers. Most of the songs celebrated the stoicism of the black community and the movement's determination to destroy Jim Crow, while projecting a pervasive, if cautious,

12 Margalit Fox, "Camilla Williams, Barrier-Breaking Opera Star, Dies at 92," *New York Times*, February 2, 2012. Stephanie Shonekan and Camilla Williams, *The Life of Camilla Williams, African American Classical Singer and Opera Diva* (New York, 2009). You can hear fragments of Williams's songs at Educational Radio Network, "Celebrity Participation in the March on Washington," August 28, 1963, WGBH Media Library and Archives, march-bc109d-celebrity-participation-in-the-march-on-washington (accessed January 5, 2014).

13 Euchner, *Nobody Turn Me Around*, 184-88 (quote 186).

14 See Eileen Southern, *The Music of Black Americans: A History*, 3rd edition (New York, 1998), 422-23.

optimism that racial justice would eventually prevail. For example, Josh White, a veteran folk and blues balladeer who had briefly sung with Bayard Rustin in the Carolinians vocal group in the early 1940s, sang "Marching Down Freedom's Road."[15]

Joining the folkies in some of the ensemble singing in the morning was Lonnie Sattin, a modestly successful black balladeer who juggled pop and light soul styles with a predilection for bossa nova beats.[16] Tellingly, Sattin was the closest the crowds on the mall came to hearing anyone within touching distance of jazz or rhythm and blues. From the same side stage, Odetta (known as "the Voice of the Civil Rights Movement"[17]) played guitar and sang the purposeful "I'm On My Way" and "Oh Freedom" accompanied by versatile African American folk guitarist and sometime country fiddle player Bruce Langhorne. For an encore, Odetta offered an a cappella medley of "No More Auction Block" and "Child of God."[18]

In the afternoon, folk continued to dominate proceedings. Straight from the heart of the Southern struggle to the steps of the Lincoln Memorial came the SNCC Freedom Singers. Formed during the Albany protests in southwest Georgia in 1962, the group, featuring Bernice Johnson Reagon, Rutha Mae Harris, Charles Neblett, and Cordell Reagon, supplemented at the march by occasional member Bertha Gober, had become useful fundraisers for the movement through albums and personal appearances around the nation. The Freedom Singers also served, in Reagon's phrase, as "a singing newspaper," performing topical songs that informed sympathetic audiences about the struggle and becoming, as SNCC's communications director Julian Bond recalled, SNCC's "public face."[19] The singers usually ended their performances with "We Shall Not Be Moved," a formula they repeated at the march, segueing into the defiant chant: "Ain't Never Gonna Stop/ Because I Want My Freedom Now."

The final song performed prior to the start of the official program was the old spiritual-turned-freedom song "Keep Your Eyes on the Prize, Hold On," led and wittily updated by African American folk singer Len Chandler ("Your butcher, your baker, your clerk,/we won't buy where we can't work"). In keeping with the integrationist ethos of the day, Chandler was joined for this rousing finale by the first couple of the folk revival, Joan Baez and Bob Dylan.[20]

Among the other white acts present was the hugely successful Peter, Paul and Mary. Having already sung Pete Seeger's "If I Had a

15 Elijah Wald, *Josh White: Society Blues* (Boston, 2000), 60, 271; *New York Times*, August 29, 1963.

16 Sattin's presence, but not what he sang, is noted in Educational Radio Network, "Interviews with participants, music from the stage," August 28, 1963, WGBH Media Library and Archives, http://openvault.wgbh.org/catalog/march-460464-interviews-with-participants-music-from-stage (accessed October 27, 2014).

17 Harry Belafonte with Michael Schnayerson, *My Song: A Memoir of Art, Race and Defiance* (Edinburgh, 2011), 210.

18 Some of Odetta's set can be heard at Educational Radio Network, "Interviews with participants, music from the stage," August 28, 1963, WGBH Media Library and Archives, http://openvault.wgbh.org/catalog/march-460464-interviews-with-participants-music-from-stage (accessed October 27, 2014).

19 Bernice Johnson Reagon, interview with Brian Ward, January 24, 1996; Julian Bond, interview with Brian Ward, March 20, 1996. See also Bernice Johnson Reagon, *We Who Believe in Freedom* (New York, 1993), 159-62; Brian Ward, *Just My Soul Responding: Rhythm and Blues, Black Consciousness and Race Relations* (London, 1998), 293-95.

20 Educational Radio Network, "Celebrity Participation in the March on Washington," August 28, 1963, WGBH Media Library and Archives, march-bc109d-celebrity-participation-in-the-march-on-washington (accessed January 5, 2014).

Hammer" from the side stage in the morning, the trio performed it again from the memorial in the early afternoon. Activist-actor Ossie Davis, who served as emcee for much of the day, introduced the group as "express[ing] in song what this great meeting is all about."[21] The trio also sang Dylan's "Blowing in the Wind" from both locations. That summer they had enjoyed a major national pop hit with the song at a time when Dylan was still relatively unknown beyond the folk fraternity.[22] "The song speaks of caring, of listening to one another," explained Mary Travers, affirming the mood of harmony and mutual respect on the mall.[23]

Shortly before the official afternoon program began, Joan Baez sang a poignant version of the spiritual "All Your Trials," sandwiched between brief remarks by Ralph Abernathy and Ralph Bunche.[24] During the morning she had harmonized with Dylan on "When the Ship Comes In" and led the crowd and many of her fellow performers in "We Shall Overcome." The song was a familiar finale to folk concerts, serving as readily understood musical shorthand for the folk revival's commitment to the freedom struggle — which helps to explain the pre-eminence of such artists at the march. A month earlier, the Newport Folk Festival had closed with an integrated line-up of the Freedom Singers, Peter, Paul and Mary, Baez, Dylan, Pete Seeger, and Theodore Bikel singing the same anthem. A July 1963 rally for SNCC workers and local activists in Greenwood, Mississippi, that featured the Freedom Singers, Dylan, Baez, Bikel, Seeger, and Chandler had ended the same way.[25]

In addition to dueting with Baez in the morning and participating in the ensemble singing that concluded the informal morning and afternoon sessions, Bob Dylan also sang "Only a Pawn in Their Game" from the steps of the memorial. While the vast majority of songs heard that day were uplifting expressions of, in Mike Marqusee's phrase, "freedom and deliverance and unity," Dylan's performances struck a different chord. "When the Ship Comes In" moved from a vision of a divinely ordained egalitarianism ("the sun will respect/ every face on the deck") that had much in common with King's "Dream," to prophecies of Old Testament-style retribution and bloody vengeance against the enemies of justice that were antithetical to King's message of love and reconciliation.[26] The main focus of "Only a Pawn" — a song about the murder of Mississippi NAACP leader Medgar Evers that Dylan had unveiled in Greenwood earlier that summer — was not Evers nor his then unnamed murderer (in

21 Ossie Davis, ibid.

22 Robert Shelton, *No Direction Home: The Life & Music of Bob Dylan*, revised and updated edition, ed. Elizabeth Thomson and Patrick Humphries (London, 2011), 125-26.

23 Mary Travers, interviewed by David Edwards, Educational Radio Network, "President John F. Kennedy Speech on the Upcoming March," August 28, 1963, WGBH Media Library and Archives, http://openvault.wgbh.org/ catalog/march-44612e- president-john-f-kennedy- speech-on-the-upcoming-march (accessed January 5, 2014).

24 "Celebrity Participation in the March on Washington."

25 For the finale of the 1963 Newport Folk Festival, see David Hadju, *Positively 4th Street: The Lives and Times of Joan Baez, Bob Dylan, Mimi Baez Farina and Richard Farina* (New York, 2001), 166; Shelton, *No Direction Home*, 132. For the Greenwood concert, see Mike Marqusee, *Wicked Messenger: Bob Dylan and the 1960s* (New York, 2005), 82.

26 Marqusee, *Wicked Messenger*, 8-9.

1994 Byron de la Beckwith was finally convicted of the crime) but the socioeconomic-political system that made poor whites victims and tools of elites and allowed violence to flourish as an instrument of racial control.[27]

Although Marqusee underestimated the nascent radicalism of King's speech before he began to dream, he was right to note that by "outlining a class-based analysis of the persistence of racism," Dylan's songs were closer in spirit to the speech of SNCC chairman John Lewis than almost any other music performed that day, with the partial exception of Chandler's re-imagined "Eyes on the Prize."[28] Dylan's celebration of retribution against those who obstructed justice in "When the Ship Comes In," like his excoriation of state complicity in racial inequality and violence in "Only a Pawn," hit radical notes unheard elsewhere in the music of the march, or in most popular black music, or in mainstream black protest politics during 1963.

Notwithstanding Dylan's portentous contrariness, the prominence of folk artists, white and black, made sense in terms of the integrated agenda of the demonstration. Contemporaries and subsequent commentators have always accorded special significance to the multiracial composition of the crowds on the mall, reading it as a public affirmation of the kind of harmony, brotherhood, and respect invoked at the end of King's speech. "It was an unbelievable feeling to see hundreds and thousands of people, black and white, sitting together, cheering," recalled Lewis.[29] The racially mixed folk line-up carried a prophetic, or at least an aspirational, dimension that helped to establish the symbolic politics of the march — accentuated by the fact that, beyond a small circle of cognoscenti who might admire Josh White and Odetta, or appreciate earlier folk-blues artists such as Leadbelly and Blind Lemon Jefferson, the folk revival was marked in the American imagination as predominantly white. Bruce Langhorne, who, with Len Chandler, was one of the few African Americans to become a fixture in East Coast clubs and coffeehouses central to the folk scene, called it a "very white scene."[30] The carefully integrated line-up at the march thus visually and audibly challenged prevailing notions of strictly segregated musical — and by extension social — worlds.

Equally important to the music's symbolic resonance was the fact that most folk artists — including many who did not perform in Washington such as Pete Seeger, the Kingston Trio, Theodore Bikel, Judy Collins, Richard Farina, and Phil Ochs — were publically supportive of the freedom struggle, artistically and personally, to a degree

27 Clinton Heylin, *Revolution in the Air: The Songs of Bob Dylan*, Vol. 1: *1957-1973* (London, 2010), 174-78.

28 Marqusee, *Wicked Messenger*, 10.

29 John Lewis, quote in Pickert, "One March," 47, 50.

30 Hadju, *Positively 4th Street*, 94.

rarely found in the early 1960s among black rhythm and blues, pop, or even jazz artists. Harry Belafonte recalled: "There was a significant array of white artists who were progressive politically...all of them came out of the folk movement."[31] The movement did not initially seek them out. Rather, they gravitated towards themes of racial justice in their music and sometimes offered practical help because of their own liberal politics and commitment to civil rights. "On the platform when these highly profiled, successful artists performed," Belafonte explained, "it wasn't just that they were sympathetic and very much involved in the ideals of the struggle, it was that that's what they really were... [they had] a moral point of view."[32]

Peter Yarrow of Peter, Paul and Mary explained, "We're here as everybody else is, to personally as individuals say that we feel that all human beings are equal, and in this case we're saying something that we've said in our songs: that the colored man in America must have today...the same rights that we enjoy as white people."[33] Joan Baez felt much the same. The daughter of Quakers with a strong commitment to social justice, Baez moved in progressive political circles that intersected with the folk revival, where her crystalline voice quickly made her its most popular female vocalist. Haunted by memories of being taunted for her strange-sounding name and called "a dirty Mexican" while growing up in California, Baez admitted that when embarking on a first tour of the South in 1961, she was "barely aware of the civil rights movement." Thereafter, she added "We Shall Overcome" and "Oh Freedom" to her regular repertoire and aligned herself closely with the struggle.[34] Echoing Yarrow, Baez told reporters she was at the March because "all men are created equal. It's as simple as that."[35]

"My Friends Don't Wear Suits": White Artists in the Black Struggle

In August 1963, Bob Dylan could not yet match Baez's commercial popularity, but he was widely touted as the most important new figure in folk. Dylan was also at the zenith of a complex and revealing engagement with the civil rights struggle that began in February 1962 when he performed at a fundraiser for the Congress of Racial Equality (CORE) in New York at the instigation of his then-girlfriend, Suze Rotolo, who worked as a volunteer for the organization. She was "into this equality-freedom thing long before I was," Dylan admitted.[36] Dylan composed his first full-blown protest song for the occasion, taking as his subject the 1955 Mississippi lynching of 14-year-old

31 Harry Belafonte, interview with Brian Ward, March 12, 1996. For connections between the folk revival and the movement, see Ronald D. Cohen, *Rainbow Quest: The Folk Music Revival and American Society, 1940*-1970 (Amherst, 2002), 204-208; Grace Elizabeth Hale, "Black as Folk: The Southern Civil Rights Movement and the Folk Music Revival," in *The Myth of Southern Exceptionalism*, ed. Matthew D. Lassiter and Joseph Crespino (New York, 2010), 121-42.

32 Harry Belafonte, quoted in Pickert, "One March," 50.

33 Peter Yarrow, interviewed by David Edwards, "President John F. Kennedy Speech on the Upcoming March."

34 Joan Baez, *And a Voice to Sing With: A Memoir* (New York, 2009), 103. See also Hadju, *Positively 4th Street*, 16, 143-44.

35 Joan Baez, interviewed by Al Hulsen, "Interviews with Participants, Music from the Stage."

36 Bob Dylan, quoted in Heylin, *Revolution in the Air*, 87.

Emmett Till.[37] Other songs followed ("The Ballad of Donald White," "Oxford Town," "The Lonesome Death of Hattie Carroll," and "Only a Pawn"), all exploring connections among racism, power, violence, and oppression.

Dylan was not alone in addressing racial matters; the folk repertoire of the early 1960s was full of such songs. Critic Robert Shelton noted how "new songs on this theme are not only weapons in the Civil Rights arsenal, but are also developing into valuable commodities in the music industry."[38] Phil Ochs's "Ballad of Medgar Evers" and "Ballad of William Worthy," Pete Seeger's "Ballad of Old Monroe" (about Robert F. Williams), Richard Farina's "Birmingham Sunday" (about the bombing of the 16th Street Avenue Baptist Church, recorded by his sister-in-law Joan Baez), Tom Paxton's "Dogs of Alabama" (about Bull Connor's violent policing of the 1963 Birmingham protests), and Paul Simon's "He Was My Brother" (written in 1963, but revised after the murder of his college friend Andrew Goodman during Freedom Summer) were among the many songs that condemned discrimination and racial violence and expressed sympathy for the movement. As a consequence, folk music and folk singers had become inextricably linked in popular consciousness with support for the freedom struggle. Shelton even reported on a coffeehouse gig in Ogunquit, Maine, where he heard an impatient young girl demanding that the performer "Sing something about segregation!"[39] This close identification with the movement virtually guaranteed that folk singers would loom large among the musicians chosen — and among those willing to be chosen — to play at the march.

Civil rights workers were generally very appreciative of the public and artistic stands made by white folkies. SNCC southern campus organizer Stanley Wise remembered seeing Bob Dylan when he was a freshman at Howard. "I remember him up there helping load trucks to take food to Mississippi. I mean, he was right there on the frontline. I don't remember that from a lot of people."[40] Dylan's trip to Mississippi in July 1963 made him acutely aware of the stark realities of Jim Crow and appreciative of the heroism of those who challenged it. Bikel, who paid for Dylan's flight south and joined him, Chandler, Seeger and the Freedom Singers for the concert-rally in Greenwood, remembered Dylan's distress at first seeing "whites only" signs at public facilities.[41] Dylan developed a deep admiration for the SNCC organizers he encountered. He cemented firm friendships with James Forman and Bernice Johnson Reagon, whom he met in New York

37 Hadju, *Positively 4th Street,* 107-108; Heylin, *Revolution in the Air,* 86-89.

38 Shelton, quoted in Cohen, *Rainbow Quest,* 204.

39 Shelton, *No Direction Home,* 124.

40 Stanley Wise, interview with Brian Ward and Jenny Walker, October 19, 1995.

41 For Bickel's recollections, see Shelton, *No Direction Home,* 129-30. For more on the significance of Dylan's 1963 Mississippi trip, see Marqusee, *Wicked Messenger,* 78-83; Ian Bell, *Once Upon a Time: The Lives of Bob Dylan* (Edinburgh, 2012), 270-72.

in 1962 and who even stayed in his apartment for a while. Reagon remembered, "We all thought, those of us in the movement and those of us in the Freedom Singers, that Dylan was fantastic as a songwriter and as a person."[42]

Although Reagon loyally maintained that "they really liked him down in the cotton country," the appeal of Dylan and other folk artists was overwhelmingly to white, largely college educated, often Northern audiences.[43] For example, when CORE's Jimmy McDonald staged a 1963 fundraiser in upstate New York he had to concede "most Negroes do not know that much about 'folk music' so that Bobby Dylan does not have that much appeal in the Negro community."[44] When Baez played movement-related events on Southern campuses including Miles College in Birmingham, Morehouse in Atlanta, and Tougaloo in Mississippi, her audience was 70 percent or more white. A black contingent sometimes had to be bused in because Baez's contract insisted that African Americans had to be admitted to her shows. "We had to call up the local NAACP for volunteers to integrate an audience for someone they'd never heard of," she recalled.[45]

Not everyone, however, was sanguine about the preeminence of white folk artists at the march. Comedian-activist Dick Gregory bluntly asked "What was a white boy like Bob Dylan there for? Or — who else? Joan Baez?" To support the cause? Wonderful — support the cause. March. Stand behind us — but not in front of us."[46] Bob Dylan sympathized. In November 1963, he wrote a column for Robert Shelton's short-lived *Hootenanny* magazine, exposing the limits of the kind of racial liberalism that he and his music were often held to personify and which the strong white presence at the march was supposed to reflect. Dylan peeled away the veneer of respectability and interracial bonhomie to focus on the material deprivations and terror that confronted African Americans, particularly in the South, and to revisit the radicalism at the heart of the movement's demands for freedom and equality. Remembering "Jim Foreman (sic) who I stood next t on a Mississippi sound truck an watched his face while he told people why they gotta go vote," Dylan "started thinkin' about John Lewis whose speech was cut down in Washington cause some people were afraid t speak on the same platform with somebody who could actually think t say 'we shall march thru the South like Sherman's Army.'"[47]

A month later Dylan was awarded the Tom Paine Award from the Emergency Civil Liberties Committee (ECLC), an organization formed to protect freedom of speech in the face of Cold War repression.

42 Reagon, quoted in Shelton, *No Direction Home*, 113.

43 Reagon, quoted in Marqusee, *Wicked Messenger*, 130.

44 Jimmy McDonald, letter to Marvin Rich, October 23, 1963, V:179, Congress of Racial Equality Papers: 1941-1967, Manuscript Division, Library of Congress.

45 Baez, *And a Voice to Sing*, 103.

46 Gregory, quoted in Hajdu, *Positively 4ᵗʰ Street*, 183.

47 Dylan's column, complete with its idiosyncratic spellings, is quoted in Bell, *Once Upon a Time*, 287. See also Shelton, *No Direction Home*, 152.

Introduction and
Prologue

**Music and
the March**

Transatlantic
Legacies

Different Views
and Voices

Visual Histories and
Cultural Memories

Resentful of the pressure to write an endless stream of topical protest songs and increasingly wary of the "spokesman for a generation" acclaim beginning to come his way, Dylan got roaring drunk and gave an extraordinary acceptance speech that offended almost everybody present. He concluded by accepting the award on behalf of Forman and again questioned the value of the march's studied respectability and claims to biracial significance. "I was on the March on Washington up on the platform and I looked around at all the Negroes there and I didn't see any Negroes that looked like none of my friends. My friends don't wear suits. My friends don't have to wear any kind of thing to prove they're respectable Negroes."[48]

Shortly after, Dylan wrote to the ECLC trying, in a verse poem, to apologize but reiterating his skepticism about efforts to wrap in the garb of middle-American respectability a movement that, as he had implied in "Only a Pawn," demanded a much more radical revision of American values and socioeconomic structures. The ubiquitous suits and ties at the march, he repeated, militated against genuine acceptance of black humanity on its own terms: "black skin is black skin/It cant be covered by clothes and made t seem/acceptable, well liked an respectable…it is naked black skin an nothin else/ if a Negro has t wear a tie t be a Negro/ then I must cut off all ties with who he has t do it for."[49]

Following the march, his ECLC experience, and another trip south to support movement activities in February 1964, Dylan steadily withdrew from making overt political gestures and virtually abandoned the kind of topical songs that had made his reputation.[50] "All I can say is that politics is not my thing at all," he explained after a set at the 1964 Newport Folk Festival heavily weighted towards his more personal songs drew the ire of some fans. "It ain't gonna work. I'm just not gonna be part of it," he added pessimistically. While some of his peers, including Baez, became increasingly enmeshed with the New Left and endorsed its broad critique of American domestic values and foreign policy, Dylan argued that efforts to change the system were futile. "I'm not gonna make a dent or anything, so why be a part of it by even trying to criticize it?" he asked.[51] Unlike many sympathetic white liberals, Dylan never pretended to fully understand, let alone articulate, the black experience. "What's a Negro? I don't know what a Negro is," an exasperated Dylan admitted to Shelton.[52] Responsibility for expressing black identity and experience, the complexities of black culture, and the aspirations of the black community did not rest with white singers like himself, Dylan insisted.

48 "Transcript of Bob Dylan's Remarks at the Bill of Rights Dinner," December 13, 1963. Bob Dylan and the ECLC, http://www.corliss-lamont.org. See also Shelton, *No Direction Home*, 142-45, and Marqusee, *Wicked Messenger*, 93-96.

49 "A Message from Bob Dylan," Bob Dylan and the ECLC, http://www.corliss-lamont.org/dylan.org. See also Hajdu, *Positively 4th Street*, 201-202.

50 Marqusee, *Wicked Messenger*, 96-99; 115-20.

51 Bob Dylan, quoted in Anthony Scaduto, *Bob Dylan: An Intimate Biography* (New York, 1971), 177.

52 Bob Dylan, quoted in Hajdu, *Positively 4th Street*, 201.

Conspicuous Silences: Jazz and Rhythm and Blues

In the world of jazz, there were many black musicians who might have filled that role at the march. Yet, as saxophonist John Handy complained at the time, "Of the large number of 'cream of the crop' Negro and white artists and entertainers present, there was not one jazz artist on the program." Handy, who had played with Charles Mingus on the seminal album *Better Git It in Your Soul*, was a longtime activist who had been imprisoned for his involvement in a New York sit-in at Woolworths. Following a move to the West Coast, he joined the San Francisco CORE chapter and picketed the Bank of America to protest discriminatory hiring practices. Handy found the absence of jazz from the program unfathomable "because jazz, along with the spirituals, has played a major role in the Negro's struggle for freedom...After all, jazz has been the Negro's artistic means of self-expression and has opened many minds and hearts to the Negro." Frustrated by the absence of jazz at the march, Handy formed his own integrated Freedom Band, which took to the road as the "musical troubleshooter for the Movement." Handy adopted "the uniform worn in the South by SNCC workers — i.e. work shirts, dark pants, denim jackets, etc." There were to be no suits and ties in the Freedom Band.[53]

Unknown to Handy, however, Washington native Duke Ellington actually had been asked to participate in the march. According to his sometime lyricist Don George, Ellington declined, moaning, "I've got sore feet. I can't walk that far."[54] But as Harvey Cohen has shown, the truth was more complex and symptomatic of the dilemmas faced by black musicians when it came to aligning themselves publically with the new, more militant, direct-action phase of the freedom struggle. For years, Ellington had been brilliantly expressing black consciousness in his art, not least in the "My People" show in the summer of 1963, when he premiered "King Fit the Battle of Alabam'" — one of his most overtly political works, dedicated to Martin Luther King Jr. and the Birmingham campaign. A life member of the NAACP who played dozens of benefits for the organization, Ellington had even joined a Baltimore sit-in in February 1960. A year later he had a non-segregation clause inserted into his contract for performances.[55] The provision was, however, unevenly applied, and Ellington drew regular criticism from activists for playing segregated shows. He was also perpetually trying to live down widely circulated comments he had made in 1951, claiming that the black community was not yet ready to mount a campaign for full citizenship due to its lack of economic power.[56] By the time of the march, Ellington had not changed his

53 John Handy, "The Freedom Band," September 14, 1964, part 1, box 7, folder 1, Congress of Racial Equality Papers, Alderman Library, University of Virginia, Charlottesville; Euchner, *Nobody Turn Me Around*, 109-10.

54 Don George, *The Real Duke Ellington* (London, 1982), 113-14.

55 For Ellington's relationship with the movement in the 1950s and 1960s, see Harvey G. Cohen, *Duke Ellington's America* (Chicago, 2010), 298-307, 379-407.

56 Ibid., 301-307.

opinion. He admired King but doubted the efficacy of direct-action tactics. He dismissed the march as a futile public relations exercise that would do nothing to raise the capital necessary to empower the black community. "The only people who did good out of the goddam parade was the people who owned businesses in Washington, the hotels and all that," he complained.[57]

If Ellington's refusal to participate rested partially on principled reservations about the value of the march and of direct-action protest more generally, his decision also reflected the fact that around 95 percent of his audience was white.[58] While this cross-racial appeal opened up potential for educating whites and persuading them to support the burgeoning movement, there was no guarantee that this would happen. Indeed, there was widespread fear that forthright civil rights advocacy might alienate white fans who had come to think of Ellington as a national treasure but rarely as a political figure. He was a man who, as Alistair Cooke once observed, often appeared "strangely apart from the troubles and recent turmoil of his race."[59]

Ellington was hardly unique among jazz musicians in his cautious approach to the movement. In 1961, white jazz critic and civil rights advocate Nat Hentoff ridiculed suggestions that jazz artists were regularly involved in civil rights activities or committed to supporting it financially. He doubted that as many as "one in five hundred even belonged to the NAACP."[60] Nevertheless, in terms of both aesthetics and thematic preoccupations, many jazz players, particularly younger musicians associated with gospel-blues soaked Hard Bop and more experimental free form New Jazz, expressed support for the struggle in their music. This was reflected most overtly in works such as Charles Mingus's "Fables of Faubus," which mocked the Arkansas governor in the wake of the 1957 Central High School crisis in Little Rock; songwriter-jazz vocalist Oscar Brown Jr.'s 1960 album *Sin & Soul*, which captured the historic black experience in "Bid 'em in" and "Work Song"; "Alabama," John Coltrane's elegy to the four girls killed in the Birmingham church bombing of September 1963; Sonny Rollins's *Freedom Suite*; and Max Roach's *We Insist! Freedom Now Suite*, which Roach insisted Candid Records offer to civil rights organizations at a discount so they could resell it to raise funds.[61]

Beyond such explicit invocations of the movement, within many forms of postwar jazz there was a quest for individual expressivity within a supportive group setting and for structural freedom (particularly harmonic and rhythmic freedom), which many heard as

57 Duke Ellington, interview with Carter Harmon, 1964, quoted in ibid., 398.

58 Ibid., 385.

59 Cooke, quoted in Derek Jewell, *Duke: A Portrait of Duke Ellington* (London, 1977), 115.

60 Nat Hentoff, "Jazz and Reverse Jim Crow," *Negro Digest*, June 1961, 70-74.

61 For the arrangements around *We Insist!*, see St. Clair Clement, letter and enclosures to John Lewis, August 7, 1963, A-I-31, Student Nonviolent Coordinating Committee Papers, Manuscript Division, Library of Congress, Washington, DC (hereafter SNCC).

a soundtrack to the black struggle for justice, freedom, and escape from the tyranny of white values.[62] Atlanta-based SNCC worker Fay Bellamy heard black pride and sympathy for the movement expressed "in how the rhythms changed in jazz," perceptively adding, "I think the mind-set a jazz person might have versus the mind-set a rhythm and blues person might have, might have been somewhat different in that period of time."[63] As Bellamy appreciated, young jazz artists tended to emerge from and work within a self-conscious cultural vanguard, where music was expected to mix with politics. There was an expectation that any credible jazz musician would be conspicuously committed to the freedom struggle: both they and their protean art were expected to challenge existing social, economic, political, and racial, as well as musical, conventions.

Hentoff's barbs notwithstanding, it is also clear that some jazz artists, veterans as well as the militant new young guns, who did speak out boldly for black pride and against racism, aligned themselves more conspicuously with the struggle. The Little Rock school crisis prompted Louis Armstrong, jazz's most revered elder statesman, to denounce Orval Faubus as an "uneducated plowboy," berate "no guts" President Eisenhower for his handling of the affair, and pull out of a State Department-sponsored goodwill tour of the Soviet Union because of "the way they are treating my people in the South."[64] Armstrong's stance drew enormous appreciation from the black public who knew the risk it posed to his career. "Armstrong knew what he was doing," explained George Perkins of Norfolk, Virginia, proudly, "and is ready to accept whatever the consequences."[65] Jazz artists also gave benefit concerts for the movement in the early 1960s, such as the SNCC "Salute to Southern Students" show at Carnegie Hall in February 1963, which spawned a lucrative double-album featuring Julian "Cannonball" Adderley, Charles Mingus, and Thelonious Monk alongside Nina Simone, one of the most heavily involved artists of the period, whose style straddled jazz, folk, blues, pop, and rhythm and blues.[66]

Ironically, however, while some promoted the New Jazz, in particular, as the sound of black pride and insurgency, the black masses in the early 1960s tended to prefer rhythm and blues, whose performers usually distanced themselves from formal identification with the struggle, either in their music or in personal terms, until later in the decade. Again, before trying to explain the absence of rhythm and blues artists from the March and their relatively low profile in

62 For the connections between ideas of freedom in jazz and in the movement, see Scott Saul, *Freedom Is, Freedom Ain't: Jazz and the Making of the Sixties* (Cambridge, MA, 2003), esp. 15-19.

63 Fay Bellamy, interview with Brian Ward, October 18, 1995.

64 Louis Armstrong, quoted in *Norfolk Journal & Guide*, September 28, 1957. See also Penny M. Von Eschen, *Satchmo Blows Up the World: Jazz Ambassadors Play the Cold War* (Cambridge, MA, 2004), 63-64.

65 George Perkins, quoted in *Norfolk Journal & Guide*, September 28, 1957.

66 "List of Sponsors for Salute to Southern Students," n.d.; James Forman, letter to Diahann Carroll, February 13, 1963, both A-IV-69, SNCC. For a sympathetic account of Simone's activism, see Ruth Feldstein, "'I Don't Trust You Anymore': Nina Simone, Culture, and Black Activism in the 1960s," *Journal of American History* 91, no. 4 (2005): 1349-79.

the early movement, it is important to acknowledge that there were exceptions to this generalization and to reaffirm that the politics and significance of African American popular music were never reducible to socially engaged lyrics or to the public activism of artists. The sound of rising black consciousness was encoded in the sounds and performance practices of rhythm and blues and in the success of some of its artists as much as in the literal meanings of its songs. As noted by Imamu Amiri Baraka, the author-activist whose liner notes, poetry, and advocacy did much to forge links between the New Jazz and the freedom struggle, even lyrically apolitical songs "provided a core of legitimate social feeling, although mainly metaphorical and allegorical for black people," which both aligned with and intensified a new black pride.[67]

Moreover, in the late 1950s and early 1960s there were some popular rhythm and blues songs that did engage with the freedom struggle and the socioeconomic realities of the black experience long before the profusion of such fare later in the decade. Like many earlier blues songs, the Silhouettes' "Got a Job" and Jerry Butler's "I'm a Telling You" addressed black economic disadvantage. Chuck Berry's "Promised Land" worked as an allegory of the 1961 Freedom Rides, while his earlier hits "Johnny B. Goode" and "Brown-Eyed Handsome Man" foreshadowed the ubiquitous "black is beautiful" songs of the late 1960s and 1970s. Nina Simone frequently touched on the intersection of racial and gender oppression and addressed the battle against Jim Crow explicitly with "Mississippi Goddam" in late 1963.[68] However, while one could undoubtedly extend this list, at the time of the march such songs were exceptional, not typical. While many folk singers and some jazz artists dealt openly with race relations in their music, such moves were much rarer among the stars of rhythm and blues who dominated black-oriented radio, black jukeboxes, black theaters, and black turntables.

Similarly, by 1963 only a few leading rhythm and blues artists had taken a bold personal and public stand in support of the movement. In 1960, Clyde McPhatter and fellow NAACP life member, organist Bill Doggett, had played a series of integrated youth rallies where McPhatter praised "the young white students who ... have stood shoulder-to-shoulder with Afro-American youth in this irresistible crusade."[69] McPhatter also participated in an Atlanta sit-in, appeared on picket lines, and performed benefits for the NAACP and SNCC. Yet the relatively unusual nature of such conspicuous commitment

67 LeRoi Jones (Imamu Amiri Baraka), *Black Music* (New York, 1968; 2010 edition), 238.

68 For a discussion of lyrical engagement with the movement in the rhythm and blues of the late 1950s and early 1960s, see Ward, *Just My Soul Responding*, 203-18.

69 Clyde McPhatter, quoted in *Amsterdam News*, July 9, 1960.

was hinted at when in April 1963 McPhatter was still being hailed in the black press as "one of the first to take an active part in a public demonstration of anger and disgust with the status quo."[70] Other rhythm and blues artists involved in early protest activities included the young Gladys Knight in Atlanta, Bunny Sigler in Greensboro, North Carolina, and Jackie Wilson, who worked hard for the Philadelphia NAACP and had for some time refused to play segregated shows. So, too, had Little Willie John, who, like black balladeer Roy Hamilton, attended the march as a private citizen and who, again like Hamilton, regularly performed at benefit concerts.[71]

Plans for the March on Washington had actually prompted a modest surge of public engagement from the world of rhythm and blues. Ray Charles and the Shirelles appeared alongside more regular movement supporters Johnny Mathis, Nina Simone, and Dick Gregory at a Miles College fundraiser that raised about $9,000 for the Council for United Civil Rights Leadership (CUCRL), which handled the financial arrangements for joint civil rights projects.[72] On August 23, 1963, even the perennially cautious Motown, a black-owned record label with a growing biracial audience that seemed to embody the predominantly integrationist agenda of the mainstream movement, allowed Stevie Wonder to appear at a benefit show at the Apollo Theater in Harlem to raise money for the forthcoming march. Significantly, the show, which generated about $30,000 with its $100 ticket price, featured well-established black and white jazz artists (Art Blakey, Carmen McCrae, Thelonius Monk, and Tony Bennett) alongside sympathetic white Hollywood celebrities such as Paul Newman and Joanne Woodward. For Motown's founder Berry Gordy, keeping this sort of company did no harm to the label's reputation as an emerging force in the wider American entertainment industry at a moment of growing optimism about the prospects for meaningful African American economic progress.[73]

Nevertheless, such public commitment was rare, and the biggest rhythm and blues artists of the day were seldom seen on the frontlines, or heard making forthright statements on behalf of the movement, or headlining benefit concerts. This reticence frustrated both activists and more militant artists. Bernice Johnson Reagon "really thought these people should be sending money. They should be doing benefits.... We thought all of them should be there. But, you know... Sometimes, I think, they couldn't quite see an interest."[74] In 1960, Harry Belafonte had condemned the timidity of many of his fellow

70 *Norfolk Journal and Guide*, April 20, 1963. Bond interview.

71 Bond interview (on Knight); *Norfolk Journal and Guide*, June 1963 (on Sigler); "The Philadelphia Fund Story," n.d., III-C-37, Papers of the National Association for the Advancement of Colored People, Library of Congress, Washington, DC, *Washington African American*, October 15, 17 (on Wilson); Roy Hamilton, letter to James Farmer, September 20, 1963, V:179, CORE Papers.

72 *Amsterdam News*, July 27, August 3 and August 10, 1963.

73 *New York Times*, August 26, 1963; *Amsterdam News*, August 24 and August 31, 1963. For Motown's local activism, see Suzanne E. Smith, *Dancing in the Street* (Cambridge, 1999), 21-53.

74 Reagon interview.

black artists, complaining "I see fear all around me and I have no respect for it." Years later he recalled how he had found it "extremely difficult" to get some of the most popular black musicians of the day involved: "When it came time for show and tell, nobody showed, they had nothing to tell." He said of James Brown, Sam Cooke, Motown, "all of those people distanced themselves from the Movement; not only once removed from it, but sometimes twenty times removed from it."[75]

All of which begs a crucial question: why, given their obvious interest in seeing the struggle for black civil and voting rights and expanded economic opportunity succeed, were so few rhythm and blues artists visible in movement activities, including the march? The most important factor was that the most successful or ambitious rhythm and blues artists were anxious to avoid potentially controversial gestures that might alienate a new, highly lucrative, young white audience from their music at a time when equal access to the economic opportunities and rewards of American consumer-capitalism was widely accepted as one of the movement's principal goals. As Belafonte put it, "I think most of them were in great danger of losing their platform ... they dreaded losing their newly found moments of opportunity."[76]

In this context it is highly significant that 1963 was an extraordinarily integrated moment for popular music, especially among American youth. The emergence of rock and roll in the mid-1950s had sparked an unprecedented crossover of black music into what had once been almost exclusively white popular music record and radio markets. By the end of 1956, one in five *Billboard* pop chart singles was by black artists. While racially specific musical preferences persisted, between roughly 1956 and 1964 it became increasingly difficult to separate black and white youth tastes. In 1958, more than 90 percent of the records on the rhythm and blues singles charts also made the pop charts, while forty-five of the eighty-six Top Ten rhythm and blues hits were actually by white artists. Between 1956 and November 1963, there were 175 Top Ten black chart hits by white artists. Just three months after the March on Washington, *Billboard* suspended its separate black charts, believing that such a racially segregated index of consumer preferences was an anachronism.[77] Although the magazine had to revive a separate black chart just fourteen months later, when white and black musical preferences began to diverge once again, the crucial point is that the march took place at a moment of striking interracial fluidity in the world of popular music.

75 Harry Belafonte, quoted in *Pittsburgh Courier*, August 30, 1960 (first quote); Belafonte interview (second quote).

76 Belafonte interview.

77 For more on this "forgotten interlude" when mass black and white teen popular music tastes were closely aligned, see Ward, *Just My Soul Responding*, 134-42, 174.

In 1963, then, there seemed to be unprecedented opportunities for black rhythm and blues artists to make the leap to mainstream success. If only a gifted and lucky few ever made that jump, fewer still were willing to jeopardize a shot at the big time, or to put their lives at risk, by appearing too militant. "The reason more artists weren't involved," according to SNCC organizer and Mississippi Democratic Freedom Party chair Lawrence Guyot, "was because a large segment of the black population wasn't involved — for the same reason, Terror." This was especially true for Southern-born acts or for those who relied on playing the region for their livelihoods. "Mostly the southern entertainers were a little reluctant to get involved because they still had to live pretty much in that region and they were a little — I don't want to say frightened — reluctant," Guyot explained.[78]

While personal ambitions and fear had a role to play in this caution, another factor was that many musicians had only limited control over where they played or what they did. Fay Bellamy had some sympathy: "They were stars to the masses, but what was really going on in their lives? Did they own their music, or were they working for Berry Gordy or some other company?"[79] As Bellamy appreciated, the basic configuration of economic and managerial power within the recording, touring, and broadcasting industries meant that rhythm and blues was an unlikely source of much forthright comment on American race relations or public support for black insurgency. The whites and a handful of African Americans in positions of real power in the industry focused on market penetration, not political mobilization. "Marvin Gaye had attempted for a number of years to just do something with us ... And I know Stevie Wonder was just trying really hard," remembered Stanley Wise. Before the later 1960s, however, public support from Motown acts tended to be, at best, covert and fleeting: "They just weren't sure how the population would accept that [activism]. Because they were trying to get to their main market and they didn't want to be viewed as militants or belligerents, or that sort of thing."[80] This contrasted with the younger generation of New Jazz players and folksingers, whose credibility and popularity might actually have been imperiled if they had not appeared sufficiently politicized.

One final context helps to explain the low visibility of rhythm and blues artists around early movement activities and at the march. This involves the movement's own confusions about whether or how to use the most popular performers of the day effectively. The civil

78 Lawrence Guyot, interview with Brian Ward and Jenny Walker, December 16, 1995.

79 Bellamy interview.

80 Wise interview.

rights movement was characterized by a genius for improvisation, and there was no grand strategy and little expertise when it came to harnessing the financial, inspirational, or propaganda potential of artists and celebrities. This was especially true when those performers came from what was considered the seamier side of black entertainment, which is how rhythm and blues was sometimes viewed. Even Mahalia Jackson, who unlike many gospel singers of her generation never flirted with secular music, was deemed far too earthy for veteran educator-writer-activist Anna Arnold Hedgeman. The only woman on the march's organizing committee, Hedgeman objected to Jackson's place on the official program, considering her too crude and ill-educated, her music too raw and emotional, for this relentlessly respectable affair.[81] Although she was outvoted on Jackson, Hedgeman's concern for propriety reflected the mainstream movement's powerful middle-class orientation with educators, students, and clergy to the fore. This could create a forbidding environment for singers of humble origins and little education whose repertoire often turned around ribald themes of lust and longing, passion and pleasure that did not accord with the decorous image the movement wished to project.

This tension, coupled with widespread inexperience in dealing with artists and celebrities, was evident at CORE, whose fundraising activities in the early 1960s were largely the responsibility of Val Coleman and Marvin Rich, two middle-aged white men whose fingers were not exactly on the pulse of the latest trends in American popular music, black or white. In theory, CORE volunteer lawyer George Schiffer, who acted as a copyright consultant to Gordy, provided some access to Motown. Yet CORE still managed to send letters asking the label to allow Stevie Wonder and the Marvelettes to play a fundraiser to the wrong management agency and later wrote to one "Berry Gardy of the Motonen Record Company."[82]

SNCC's membership was generally younger and hipper, so it might have been expected to be better at courting black musicians. But as late as 1965, Betty Garman admitted that SNCC's use of popular artists was still a "kind of hit and miss operation," while experience persuaded Julian Bond "that you can't appeal to this class of entertainers… If you are going to get help it's going to be the Belafontes, the Dick Gregorys, the folk people."[83] As Stanley Wise put it, "there was never any real effort on our part unless the artists themselves pushed it. In other words, artists had to do something for us despite

81 Euchner, *Nobody Turn Me Around*, 155.

82 Marvin Rich, letter to Barry Gardy (sic), May 4, 1964, V:179, Congress of Racial Equality Papers, 1941-1967, Manuscript Division, Library of Congress, Washington, DC.

83 Betty Garman, letter to Dick Perez, July 14, 1965, A-IV-70, SNCC Papers. Bond interview.

our hesitancy."[84] This attitude created a stultifying cycle of inactivity. Few black artists were likely to step forward without encouragement from the movement. And even when such encouragement was forthcoming, there was often a sense that musicians were not really respected, consulted properly, or treated as a significant part of the movement beyond a crude fundraising or publicity function. "Those niggers don't ever bother with me until they want something," Mahalia Jackson once fumed to Coretta Scott King about her treatment by the SCLC.[85]

Here, the perspective of Junius Griffin, who worked as director of public relations at the SCLC before joining Motown's publicity department, is revealing. Griffin could recall "no concerted efforts to court soul artists during [my] years with SCLC." Moreover, he agreed that those artists who did appear at rallies or fundraisers thanks to ad hoc arrangements or personal connections were often treated insensitively and left disillusioned. Berry Gordy's sister and Motown executive Esther Gordy once explained to Griffin that "Motown was reluctant to allow its artists to participate in Movement events and activities because they were used as mere addendums to programs and never as an integral part of activities." Invited to swell attendances and income at benefits and rallies, these artists often performed in the aftermath of endless speeches, usually using inferior sound systems that failed to showcase their music effectively. And, recalled Griffin, "when they were ready to leave the next morning, no one was present to say goodbye. Artists and management were highly offended by this practice."[86]

In the final analysis what civil rights organizations wanted most from artists and celebrities was revenue and publicity, and there were always richer, more reliable pickings available in other areas of entertainment than in rhythm and blues. Artists of the stature of Ray Charles or James Brown were attractive propositions, not least because their endorsements might have done much to raise black morale and maybe even some cash. But such artists were usually deemed less effective than jazz musicians, folksingers, or Hollywood stars for reaching the middle-class whites whose consciences and wallets the movement most needed to pry open. These pragmatic and fiscal priorities meant that civil rights organizations were hardly precious about who they approached. SNCC was equally happy courting James Brown and the Beatles, whom Constancia "Dinky" Romilly initially tried to contact through Bobby Dillon (sic) and Joan

84 Wise interview.

85 Coretta Scott King, telephone conversation with Stanley Levison, May 24, 1969, Martin Luther King, Jr. FBI File, Part II: The King-Levison File, Alderman Library, University of Virginia, Charlottesville.

86 Junius Griffin, interview with Brian Ward, July 22, 1996.

Baez. Romiley made no distinction between soul brother number one and the fab four in terms of their fundraising and publicity potential, which was how their usefulness to the movement was primarily conceived.[87] Not that income from most benefit concerts was particularly impressive. SNCC reckoned benefits "seldom net more than 10% to the beneficiary" and listed them among the more "unwise or questionable" methods of fundraising at its disposal.[88]

Conclusion

The music made and shared in Washington on August 28, 1963, generally spoke to the ideas of individual and collective freedom, and to the desire for more harmonious and respectful race relations that permeated the early movement. Of course, the emotional and motivational qualities of music are difficult to capture, even in the most lyrical prose; its political significances and influences are harder still to quantify. Yet, while the emphasis on white folk and the absence of some forms of black music irked some, we know that the music played, sung, and heard at the march profoundly moved many participants and observers. Music somehow captured the essence of the moment, articulating and enhancing the feelings of solidarity and purposefulness, determination and guarded optimism that most marchers felt that day. "When I began to really feel good was when Joan Baez sang 'We Shall Overcome'," recalled Berl Bernhard, white staff director of the Civil Rights Commission. "You just felt 'this is it, this is OK…You could just feel everybody going 'Yes!'"[89] Julian Bond, a self-professed Bob Dylan fan, arrived on the mall eager to hear him and Baez sing, and still managed to sound giddy with excitement half a century later when recalling Mahalia Jackson's performance: "That was a big, big treat," he purred. Equally memorable, however, was a moment late in the afternoon, after the official events had concluded and the professional singers had departed, when Bond joined hands with his SNCC colleagues to sway and sing along in a final rendition of "We Shall Overcome." This reminds us, not just of the significance of that particular song in the movement and at the march, but also of how those who sang as they made their way to, along, and away from the mall helped to create the soundtrack to the event and thereby shape its meanings.[90]

Brian Ward is Professor in American Studies at Northumbria University. His major publications on the US South, the African American experience, and popular music include *Just My Soul Responding: Rhythm and Blues, Black Consciousness and*

87 "SNCC Guide to Fundraising," n.d., C-I-151; Dinky Romilly, letters to Joan Baez and Bobby Dillon (sic), July 9, 1965, B-I-52, both SNCC.

88 "Unwise or Questionable Fund Raising Methods," n.d., A-IV-13, SNCC. A Westbury, NY, "freedom concert" for SNCC in June 1964 generated $2,800, but by the time headliner Nina Simone, the supporting acts, and the venue were paid for, the net profit was under $600. That same summer, when Joan Baez and Pete Seeger waived their fees for another SNCC benefit in New York, the organization netted over $1,300 profit. "New York Friends of SNCC: Balance Sheet (May 1 — Sept. 30, 1964)," A-VI-6, SNCC. Andrew B. Stroud, letter to Jim McDonald, August 16, 1965, E-II-44, CORE-Addendum.

89 Berl Bernhard, interviewed in *Martin Luther King and the March on Washington*, dir. John Akomfrah (Smoking Dog Films, 2013).

90 Julian Bond, "On the Music of the March," August 2013, Witnify: First Person Accounts of the World, http://witnify.com/experience/julian-bond-on-the-music-of-the-march/.

Race Relations (1998); *Radio and the Struggle for Civil Rights in the South* (2004); *The American South and the Atlantic World, Creating Citizenship in the Nineteenth-Century South* (both 2013), and *Creating and Consuming the American South* (2015). He is currently working on two projects: the first about A&R (Artists and Repertoire) workers in the early US recording industry; the second on the Beatles' experiences in the US South.

Transatlantic Legacies

MARTIN LUTHER KING JR.'S RECEPTION AS A THEOLOGIAN AND POLITICAL ACTIVIST IN GERMANY – EAST AND WEST

Michael Haspel

During the past few years I have given several talks on Martin Luther King Jr. as a theologian, especially his understanding of the *Imago Dei*, and how he derived the concepts of human dignity and human rights from his understanding of all people being created in the image of God. I have argued that King should be seen not only as an influential civil rights activist and global freedom icon but also as a serious theologian.[1] Certainly, I have had to deal with the problems of plagiarism in King's past in order to identify what really was his authentic contribution. Yet the really interesting thing for me about these talks has been the different reactions of the audiences in the former West and East German areas. Whereas people in the former states of West Germany, even theology students, remarked that they never thought of King as a theologian but as a political activist, the church-affiliated audiences in the former states of East Germany were astounded that King's status as a theologian was ever in doubt: "Why are you trying to prove that King was a theologian? This is crystal clear. We never perceived him differently."

It is remarkable that King, who became a global celebrity after delivering his famous "I Have a Dream" speech, was perceived by many primarily as a political activist, even though he was an ordained minister, and the Southern Christian Leadership Conference he founded and led was, obviously, a Christian, church-based organization.

A number of activists and scholars, especially referring to his "I Have a Dream" speech, doubt whether King simply used religious rhetoric to mobilize people for his political agenda. Yet, with few exceptions, it took a rather long time before more extensive and qualified research was done on him as a theologian. In the current literature on King, there still seems to be a gap between analysis of his role as a political activist and of his profession as a theologian.

So, why did and do the East German church folk perceive King differently, and first and foremost as a theologian? And does this perception contribute to our understanding of King's dream fifty years ago and, in turn, to our understanding of the unfulfilled dream today? At least it seems to be one of the many untold stories of the March on Washington.

1   See Michael Haspel, "Gottebenbildlichkeit und Menschenwürde. Implikationen für Bildung und öffentlichen Diskurs in Martin Luther King, Jr.'s Konzeption 'Öffentlicher Theologie'," *Zeitschrift für Pädagogik und Theologie* 64, no. 3 (2012): 251-64.

Different Perceptions of King in East and West Germany

Let me start with the question of why King was perceived differently in East Germany and West Germany. King visited Berlin, including East Berlin, on September 12 and 13, 1964. Willy Brandt, who was then the mayor of West Berlin before becoming the secretary of state and later chancellor of the Federal Republic, had invited him to visit West Berlin. Church officials from the East invited him to visit the Eastern part of town as well. It is said that the U.S. State Department took his passport away to prevent him from going to the East, but for reasons not entirely clear, the East German border police let him pass with his American Express card as proof of his identity.[2]

After preaching at the Waldbühne amphitheater in the Western part of the city earlier on September 13th, King was scheduled to preach at the Protestant St. Mary's Church in East Berlin that evening. So many people wanted to listen to King that an additional appearance in the Church of St. Sophia was spontaneously arranged that evening, and this location was also packed. His visit made an enormous impression on the Protestant churches in East Germany, which had been cut off from the Protestant churches in West Germany since the Berlin Wall had been erected in 1961. They were in a process of defining their way as churches not for or against but simply within a supposedly socialist society.[3] Pressure from the communist regime increased on Protestant churches after the Wall was built and it became nearly impossible to leave the country. Thus, East German Protestants were looking for their own way in the tradition of the Confessing Church, which had resisted the influence of National Socialism on the church during the 1930s and 1940s. They were also trying to build strong ecumenical relations, especially with countries that were also under communist rule, or with churches that were affiliated with the anti-colonial and anti-apartheid struggle. King was an ideal model for them of a theologian struggling for freedom and justice — and the communist rulers were not suspicious of him or his ideas because they saw him as a political activist fighting against the oppression, exploitation, colonialism, and imperialism of the capitalist superpower, as a representative of the "other America." This, in turn, made the U.S. government wary of him during the Cold War with its pronounced anti-communist tendencies.

It was the Christian Democratic Union (CDU) in East Germany seeking contact with King and publicly endorsing his actions in the civil rights protests of 1963 that made him a global icon. This party was created in

2   There are various versions of this story. For the most accurate account, see Maria Höhn and Martin Klimke, *A Breath of Freedom: The Civil Rights Struggle, African American GIs, and Germany* (New York, 2010), 100. Given the political situation and the character of the regime in East Germany, it is very unlikely that a border guard and his immediate superior could have made a decision of such importance on their own. It is more likely that GDR intelligence agents were informed that King planned to visit East Berlin and decided to let him enter to avoid negative publicity. Perhaps secret talks between church and government officials had also taken place to come to an agreement about how the visit could and should unfold. Unfortunately, we do not yet know of any documentation for these theories.

3   For the history and the development of theological reflection of the Protestant churches in East Germany, see Michael Haspel, *Politischer Protestantismus und gesellschaftliche Transformation. Ein Vergleich der evangelischen Kirchen in der DDR und der schwarzen Kirchen in der Bürgerrechtsbewegung in den USA* (Tübingen, 1997).

the so-called Democratic Bloc to attract Christians and, by this token, to include them in the system of communist rule. Several other parties besides the ruling Socialist Unity Party (SED) were permitted in order to make the political system look diverse. However, the whole Democratic Bloc was strictly controlled by the communist regime.[4]

Gerald Götting, a CDU party functionary, had tried to invite King to officially visit East Berlin during the dates he was supposed to be in the Western part of the city. We can assume that he did not take this action without previously consulting with the communist authorities. For the East German state it would have been prestigious to host King officially in East Berlin and thus gain legitimacy in the international public arena. Though King replied courteously, he declined the invitation. There was further correspondence between Götting and King.[5] However, King apparently never accepted another invitation to a communist country, including East Germany.

It is remarkable that even though King had refused the official invitation on the grounds of time constraints, he did change his mind later and not only visited East Berlin but even delivered two sermons there. He probably wished not to be an official "guest of the Communist state" but rather a guest of a Christian church audience. We still know rather few details of this visit, which is barely mentioned in literature on King and the civil rights movement.[6] At home quarrels about the Mississippi Freedom Democratic Party and the upcoming Democratic National Convention were in full swing. Sometimes, the literature mentions only that King went to Europe for a couple of days and places more emphasis on the audience King, his wife Coretta Scott King, and Ralph Abernathy had with the pope. For example, Peter Ling, after going into the details of the domestic political turmoil, reports briefly:

> In mid-September, King, Coretta, and the attention-craving Abernathy went on a short European tour that included Berlin, Rome, Madrid, and London. The SCLC preachers had an audience with Pope Paul VI but, apart from two days in Spain, there were too many speeches and press conferences for this to be a vacation.[7]

5 Sekretariat des Hauptvorstandes der Christlich-Demokratischen Union Deutschlands, ed., *Martin Luther Kings Vermächtnis* (Berlin, 1968).

6 Though King emphasized during his visit how special the experience was for him, he did not refer extensively to it afterwards, either. This is surprising because his father had been in Berlin exactly thirty years before him to attend a world conference of Baptist ministers—an experience that moved him to change his and his son's name from Michael to Martin Luther. In other words, after that visit to Berlin, Michael King Jr. had become Martin Luther King Jr. Whereas his father had visited during the Nazi period, King himself faced the dividing line of the Cold War. See inter alia Peter J. Ling: *Martin Luther King, Jr.* (London, 2011), 11.

7 Ling, *King*, 174-75. There is also a brief account in David J. Garrow, *Bearing the Cross: Martin Luther King, Jr., and the Southern Christian Leadership Conference* (New York, 1988 [1986]), 351. Taylor Branch gives more details about the Berlin visit but also puts the emphasis on the audience with the pope in *Pillar of Fire: America in the King Years 1963-65* (New York, 1999), 483-85. Even the FBI seems to have been more concerned with King's audience with the pope, which Hoover wanted to inhibit, than with his visit to Berlin. See David J. Garrow, *The FBI and Martin Luther King, Jr.* (New York, 1983 [1981]), 121. See also Höhn and Klimke, *A Breath of Freedom*, 104.

4 For the development of the Christian Democratic Union in the GDR, see Michael Richter and Martin Rißmann, *Die* *Ost-CDU. Beiträge zu ihrer Entstehung und Entwicklung* (Weimar, 1995); "Sozialismus aus christlicher Verantwortung? Die Ost-CDU und die Kirchenpolitik in der DDR," *epd-Dokumentation* 20 (2012).

It seems that something extraordinary happened on September 13, 1964, when King preached in two churches in East Berlin. The communist state *via* the Christian Democratic Party endorsed King's political claims. After he was murdered, they organized memorial speeches and rallies at universities and other public venues. For them, King was a fighter against the capitalist colonial powers, which allegedly oppressed the working class in the non-communist countries. He was seen as a popular witness against the capitalist enemy. His Christian motivation was termed "humanist heritage" and was regarded as compatible with the communist ideology. Since he was a Christian minister struggling, in their understanding, as a political activist against racist oppression and capitalist exploitation, he could be presented to the so-called reactionary or bourgeois Christians as a role model, and in this function also communicate that Christians as humanists could and should struggle against capitalism and support the construction of a socialist society.[8] Interestingly, this was similar to West German protesters' interpretation of King. Among them, King was mainly viewed as a political activist and as a leader of a protest movement against injustice and oppression. He was seen through a political rather than a theological lens.

That King was endorsed by the communists and their forced allies constituted both a chance and a problem for the Protestant churches. On the one hand, it was safe for them to refer to King and his liberating philosophy and activism because the regime did this also. On the other hand, it was dangerous to challenge the party's authority with regard to the political interpretation of King. This made it possible and nearly necessary to interpret King differently from the official line without conflicting with it. Thus, the churches interpreted King as a "progressive" religious leader and theologian:

> In the shorter term, the repercussions of King's visit were felt primarily in the religious sphere. East German publishing houses thus considered it politically safe to extensively publish texts by and about him in the following years. In this way, these publishers helped incorporate King into official doctrine by insisting that "Christianity and the humanistic goals of socialism" were not opposed to one another.[9]

Interpreting King as a Christian and theologian was a very appropriate solution — though it might not have been a conscious and strategic

8   See Sekretariat des Hauptvorstandes der Christlich-Demokratischen Union Deutschlands, ed., *Martin Luther Kings Vermächtnis* (Berlin, 1968).

9   Höhn and Klimke, *A Breath of Freedom*, 104.

decision. The circumstances forced the Protestant churches in East Germany to interpret King this way, yet they may have found a deeper truth in doing so. His theological understanding of human dignity and human rights provided a sound basis for Christians in East Germany—who were confronted with a communist regime violating basic human rights every day, oppressing Christians and the Christian churches in all venues of public life—to engage in theological reflection. King's emphasis on the biblical concepts of justice and peace influenced the church-based peace movement and the civil movement, which was crucial to the Peaceful Revolution of 1989. Höhn and Klimke conclude in their treatise on King's visit to Berlin:

> King's writings and actions, as well as his theology, did undoubtedly serve as an inspiration for the East German opposition movement in the long run. Yet the exact ways in which his reception and the civil rights movement of the early 1960s, among a multitude of other factors, contributed to the emergence of a civil society based in East German churches that would eventually bring down the communist regime in 1989 remains to be explored.[10]

However, there are many reports of how King was present in spirit in the protests in East Germany through readings of his texts, applications of his methods, and songs from the movement.[11] Heinrich W. Grosse, one of the first scholars in Germany to study King and translate his works, reports that on November 9, 1989, the day the Berlin Wall was opened, a minister from East Germany made this connection explicit in writing to him: "Finally, the wall is unnecessary. One of my sons started from October 2 [to participate in the demonstrations] every Monday in Leipzig. I think many were thinking of Martin Luther King as an example."[12]

Was King a Theological Thinker in His Own Right?

Was King a theologian in the sense of being a productive theological thinker?[13] To be sure, King received a doctorate in systematic theology. But in exploring this question, one has to consider two facts: It is beyond any doubt that King used other scholars' material excessively for his academic work, public speeches, sermons, and publications. So was he only reproducing and compiling material from others or generating something unique? The second issue is the claim that

10 Ibid.

11 See Britta Waldschmidt-Nelson, "'We Shall Overcome': The Impact of the African American Freedom Struggle on Race Relations and Social Protest in Germany after World War II," in *The Transatlantic Sixties: Europe and the United States in the Counterculture Decade*, ed. Grzegorz Kosc, Clara Juncker, Sharon Monteith, and Britta Waldschmidt-Nelson (Bielefeld, 2013), 66-97, 77.

12 See Heinrich W. Grosse, "Die Macht der Armen. Martin Luther Kings Kampf gegen Rassismus, Armut und Krieg," in *Martin Luther King: Leben, Werk und Vermächtnis*, ed. Michael Haspel and Britta Waldschmidt-Nelson (Weimar, 2008), 15.

13 I avoid the term "original" here since Keith D. Miller convincingly makes the point that we should differentiate between "originality" and "creativity" in light of his analysis of King's oratory, in which he borrows heavily from other sources yet creates something new out of it (see Keith D. Miller, *Voice of Deliverance: The Language of Martin Luther King, Jr., and Its Sources* [Athens, 1992], 9).

many of his publicized works were actually largely written by his friends and coworkers.

King's use of other authors' material has been widely discussed.[14] Though it is evident that King did not always follow academic rules adequately, I don't think that the charges against King are strong enough to disregard his theological thought. Keith D. Miller and Richard Lischer in their analyses amply demonstrated that King used material from sermon textbooks for many of his sermons and speeches, including the "I Have a Dream" oration. However, they showed equally convincingly that King's overarching achievement was to synthesize the material and make new texts from these elements, creating a new artwork, so to speak, that served a special purpose.[15] Miller emphasized that King was perhaps the first ever to synthesize the black oral and white written oratory and preaching traditions, which both included certain classic and common motifs and formulations. One could compare King's accomplishments to those of a chef. While most dishes may be based on the same basic ingredients, the outcome of his recipes might be quite distinct:

> King adapted material in a highly creative way. No matter what he borrowed or how often, after leaving Boston University, he managed never to sound stilted and artificial. Instead, he paradoxically, but invariably, sounded exactly like himself. His long training in the folk pulpit accounts for his extraordinary ability to use others' language to become himself. This training also explains why his audiences never objected to his borrowing and why an entire generation of scholars failed to guess that he mined sources frequently. His skill in transporting procedures of folk preaching into print ensured that his borrowed lines fit his persona more closely than did the words of ghostwriters.[16]

This insight can also be applied to King's theological work as a whole. He used others' material extensively, but his original synthesis and recreation of that material generated some of the most significant theological texts of the twentieth century. As Richard Lischer put it, "Most scholars would have published their thoughts on justice and history in learned journals. But the circumstances and choices of King's life were such that the only verbal medium he had at his disposal was the sermon. He hammered out his Christian theology on the anvil of the pulpit."[17]

14 Lischer's assessment of King's student papers is very blunt: "King's Crozer papers reveal a highly derivative style of thinking and a pattern of citation that often transgresses the boundary between mere unoriginality and outright plagiarism." Richard Lischer, *The Preacher King: Martin Luther King, Jr. and the Word That Moved America* (New York, 1995), 62. For the history of the discovery of King's plagiarism, see Clayborne Carson, *Martin 's Dream: My Journey and the Legacy of Martin Luther King Jr.: A Memoir* (New York, 2013), 123-33. King's dissertation was subjected to a formal investigation after his death. It is reprinted in Clayborne Carson, ed., *The Papers of Martin Luther King, Jr.*, 6 vols. (henceforth *Papers of MLK*) (Berkeley, 1994), 2:339-544, where King's usage of other material is indicated, as well as in the introduction to the volume (25-26) and the introduction to the reprinted document (339).

15 See Miller, *Voice of Deliverance*; Lischer, *The Preacher King*.

16 Miller, *Voice of Deliverance*, 195. In this mention of ghostwriters, Miller refers not to King's sermons but to his policy statements. See ibid., 193.

17 Lischer, *The Preacher King*, 8.

Introduction and
Prologue · Music and
the March · **Transatlantic
Legacies** · Different Views
and Voices · Visual Histories and
Cultural Memories

Some of the published versions of King's sermons and speeches differed significantly from the originals, prompting some observers to claim that the published King was not the original King. This was first discovered when the published version of the homily King delivered spontaneously at the first mass meeting that sparked the Montgomery bus boycott at Holt Street Baptist Church, which happened to be recorded on tape, did not match the original wording.[18] The emphasis had shifted from justice to freedom. Some argue that this must have been intentional to make it more appealing to a broader white audience.[19]

The sixth volume of the King papers, published in 2007,[20] documents the contents of a private file of sermon materials that King had kept in his study, which were later discovered in his basement. His widow made them available in 1997. It provides evidence that King penned his own sermons.[21] He was the one creating the theology of his sermons and mass meeting speeches. The editors describe King's process:

> King continually revised his favorite sermons to increase their rhetorical effectiveness as well as to incorporate new themes and contemporary references. The documents illustrate his characteristic ability to weave together biblical texts and ideas from various sources — the sermons of other ministers, the insights of philosophers, passages from literature and Christian hymns, contemporary news and set pieces — into a coherent, persuasive presentation.[22]

It is also clear that the published material, including his sermons in *Strength to Love*, were edited supposedly to make them less provocative to a broader public. The editors of the King papers argue that while officials of the original publisher, Harper, "agreed with King's broad view of race relations and may have privately cheered his methods and his language calling for the attainment of social justice, in their editing of King's sermons, they reworked his sentences with the purpose of toning down what they saw as the militant character of his speech."[23]

All in all, one can conclude that King used others' material extensively and often without adequate citation. Yet his theological and other writings are authentic because he created new texts out of the given material, including sound theological analyses and arguments.

18 See the published sections in Martin Luther King Jr., *Stride Toward Freedom: The Montgomery Story* (New York, 1958), 61-63, with the transcribed version (Carson, ed., *Papers of MLK* (Berkeley, 1996), 3:71-79, and see the introductory note on p. 5.

19 See James H. Cone, "Martin Luther King, Jr.: Black Theology — Black Church," *Theology Today* 40 (1984): 409-20, 410-12; idem, "The Theology of Martin Luther King, Jr.," *Union Seminary Quarterly Review* 40, no. 4 (1986): 21-39, 32; David J. Garrow, "The Intellectual Development of Martin Luther King, Jr.: Influences and Commentaries," *Union Seminary Quarterly Review* 40, no. 4 (1986): 5-20, 6; idem, *Bearing the Cross: Martin Luther King, Jr., and the Southern Christian Leadership Conference* (New York, 1988 [1986]), 111-12.

20 Carson, ed., *Papers of MLK* (Berkeley, 2007), vol. 6.

21 See ibid., 2-3.

22 Carson, "Introduction," in ibid., 3.

23 Ibid., 40. See also 36-44. King also received assistance from his staff, especially in drafting policy statements.

Without casting doubt on the support provided by his own staff and professional editors, we can still claim from the strong evidence that King himself was the mind behind the published work. The published papers and available archival material provide a solid ground for an account of his theology.[24]

King's Theology as the Foundation of His Political Activism

Various facets of King's theological thought and its relationship to his political activism can be discerned.[25] One is his understanding of human dignity based on the biblical image of all human beings created in the image of God. The second is his understanding of the church, which includes the mission of promoting justice in this world grounded in the biblical vision of the Kingdom of God. A third dimension is King's application of the concepts of civil religion while simultaneously acting as a prophet of Protestant theology and the religion of the republic. Finally, one needs to look at King's homiletics, his paramount emphasis on freedom, human rights, and human dignity, as well as his universalizing tendency, as fundamental features of his theology. These stem from the American branches of Reformed and non-conformist theology and the African American theological and church traditions and have no parallels in European theological discourse. His synthesis of liberal Boston Personalism and Niebuhr's Christian Realism is especially interesting. It is important to note that his social theory and anthropology were deeply grounded in theology. As King stated:

> Personalism's insistence that only personality — finite and infinite — is ultimately real strengthened me in two convictions: it gave me metaphysical and philosophical grounding for the idea of a personal God, and it gave me a metaphysical basis for the *dignity and worth of all human personality*.[26]

King's call to engage in the political struggle for human dignity and human rights cannot be separated from the theological concept of *Imago Dei*, which is a fundamental component of black religion and

24 The editors of the published sermon material in *Papers of MLK*, vol. 6, claim to have gleaned novel insights from this material (see, in addition to the "Introduction," 1-44, also Carson, *Martin's Dream*, 173-83). While its publication is undoubtedly advantageous for research, similar evidence was previously available in the documents in the Martin Luther King, Jr., Archive at Boston University (BU), including drafts of *Strength to Love*. The list of documents I consulted and excerpted in the early 1990s is documented in Michael Haspel, *Politischer Protestantismus*, 374. However, I have not yet been able to systematically compare the documents at BU with the published documents in Carson, ed., *Papers of MLK*, vol. 6.

The example of the sermon "The Death of Evil upon the Seashore" seems to sustain my impression. It was available at BU (Martin Luther King, Jr., "The Death of Evil upon the Seashore (Exodus 14:30), Sermon to be Delivered at the Cathedral of St. John the Divine. NYC, Thursday, May 17, 1956." BU Box 119 A, Folder XVI-16, 2 of 2, 6) and was already printed in *Papers of MLK*, 3:256-62. Also several versions of the draft of this sermon for *Strength to Love* are at BU and one of them is printed in *Papers of MLK*, 6:504-14. Thus, it seems that even before the basement discovery a sufficient number of documents was accessible to reconstruct King's theological thinking and concepts. This does not diminish the value that the additional material and its publication provide in broadening the basis for research and reconstruction. The major conclusion the editors of the King papers came to was that King's faith, theology, and pastoral identity formed the foundation of his civil rights activism and leadership. This conclusion had already been elaborated in the 1990s in theological work such as Miller, *Voice of Deliverance*; Lischer, *The Preacher King*; and Haspel, *Politischer Protestantismus*. Carson's introduction to *Papers of MLK*, vol. 6, is actually a fine theological account of King's work.

25 For a more comprehensive analysis, see Michael Haspel, *Politischer Protestantismus*, 258-83; Michael Haspel, "Martin Luther King, Jr. — Die theologischen Wurzeln seines sozialen Handelns," *in respect* 1 (2007): 24-31.

26 King, *Stride Toward Freedom*, 100. Italics added.

abolitionist theology. King argued: "All men, created alike in the image of God, are inseparably bound together. This is at the very heart of the Christian gospel."[27] His theological critique of segregation follows from this understanding: "Racial segregation is a blatant denial of the unity which we have in Christ; for in Christ there is neither Jew nor Gentile, bond nor free, Negro nor white."[28]

These aspects of human dignity based in the ideas of all human beings being created in God's image and being interrelated find their expression in King's concept of the "beloved community," which refers to a vision of a society in which people live together with fundamental respect, overcoming hatred and violent conflict. This grounds his claims for justice and reconciliation in the integration of the voices of biblical prophets and Jesus's teaching of loving one's enemy. Richard Lischer argues:

> Much traditional theology, including his own Baptist heritage, isolated "faith" and "love" as successive moments in the life of the believer. In King's vocabulary the two are inseparably joined. There can be no discussion of faith as the intellectual or spiritual preparation for love, or of love as the inevitable response to faith. Faith assumes two modalities at the same time: trust and love.[29]

Closely related to the concept of the beloved community is King's understanding of "redemptive suffering." Although his contemporaries and other theologians also often criticized this idea,[30] it was essential to his understanding and justification of nonviolence, as the following quotations in *Stride Toward Freedom* make clear: "Through nonviolent resistance the Negro will be able to rise to the noble height of opposing the unjust system while loving the perpetrators of the system";[31] and "The way of nonviolence means a willingness to suffer and sacrifice.... The answer is found in the realization that unearned suffering is redemptive."[32] This latter statement, in turn, is grounded in his belief that God is on the side of justice in the end: "Let us realize that as we struggle for justice and freedom we have cosmic companionship."[33]

28 King, *Stride Toward Freedom*, 205.

29 Lischer, *The Preacher King*, 229. On the development of King's terminology from "beloved community" to the "Kingdom of God," see 234.

30 See Anthony B. Pinn, *Why, Lord? Suffering and Evil in Black Theology* (New York, 1995).

31 King, *Stride Toward Freedom*, 214.

32 Ibid., 216, 103.

33 Martin Luther King Jr., "A Look to the Future. Address Delivered at the Highlander Folk School's Twenty-Fifth Anniversary Observance. September 2, 1957." BU Box 54, Folder VII-14, 13 (*Papers*, 4:269-76). See also "Annual Address Delivered at the First Annual Institute on Non-Violence and Social Change under the Auspices of the Montgomery Improvement Association, 3 December 1956, Holt Street Baptist Church, Montgomery, Alabama." BU Box 2, Folder I-11, 14 (*Papers*, 3:451-63).

27 Martin Luther King, Jr., "For all — A Non-Segregated Society. You Are All One in Christ Jesus (Galatians 3, 28)." BU Box 3, Folder I-11, 5 of 9, 1 (*Papers of Martin Luther King, Jr.*, 4:123-25). On King's understanding of the *Imago Dei*, see Richard W. Wills, *Martin Luther King, Jr. and the Image of God* (Oxford, 2009). Though I basically do agree with Wills's analysis, his methodology is flawed in that he refers to King's student papers, which are basically reproductions of other texts, as we have discussed above, as material proving some of King's theological concepts as if they were his original work.

34 Martin Luther King Jr., "The Death of Evil upon the Seashore (Exodus 14:30)." Printed in Papers of MLK 3:256-62, quotation on 261-62. This sentence is not in the published version of the sermon in Martin Luther King Jr., Strength to Love (Philadelphia, 1981), 77-86, nor in the approved typescript printed in Papers of MLK 6:504-14.

35 King, Stride Toward Freedom, 36. See also "What Is Man? An Address Delivered before the Chicago Sunday Evening Club. Orchestra Hall, January 12, 1958. Broadcast over Station WIND." BU Box 1, Folder II, 1-2.

36 Martin Luther King Jr., "The Mission to the Social Frontiers." BU Box 119 A, Folder XVI-17, 3 of 6, 8-9.

37 King, Stride Toward Freedom, 205.

38 Ibid, 207-208.

39 See Lewis Baldwin, The Voice of Conscience: The Church in the Mind of Martin Luther King, Jr. (Oxford, 2010); C. Eric Lincoln and Lawrence H. Mamiya, The Black Church in the African American Experience, 5th ed. (Durham, 1992 [1990]); Doug McAdam, Political Process and the Development of Black Insurgency 1930-1970 (Chicago, 1985 [1982]); Aldon D. Morris, The Origins of the Civil Rights Movement: Black Communities Organizing for Change (New York, 1984); Michael Haspel, "Martin Luther King, Jr. als ökumenischer Sozialethiker," ÖR 47, no. 3 (1998): 375-82; idem, "Martin Luther King Jr. als Theologe, Kirchenführer und Bürgerrechtler. Die Kontextualisierung Schwarzer Theologie und die Mobilisierung der schwarzen Kirchen in der Bürgerrechtsbewegung," in Martin Luther King: Leben, Werk und Vermächtnis, Scripturae 1, ed. Michael Haspel and Britta >>

>>Waldschmidt-Nelson (Weimar, 2008), 67-86.

40 Cf. Robert N. Bellah, "Civil Religion in America," Daedalus 96, no. 1 (1967): 1-21.

"God has a great plan for this world. His purpose is to achieve a world where all men will live together as brothers, and where every man recognizes the dignity and worth of all human personality."[34]

Against this backdrop, King developed his theological concept of the church. In King's ecclesiology, it is crystal clear that the church not only has to deal with otherworldly affairs but also with questions of justice, equality, and freedom in this world. King declared repeatedly: "Any religion that professes to be concerned with the souls of men and is not concerned with the slums that damn them, the economic conditions that strangle them, and the social conditions that cripple them is a dry-as-dust religion. Such a religion is the kind the Marxists like to see — an opiate of the people."[35]

From the very beginning of his ministry in Montgomery, King's church, as a religious and a civic institution, took part in the struggle against segregation. Again, this was not only in an instrumental sense but also in his theological understanding of the church, which was deeply rooted in the tradition of the urban black church and had been handed down to him by his father and his predecessor in the pulpit in Montgomery. As King put it: "Whenever a crisis emerges in society the church has a significant role to play."[36] He leaves no doubt about what the task of the church is: "The church ... must face its historic obligation in this crisis. In the final analysis the problem of race is not a political but a moral issue. ... The task of conquering segregation is an inescapable *must* confronting the church today."[37] For King, theology has to be transformed into action: "It is not enough for the church to be active in the realm of ideas; it must move out into the arena of social action."[38] This ecclesiology was critical to the success of the modern southern civil rights movement when other civil rights organizations were made illegal in the South.[39]

The third dimension of King's theological identity was his use of concepts from two religions: Christianity and civil religion. Robert Bellah's concept of civil religion describes the religious strands in the philosophy and rituals of the American republic.[40] Within this civil religion, there is a belief shared by most Americans that all people are created equal by God, independent of their religious orientation. This concept had been widely accepted in the last several decades and was also applied to the interpretation of King's public oratory. Some scholars have thus concluded that King's use of religious language was only a rhetorical tool.

Yet I believe King's religious language was also a matter of conviction, and that Winthrop Hudson's concept of "two religions" can be applied to understanding and interpreting King's theology. One religion is evangelical Protestantism, which was so pervasive in the eighteenth and nineteenth centuries that even non-Protestant denominations were modeled upon it. The other he calls the "religion of the republic."[41] Hudson's differentiation between the two religions is still useful because it reminds us that the "religion of the republic" did not emerge in a situation of religious pluralism. The religion of the republic bridged mainly the differences among Protestants and the gap between believers and non-believers. Since the American myth starts with people longing for the freedom to practice their religion, it is sometimes overlooked that most colonists did not view religion as a major concern. In this context, the "religion of the republic" emerged as the original form of civil religion, embraced by an overarching majority of the people as part of their culture, as a source of the guiding principles of the commonwealth, and as a truly American phenomenon.

What was later termed civil religion can be found in King's very first public appearance. He based his central concept of human dignity on the fundamental civil religious principle of all men being created equal, quoting Lincoln and appealing to his unfulfilled legacy. To be sure, King used this widely accepted code not only strategically but also as a fundamental part of his theology, along with the other basic convictions of the religion of the republic. He used biblical sources as well as the rhetoric and iconography of civil religion. His use of President Abraham Lincoln and the United States Constitution is legion.[42] But he also critically engaged with the ideology of civil religion throughout his career, invoking its promises and referring to those that were broken. In other words, "[King's] civil religion was succeeded by its demythologization."[43] He used the major symbols of civil religion to criticize the current injustices in contemporary politics, turning civil religion into normative arguments in a conflict rather than simply as a means to reduce conflict by means of a shared set of symbols.

All in all, the examples cited here show that King's religious language was not merely a rhetorical tool to communicate his political claims. The biblical grounding and theological foundation are actually

41 Winthrop S. Hudson, *Religion in America: An Historical Account of the Development of American Religious Life*, 2nd ed. (New York, 1973), 109-30.

42 For Lincoln's relation to religion and its reception, see Jörg Nagler and Michael Haspel, eds., *Lincoln und die Religion. Das Konzept der Nation unter Gott*, Scripturae 2 (Weimar, 2012).

43 Lischer, *The Preacher King*, 11.

the prevalent and predominant dimensions in King's thought. He employed the language of civil religion to lend more weight to his argument; the legal arguments were important for him, the founding fathers of the United States and the Constitution were significant. But most fundamental was his Christian conviction that God had created all human beings to be equal in His or Her image.

We can see this in the fourth dimension of his theological *gestalt*, his homiletic and oratorical style, which I want to illustrate briefly using King's "I Have a Dream" speech, drawing upon Keith D. Miller's persuasive analysis of it in *Voice of Deliverance*. Miller argues that the address was actually not a speech but a sermon, evoking in the decisive passage no less than three biblical references — to the prophets Amos, Isiah, and Daniel. He not only shows which material King used and how he combined and arranged it but also argues convincingly that the dream part of the speech was even a folk sermon. After all the inductive arguments in the other speeches at the March on Washington, which started from the experiences of oppression, King arranged his oratory deductively, first referring to secular authorities such as Abraham Lincoln and Thomas Jefferson, then referring to biblical authorities. The references to the secular authorities actually did not describe a dream — they resulted in the description of a nightmare. Only when he started to refer to Amos — "Let justice roll down like waters and righteousness like a mighty stream!" — did the dream unfold — and the mode of the talk changed into a sermon. King abandoned the written typescript and began extemporizing. Miller states:

> As he catalogued an American nightmare, King essentially argued that the finest secular presences, including Jefferson and Lincoln, had failed miserably. The "architects of our republic" offered a "promissory note" that pledged liberty. But for blacks the note proved "a bad check," a check "marked insufficient funds." By introducing divine authority after secular authority, which had proven inadequate, this new Biblical prophet suggested that an impatient God would now overrule secular forces and install justice without delay. When God ordains for justice to roll down like waters, the flood must eventually cross the Mason-Dixon line. When valleys are exalted, racism will end. When the stone of hope emerges from the mountain, it will smash the flawed kingdom of segregation.[44]

44 Miller, *Voice of Deliverance,* 145-46.

King did not make a concrete political claim, but he provided a biblical vision of justice that was ultimately radically political.

King as a Contextual Theologian and Thus Political Activist

Ultimately, King's theology can be qualified as *contextual* theology. Analysis of the cultural, social, and societal context is built into the very concept of his theology. Therefore, King's theology focuses not only on political and social action but also provides the categories for linking theological interpretation, ethical orientation, and political action.

Most models of contextual theology emphasize one aspect of a given social context as the criterion for contextualization. In many feminist approaches, it is the (subjective) experience of women. In African and Asian models of enculturation, it is the respective culture. Liberation theology focuses on a certain kind of societal structure.[45] Elsewhere I have argued that these models may produce inadequate results since they only pay attention to one level of society. The concept of theological contextualization I have suggested draws on the elements of the "life-world" developed by Jürgen Habermas in his *Theory of Communicative Action*.[46] Methodologically, contextualization is structured according to the subjective, objective-cultural, and social world relations. I suggest that with these three dimensions one can sufficiently analyze a social context and reconstruct theology in a way fitting its communicative, cultural, and political challenges while remaining true to its original intention.

With regard to King's theology, my claim is twofold: First, I want to propose that King actually employed such a method of contextualization. Second, I argue that this was a necessary, though not sufficient, precondition for his contribution to the civil rights movement and its success.

King was prepared enough to arrange his contextual theology to support the civil rights movement. His academic training equipped him with the intellectual and theological tools to analyze the mental, ideological, economic, and political schemes underlying racism and exploitation. While at Boston University he took sociology classes in summer school at Harvard. King was fully aware that segregation and racism were structurally caused and also had subjective psychological effects:

45 See Stephen B. Bevans, *Models of Contextual Theology* (Maryknoll, NY, 2002).

46 See Michael Haspel, *Sozialethik in der globalen Gesellschaft. Grundlagen und Orientierung in protestantischer Perspektive* (Stuttgart, 2011), 57-61.

This is the ultimate tragedy of segregation. It not only harms one physically but injures one spiritually. It scars the soul and degrades the personality. It inflicts the segregated with a false sense of inferiority, while confirming the segregator in a false estimate of his own superiority.[47]

Moreover, he systematically combined the subjective experience of segregation with its objective-cultural and societal causes: "Men convinced themselves that a system which was so economically profitable must be morally justifiable. ... This tragic attempt to give moral sanction to an economically profitable system gave birth to the doctrine of white supremacy."[48] And he was clear about the social preconditions of the civil rights movement:

The last half century has seen crucial changes in the life of the American Negro. The social upheavals of the two world wars, the great depression, and the spread of the automobile have made it both possible and necessary for the Negro to move away from his former isolation on the rural plantation. The decline of agriculture and the parallel growth of industry have drawn large numbers of Negroes to urban centers and brought about a gradual improvement in their economic status.[49]

King's concept of theology stressed that religion had to start with people's social reality in order to change it according to the prophetic visions of freedom and justice:

Certainly, otherworldly concerns have a deep and significant place in all religions worthy of the name. ... Religion, at its best, deals not only with man's preliminary concerns but with his inescapable ultimate concern. ... But a religion true to its nature must also be concerned about man's social conditions.[50]

King employed a complex method of theological contextualization that centered on analyses of the subjective, objective-cultural, and social-societal world relations. This enabled him to start his theology from social reality and aim to change it. His ability to fulfill this theological enterprise so brilliantly fueled the civil rights movement with intellectually sound and emotionally moving visions and spurred action accordingly. Thus, the East German understanding of King

47 King, *Stride Toward Freedom*, 37.

48 King, *Strength to Love*, 44.

49 King, *Stride Toward Freedom*, 189-90. King concludes: "And so [the Negro's] rural plantation background gradually gave way to urban industrial life" ("The Mission to the Social Frontiers," BU Box 119 A, Folder XVI-17, 3 of 6, 5). See also "Annual Address Delivered at the First Annual Institute on Non-Violence and Social Change," 7. Cf. Baker-Fletcher, *Somebodyness*, 45-56.

50 King, *Stride Toward Freedom*, 36. This new approach was shared by other ministers such as Wyatt Tee Walker, who stated: "I didn't see that preaching, visiting sick, praying with troubled people, and burying the dead was the fulfillment of the ministerial responsibility. I had to be concerned about whether people had enough to eat, what kind of homes they lived in, etc." (Interview, Moorland-Spingarn Research Center, Manuscript Division, Howard University [Washington, DC, 1967], 7).

as a theologian might actually lead us to a better understanding of King the civil rights leader. In the words of James Cone, one of the greatest articulators of Black Liberation Theology: "... if one wishes to know what it means to be a theologian, there is no better example than Martin Luther King, Jr."[51]

51 James H. Cone, *The Theology of Martin Luther King, Jr.*, 36.

Michael Haspel is Executive Director of the Evangelische Akademie Thüringen in Neudietendorf near Erfurt, Thuringia, and holds an extraordinary professorship in systematic theology at the Friedrich Schiller University in Jena. His research interests include social ethics, peace ethics, human rights, and church and society. In his dissertation, he compared the role the Protestant churches in former East Germany played in the democracy movement to the role of black churches in the civil rights movement.

THE MARCH ON WASHINGTON AND THE AMERICAN CIVIL RIGHTS MOVEMENT AS AN INSPIRATION FOR SOCIAL PROTEST MOVEMENTS IN WEST AND EAST GERMANY

Heinrich Grosse

In memory of Ulli Thiel (1943-2014),
a "drum major for peace"

The March on Washington and Its Echo in the West German Media

In August 1963, the leading national newspapers of West Germany, as well as many local ones, published front-page articles on the goals, the preparation, and performance of the March on Washington.[1] Conservative newspapers like *Die Welt* and liberal newspapers like the *Frankfurter Rundschau* essentially agreed that the fight against racial discrimination and the demand for equal rights for African Americans in the U.S. were justified. The journalists, even though some of them were probably not entirely free of racial prejudices themselves, praised the March for being such a positive event without any of the anticipated outbreaks of violence. The correspondent of *Die Welt*, for example, wrote, "A big and dignified demonstration... the 'March for Jobs and Freedom' of the black citizens of America, in which also many thousands of whites participated, the biggest mass demonstration for political and social demands that ever took place in the capital, proceeded in a dignified manner, peacefully, without violent incidents."[2]

Several newspapers also emphasized the fact that leading representatives of Protestant and Catholic churches, and of Jewish organizations, were key in the March.[3] Martin Luther King Jr. was distinguished as "the most prominent of all Negro leaders,"[4] and as a "champion of the freedom movement" who "drove the demonstration to its emotional peak"[5] and garnered the greatest applause. Some newspapers and church-related periodicals also published quotes or passages of his "I Have a Dream" speech with its integrationist vision.[6]

Most Germans heard the news about the march from their regional radio stations. Although in 1963 only 7 out of the 58 million West German citizens owned a television set (compared to 17 million radio owners), this new medium played an essential role in spreading the

[1] As freedom of the press did not exist in East Germany (GDR) at the time of the March on Washington, I confine my analysis to West German media. If not noted otherwise, translations of original German sources are my own.

[2] "Eine große und würdige Demonstration," *Die Welt*, Aug. 29, 1963: 1. Surprisingly, the influential political magazine *Der Spiegel* did not mention the March on Washington in its editions of August and September 1963. On the other hand, an article with quotes by Malcolm X did appear under the title "Unity and a Razor-Blade — By Malcolm X, Chief Propagator of the Black Muslims in America" (Sept. 25, 1963: 80).

[3] For example, *Frankfurter Allgemeine Zeitung* (FAZ), Aug. 23, 1963: 4; *Frankfurter Rundschau*, Aug. 26, 1963: 2.

[4] *Die Welt*, Aug. 29, 1963: 4.

[5] *FAZ*, Aug. 30, 1963: 2 and 3.

[6] E.g., *Junge Kirche* 24 (1963): 501-502.

information, sounds, and images of the march throughout Germany. Via the news satellite "Telstar" many German citizens were able to view parts of the demonstration live. On the eve of the march, in a "Meet the Press" telecast, they could watch Roy Wilkins of the National Association for the Advancement of Colored People (NAACP) and Martin Luther King Jr. being interviewed by German journalists in Washington, DC. On August 30, a second interview with King was shown on German TV, followed by an interview with the segregationist Alabama Governor George Wallace.[7]

When German citizens learned about the march, many of them remembered the disturbing pictures of the brutal attacks on peaceful demonstrators in Birmingham, Alabama, only a few months earlier. Some newspapers and especially church publications in West Germany had published quotes from King's prophetic "Letter from Birmingham Jail" during the preceding months.[8] The impact of the march on Germans can therefore only be evaluated if it is not seen as an isolated event but as an important milestone of the American civil rights movement. The news media in Germany reported extensively on the sequence of events that began with the Montgomery Bus Boycott (1955-1956) and proceeded through the sit-ins (1960), the Freedom Rides (1961), the Birmingham Campaign, the March on Washington (1963), and the Mississippi Freedom Summer (1964) to the Selma Voting Rights Campaign (1965). In the summer of 1963, many Germans perceived the march as the culmination of all the previous efforts in the civil rights struggle and Martin Luther King Jr. as the undisputed and charismatic leader and icon of this movement.

The Goals of the March on Washington and the Political and Economic Situation of West Germany in 1963

The March on Washington was intended as a march "for jobs and freedom" that was to promote comprehensive civil rights legislation. From the perspective of West Germans, the march dealt with specific problems of the United States: the lack of employment, decent jobs, and equal rights for the black minority. In West Germany, in contrast, the early 1960s were a time of full employment thanks to the so-called economic miracle. In fact, the country was so prosperous that migrant workers from Spain, Greece, and Turkey were needed to fill positions in there.[9] Germans could thus not relate to the U.S. job situation, and, although they understood the demand for freedom, their understanding of this was different from that of the African American

7   See *Hamburger Abendblatt*, Aug. 28, 1963: 4, and Aug. 31, 1963: 4. In the telecast of Aug. 30, King was presented as the "Gandhi of Alabama." Alabama Governor George Wallace (1919-1998) was interviewed because he had gained international notoriety as an outspoken defender of segregation. In his 1963 inaugural address he pledged: "Segregation now! Segregation tomorrow! Segregation forever!" In June 1963 he stood in a schoolhouse door and later at the entrance to the University of Alabama to block the admission of African American students. Unfortunately, no audio or written version of the "Meet the Press" interviews with King and Wallace have yet been found (Stefan Hertrampf, archivist of the Zweites Deutsches Fernsehen, in a letter to the author, July 23, 2014).

8   E.g., *Junge Kirche* 24 (1963): 504-508; *Der Stern*, Sept. 1, 1963: 133-35.

9   In the 1960s they were called *Gastarbeiter* (guest workers).

minority as postwar Germany had no comparable underprivileged minority. When West Germans spoke of the lack of freedom, they primarily thought of their countrymen living in East Germany, the German Democratic Republic (GDR), under a communist regime. The erection of the Berlin Wall in 1961 symbolized this oppression to the West Germans.

Despite these differences in perception between the U.S. and West Germany, the West German media coverage of the march undoubtedly increased West Germans' knowledge about the situation of African Americans and white racism in the U.S. And in some cases it may have positively influenced their perception of the black minority in the U.S. especially as the German nation was still grappling with its own racist past. One must keep in mind that until the end of the Nazi regime in 1945, the German people had been indoctrinated with racist stereotypes of *Neger* (Negroes) or *Schwarze* (blacks). Not all Germans had renounced these racist stereotypes by 1963, although some did speak out against them and dedicated themselves to fighting racial injustice wherever it occurred. Prominent among them was the Protestant minister and church leader Heinrich Grüber (1891-1975).[10] An active opponent of the Nazi regime who had been imprisoned in two concentration camps (1940-1943), Grüber testified during the Adolf Eichmann trial in 1961. Two years later, after he had witnessed the civil rights struggle in the U.S., he invited Martin Luther King Jr. to visit Berlin. Grüber exchanged letters with King in which he compared King's fight against racism to his own fight during the Nazi regime: "I write in the bond of the same faith and hope, knowing your experiences are the same as ours were. ... During the time of Hitler, I was often ashamed of being a German, as today, I am ashamed of being white. I am grateful to you, dear brother, and to all who stand with you for this fight of justice, which you are conducting in the spirit of Jesus Christ."[11]

The March on Washington and the American Civil Rights Movement as an Inspiration for Social Protest Movements in West Germany

In the second half of the 1960s, West Germany, like many other countries, was shaken by unprecedented student protests.[12] They were characterized by sharp controversies about activists' use of violent means to change societal conditions.[13] In many cases, the German student protest movement adopted techniques of the civil rights movement, as well as the student and anti-war movement in the U.S.

10 See Heinrich Grüber, *Erinnerungen aus sieben Jahrzehnten* (Cologne, 1968); Jörg Hildebrandt, *Bevollmächtigt zum Brückenbau. Heinrich Grüber. Judenfreund und Trümmerpropst* (Leipzig, 1991).

11 Heinrich Grüber to Martin Luther King Jr., July 15, 1963, cited in Maria Höhn and Martin Klimke, *A Breath of Freedom: The Civil Rights Struggle, African American GIs, and Germany* (New York, 2010), 92. For the relationship between King and Grüber, see the informative analysis by Höhn and Klimke, *A Breath of Freedom*, 89-105. Grüber wrote the afterword to the German edition of King's book on the Montgomery bus boycott (Martin Luther King, *Freiheit*, Kassel, 1964, 203-205) and included King in the dedication to his memoirs *Erinnerungen aus sieben Jahrzehnten*.

12 See Norbert Frei, *1968. Jugendrevolte und globaler Protest* (Munich, 2008); Martin Klimke, *The Other Alliance: Student Protest in West Germany and the United States in the Global Sixties* (Princeton, 2010).

13 See Volker Hornung, "Amerikanische Bürgerrechtsbewegung und Black-Power-Revolte," in *Ziviler Widerstand*, ed. Theodor Ebert, 32-56 (Düsseldorf, 1970), who stated: "Since Easter 1968 parts of the extra-parliamentary opposition in West Germany have gone over to justifying the use of violence" (33). Student leader Daniel Cohn-Bendit declared: "The great comrade Martin Luther King is no longer in demand," qtd. in *Der Spiegel* 23/7, Feb. 2, 1969: 30.

(e.g., direct action: sit-ins, teach-ins, go-ins).[14] However, not all of the German activists believed in the power of nonviolence as much as King did.[15] Within the Sozialistischer Deutscher Studentenbund (SDS — German Socialist Student League), a leading organization in the student protests in the 1960s originally inspired by the SNCC and the American SDS, there were always pronounced and controversial discussions about the use of violence.[16]

In response to this situation, Theodor Ebert (b. 1937), a Christian pacifist and lecturer on politics, initiated a working group of students and assistant professors of the Kirchliche Hochschule and of the Otto-Suhr-Institut of the Free University in West Berlin to discuss how the "extra-parliamentary opposition" could "translate" and "make use of" the practices of the American civil rights movement.[17] Ebert used teach-ins and other means of communication to pass on the experiences of the civil rights movement in the planning and execution of strictly nonviolent demonstrations and acts of civil disobedience. Shortly after the assassination of Martin Luther King Jr., Ebert, together with the Protestant theologian Hans-Jürgen Benedict (b. 1941), published a collection of essays: *Macht von unten: Bürgerrechtsbewegung, außerparlamentarische Opposition und Kirchenreform* (Power from Below: civil rights movement, Extra-Parliamentary Opposition and Church Reform).[18] In this book, the Protestant theologian Rüdiger Reitz (b. 1938), who had spent two years at the Christian Theological Seminary in Indianapolis, Indiana, analyzed the role Christian ministers played in the civil rights movement.[19] His essay "The Minister as a Public Demonstrator" focuses on the lessons of the civil rights marches in the years between 1955 and 1968, especially including the March on Washington. Reitz's intention was "to make the American experiences fruitful" for ministers and churches in Germany, challenging pastors who were content to live comfortably within the traditional church-state relationship.[20] He reminded them of King's words in a speech at the beginning of

14 See Martin Klimke, "Sit-in, Teach-in, Go-in. Die transnationale Zirkulation kultureller Praktiken in den 1960er Jahren am Beispiel der direkten Aktion," in *1968. Handbuch zur Kultur- und Mediengeschichte der Studentenbewegung*, ed. Martin Klimke and Joachim Scharloth, 119-31 (Stuttgart, 2007). See also Martin Klimke, "The African American Civil Rights Struggle and Germany, 1945-1989," *GHI Bulletin* 43 (Fall 2008): 91-106.

15 See Theodor Ebert, *Gewaltfreier Aufstand. Alternative zum Bürgerkrieg*, 4th ed. (Berlin, 1970), 239-41; and Alexander Christian Widmann, *Wandel mit Gewalt? Der deutsche Protestantismus und die politisch motivierte Gewaltanwendung in den 1960er und 1970er Jahren* (Göttingen, 2013), 161-297.

16 See Klimke, *The Other Alliance*. In the 1970s, some former members of the German SDS turned to violence and eventually founded the terrorist organization, the Red Army Faction (RAF).

17 Theodor Ebert and Hans-Jürgen Benedict, eds., *Macht von unten. Bürgerrechtsbewegung, außerparlamentarische Opposition und Kirchenreform* (Hamburg, 1968), 6.

18 Hans-Jürgen Benedict's and my doctoral adviser was Hans-Eckehard Bahr (b. 1928), a professor at the Ruhr University of Bochum, who met Martin Luther King Jr. in Chicago in 1966. He motivated us to study and to write about the relevance of the American civil rights movement in Germany and to translate

some of King's sermons and speeches. See, e.g., Hans-Jürgen Benedict and Hans-Eckehard Bahr, eds., *Kirchen als Träger der Revolution* (Hamburg, 1968); Heinrich Grosse, *Die Macht der Armen. Martin Luther King und der Kampf für soziale Gerechtigkeit* (Hamburg, 1971); Hans-Eckehard Bahr and Heinrich Grosse,

eds., *Martin Luther King. Ich habe einen Traum* (Düsseldorf, 2003).

19 "German church groups in particular were very much influenced by the integrationist vision of the African American struggle after some of their ministers and priests had taken part in

the civil rights demonstrations within the US." (Klimke, *The African American Civil Rights Struggle*, 103).

20 Rüdiger Reitz, "Die Rolle des Pfarrers in der Bürgerrechtsbewegung," in *Macht von unten*, ed. Ebert and Benedict, 46-59, 59.

the bus boycott in Montgomery: "We will only say to the people, 'Let your conscience be your guide.'"[21]

Influences on German Activism

While King's death in 1968 is often regarded as marking the end of the American civil rights movement, the new West German social movements were just entering a peak phase that would continue throughout the late 1960s, the 1970s, and 1980s.[22] The initial impetus for these movements was student opposition to former Nazis holding respectable positions in the West German government and judiciary and to the emergency laws of 1968.[23] In the ensuing decades, protests against the use of nuclear energy for military or civilian purposes and protests against the arms race, especially the installation of missiles with nuclear warheads, stood at the center of these social movements. These protests formed the environmental movement and the peace movement in West Germany and took a great deal of inspiration from the American civil rights movement.

In the mid-1970s self-proclaimed citizen initiatives successfully blocked the erection of a nuclear plant in Wyhl in southwestern Germany. They used nonviolent action techniques and forms of civil disobedience while occupying the construction site. A key figure in the resistance was Wolfgang Sternstein (b. 1939), a peace researcher and activist who was strongly influenced by the ideas and actions of King, Mahatma Gandhi, and Philip and Daniel Berrigan.[24] In spite of some opposing groups who refused to renounce violence as a means to reach their goal, Sternstein, in the tradition of Gandhi and King, always held fast to his conviction: "The way and the goal, means and ends, must correspond if the goal is to be reached."[25]

24 In his autobiography, *Mein Weg zwischen Gewalt und Gewaltfreiheit* (My Way between Violence and Nonviolence [Norderstedt, 2005]), Sternstein spoke of these figures as his "spiritual sources" (385). The brothers Daniel (b. 1921) and Philip Berrigan (1923-2002), both ordained Roman Catholic priests (Philip later married and founded a family), became radical peace activists. They engaged in courageous nonviolent actions against the Vietnam War and against nuclear weapons. For example, in 1968, in Catonsville, MD, they doused draft cards in napalm and burned them in a group of nine activists ("The Catonsville Nine"). In 1980, they hammered on nuclear warhead nose cones in King of Prussia, PA, and poured blood on military documents. This marked the beginning of the Plowshares Movement against (nuclear) weapons. Daniel and Philip spent many years in prison for their acts of civil disobedience. See Murray Polner and Jim O'Grady, *Disarmed and Dangerous: The Radical Life and Times of Daniel and Philip Berrigan* (New York, 1997).

25 O'Grady, *Disarmed and Dangerous*, 255. Because of various acts of civil disobedience Sternstein was imprisoned several times, spending more than one year total in prison.

21 Martin Luther King Jr., *Stride toward Freedom* (New York, 1964), 48.

22 See Roland Roth and Dieter Rucht, eds., *Neue soziale Bewegungen in der Bundesrepublik Deutschland*, 2nd ed. (Bonn, 1991); and Dieter Rucht, "The Study of Social Movements in West Germany: Between Activism and Social Science," in

Research on Social Movements: The State of the Art in Western Europe and the USA, ed. Dieter Rucht, 175-202 (Frankfurt/Main, 1991). As Rucht observed in this article, "there are large overlaps between the adherents of various movements" (187).

23 The Emergency Acts were passed by the West

German parliament on May 30, 1968, as an amendment to the Basic Law to ensure the government's ability to react to crises like uprisings or war. The Free Democratic Party, student groups, and labor unions were strongly opposed to these laws because they limited civil rights in an emergency.

In 1975, environmental movement activists organized resistance to the building of a nuclear plant in Brokdorf (at the Elbe River near Hamburg).[26] When at the end of 1976 conflicts around the construction site escalated, a group of Christian ministers and lay people founded the "Hamburg Initiative of Church Employees and Nonviolent Action."[27] To prepare for protest activities, they watched Ely Landau's documentary film on King. Benedict, one of the pastors of the Martin Luther King congregation in Hamburg, described his reaction to the film: "All of this stirs me up, but it also strengthens my commitment. I realize the difference of our experiences compared to those of oppressed blacks in the U.S. — we protest as privileged and economically secure church officials. But I also see the parallels. To me the fight against nuclear energy — like King's actions — is a protest of love for life and social justice."[28] The Hamburg initiative organized nonviolent demonstrations against the nuclear plant and tried to prevent demonstrators from using violence against policemen. Yet in some cases they could not hinder the small minority of demonstrators in self-proclaimed "autonomous groups" from violently attacking their opponents. Benedict also drafted and distributed a flyer for the police: "Even if you hit us, you remain our human brother. We will not insult you or hit back." Expecting the use of water guns by the police, the members of the initiative sang the protest song "We Shall Overcome."[29]

Plans for a new runway at the Frankfurt Airport (Startbahn West) became a central issue for the environmental movement in West Germany in the 1970s and 1980s. When the beginning of construction work led to war-like battles between the police and groups of demonstrators, citizens living in the vicinity (many of them active members of Christian congregations) organized nonviolent demonstrations, sit-ins, and special worship services. In the context of the "People's Free University Startbahn West," Egbert Jahn (b. 1941), a political scientist and peace researcher, delivered a speech entitled "Nonviolent Resistance in Parliamentary Democracies: The Experiences of Martin Luther King and the American Civil Rights Movement."[30] Jahn described the "six basic aspects of nonviolent resistance" King had developed. Invoking the example of the American civil rights movement, he emphasized the legitimacy of nonviolent resistance and civil disobedience in the German democratic system and underlined the necessity of intensive training in nonviolent methods for activists.[31]

The NATO decision to locate cruise missiles in Western Europe, codified in its 1979 Double-Track Decision, led to unprecedented

26 See Ulfried Kleinert, ed., *Gewaltfrei widerstehen* (Hamburg,1981).

27 "Hamburger Initiative kirchlicher Mitarbeiter und für gewaltfreie Aktion." The philosophy and actions of this group are described in Kleinert, *Gewaltfrei*, 139-52.

28 Ibid., 117.

29 See Kleinert, *Gewaltfrei*, 116-17.

30 Egbert Jahn, "Gewaltfreier Widerstand in parlamentarischen Demokratien — Die Erfahrungen Martin Luther Kings in der amerikanischen Bürgerrechtsbewegung," *psychosozial* 2, no. 82 (1982): 124-37.

31 See Reiner Steinweg, ed., *Friedensbewegung* (Frankfurt/Main, 1977); idem, ed., *Die neue Friedensbewegung* (Frankfurt/Main, 1982); Ulrike C. Wasmuht, "Von den Friedensbewegungen der 80er Jahre zum Antikriegsprotest von 1991," in *Neue soziale Bewegungen*, ed. Roth and Rucht, 116-37.

mass demonstrations in the German peace movement. On October 10, 1981, about 300,000 concerned citizens gathered in Bonn, then the capital of West Germany, demonstrating against the installation of missiles with nuclear warheads. The most-applauded speaker during this rally was Dr. King's widow, Coretta Scott King. She had flown to Germany for this special event and told her German audience: "It is the spirit of peace and nonviolence that brings you together today. I can assure you that you have strong moral support in the United States. ... Our fight is your fight; our movement is your movement." Mrs. King emphasized that her experience had taught her that a nonviolent mass movement can be successful.[32] Huge peace marches at the biannual church conventions in Hamburg in 1981 and in Hanover in 1983, and the annual peace weeks in more than 3,000 congregations, showed that Protestant laypersons and clergy were crucial to the peace movement of the 1980s.[33] In the urban congregation I ministered to in the "Volkswagen City" of Wolfsburg, for example, I organized a seminar on the ideas and actions of Henry David Thoreau, Gandhi, King, and the Berrigans,[34] and we got training in the use of nonviolent techniques in workshops. The church council and other members of this liberal, peace- and justice-oriented (Lutheran) congregation with a tradition of community organizing participated in peace demonstrations and conducted "peace weeks."

In the movement against nuclear rearmament, activists organized blockades of military installations of the U.S. Army in southwestern Germany — specifically, in Mutlangen, Großengstingen, and Büchel where nuclear missiles or bombs were stored. In Großengstingen all participants of the blockade were organized in small local groups and had to undergo thorough training in the theory and practice of nonviolent action.[35] Sternstein declared: "The blockade of Großengstingen stands in the tradition of civil disobedience against an unjust government as it was initiated by H. D. Thoreau, M. K. Gandhi and M. L. King."[36] In 1983 and 1986 a small group around Sternstein even intruded into U.S. Army locations with symbolic actions following the example of the "Plowshares" movement in the U.S. They also sang "We Shall Overcome."[37]

It was a dedicated Christian pacifist and conscientious objector, teacher Ulli Thiel (1943-2014) from Karlsruhe in southern Germany, who

» Volkmar Deile of Berlin, in an e-mail to the author on July 7, 2014, indicated that the organizers of the Bonn demonstration could not say who had invited Mrs. King nor could they provide a complete English text of her speech. A second speaker from the U.S. that day was Randall Forsberg of the Nuclear Freeze Campaign.

33 They were, of course, a minority within their congregations, but a relatively big one. The involvement of the Catholic, generally more conservative, community didn't reach the Protestant level in West Germany. See Helmut Zander, *Die Christen und die Friedensbewegungen in beiden deutschen Staaten* (Berlin, 1989).

34 See note 24.

35 See Sternstein, *Mein Weg*, 282- 98.

36 Wolfgang Sternstein, "Schwerter zu Pflugscharen. Die Blockade des Atomwaffenlagers bei Großengstingen," *gewaltfreie aktion* 53/54 (1982): 15-34, 27.

37 See Ulrich Philipp, *Politik von unten. Wolfgang Sternstein — Erfahrungen eines Graswurzelpolitikers und Aktionsforschers* (Berlin, 2006), 110-17. Sternstein's radicalism was atypical for the German peace movement in the 1970s and 1980s. In retrospect, Sternstein wrote: "The German peace movement was miles away from the radicalism and readiness to make sacrifices of the campaigns for independence in India or the civil rights movement around Martin Luther King." (Sternstein, *Mein Weg*, 265).

32 See Aktion Sühnezeichen/ Friedensdienste, Aktionsgemeinschaft für den Frieden, ed., *Bonn*

10.10.1981. Friedensdemonstration für Abrüstung und Entspannung in Europa (Bornheim, 1981).

For the German translation of Coretta Scott King's speech, see ibid., 99-100. »

coined the motto of the German peace movement — *Frieden schaffen ohne Waffen* (create peace without weapons) — and who initiated human chains as a mass signal against the arms race in 1983.[38] The fiftieth anniversary of the March on Washington in 2013 prompted him to write an article with the title "Prägung durch Martin Luther King" (Inspired by Martin Luther King). The autobiographical statement begins with the words: "Nobody has influenced my thinking and acting as much as the US-American civil rights activist Martin Luther King. For me, his nonviolent direct actions ... have always been an important orientation for the planning and execution of local as well as supra-regional peace actions."[39]

From the American civil rights movement, German peace and environmental activists learned that in order to be successful, nonviolent direct actions must be thoroughly planned and must include prior training. To that aim, courses or centers for learning about and training in nonviolent direct action were founded throughout Germany, as the following two examples illustrate. In 1980, the Bildungs- und Begegnungsstätte für gewaltfreie Aktion (Center for Education and Training for Nonviolent Action) was established in Wustrow, a small village in northeastern Lower Saxony. This institution grew out of the protests against the nuclear waste disposal site in nearby Gorleben. The center aims to "to help to translate concern about military conflicts, ecological destruction and social injustice into nonviolent action."[40] The Werkstatt für gewaltfreie Aktion Baden (Workshop for Nonviolent Action in Baden) was founded in 1984, after nuclear missiles were installed on German soil in 1983. The initiative offered (and still offers) seminars and training sessions. Centers like these were established because "many [German] activists who conducted training sessions in nonviolent action had come into contact with people who lived and practiced nonviolence in the USA. ... The contact with American trainers like Bill Moyers, who had still worked with Martin Luther King Jr. himself, with their enthusiasm and creativity, inspired and animated the then still nascent nonviolent movement in West Germany."[41] Benedict even goes further in expressly linking the civil rights movement to the use of direct action techniques in German protest movements, though he also notes the absence of spirituality in the German adoption of many of them: "Manifold and imaginative actions of civil disobedience have been developed in the environmental movement and in the peace movement. This variety directly and indirectly is an effect of the nonviolent actions

38 The most famous human chain with probably more than 400,000 participants on Oct. 22, 1983, stretched over 67 miles from Stuttgart to Neu-Ulm.

39 Ulli Thiel, "Prägung durch Martin Luther King. Die Bedeutung des Vorkämpfers für Gewaltfreiheit und Zivilen Ungehorsam für die eigene Friedensarbeit," *Forum Pazifismus* 38, no. 2 (2013): 35-38, 35.

40 See http://www.kurvewustrow.org/78-0-wofuer-wir-stehen.html.

41 Werkstatt für Gewaltfreie Aktion, Baden, ed., *25 Jahre Werkstatt für Gewaltfreie Aktion, Baden. Festschrift zum 25jährigen Jubiläum 2009* (Heidelberg, 2009), 19.

of the American civil rights movement and the peace movement. The spiritual dimension of most of King's actions was, however, not adopted in many cases. The corresponding spirituality does not exist in many of the nonviolent groups (in Germany)."[42]

In addition to these written manifestations of the influence of the American civil rights movement and the obvious adoption of its techniques, we must not forget or underestimate its cultural influence, especially in the field of music: freedom songs and black music were critical inspiration and motivation for West German protest movements. Joan Baez, Pete Seeger, Harry Belafonte, Bob Dylan, and others gave live concerts in West (and less often in East) Germany in front of enthusiastic crowds. Their records and CDs — for example, the live recording of Pete Seeger's famous Carnegie Hall Concert of June 8, 1963, with many songs referring to the civil rights movement in the South — were very popular. Songs like "Where Have All the Flowers Gone," "Blowing in the Wind," "This Land Is Your Land," and, of course, "We Shall Overcome" were often sung by peace and environmental activists. Joan Baez even participated in the anti-military "Easter Marches" in West Germany.[43]

The March on Washington and the American Civil Rights Movement as an Inspiration for Social Protest in East Germany

The political rulers of the German Democratic Republic (GDR) were ambivalent about the American civil rights movement. As they regarded the U.S. as an exponent of racism and imperialism, they officially expressed solidarity with this movement as well as with the American peace movement to end the war in Vietnam. GDR party leaders praised King as a hero of international anti-imperialism.[44] On the other hand, the government feared that the message of nonviolent methods for conflict resolution would undermine the official doctrine of the necessity of military means for the protection of socialism.[45] This ambivalence became especially obvious in September 1964, when King visited West and East Berlin. King, the

» German CDU, Gerald Götting, spoke of "the simple truth that race war equals class war and that both, like the struggle for world peace, are directly connected to the revolutionary fight against imperialism" (Gerald Götting, "Ein Leben für Menschlichkeit und Brüderlichkeit," in *Martin Luther Kings Vermächtnis*, ed. Sekretariat der Christlich-Demokratischen Union Deutschlands [Berlin, 1968], 9). In her memoirs, Anneliese Kaminski (née Vahl) reports that she was asked by the CDU in 1974 to write an article about "Martin Luther King as a communist leader in the USA." She declined and emphasized that "Martin Luther King had acted as a committed Christian." See Anneliese Kaminski, *Erfülltes Leben* (Berlin, 2007), 53; and her King biography: Anneliese Vahl, *Martin Luther King. Stationen auf dem Wege, Berichte und Selbstzeugnisse* (Berlin, 1968).

45 In retrospect, Günther Wirth, an influential member of the East German Christian Democratic Union (CDU) and chief editor of the state-owned publishing house Union-Verlag in the 1960s, wrote: "In the GDR, the nonviolence of Martin Luther King ... generally stood under the ideological verdict of being close to 'feeblish pacifism'." (Günther Wirth, "Die neue Richtung unseres Zeitalters — Martin Luther Kings Traum von Gerechtigkeit, Gleichheit und Gewaltlosigkeit," Jan. 15, 1999, 2-3, http://www.kingzentrum.de. The motto of the state-controlled youth organization Freie Deutsche Jugend was: "Peace must be defended — peace must be armed."

42 Hans-Jürgen Benedict, "Zu Martin Luther Kings aktueller Bedeutung," *Pastoraltheologie* 78 (1989): 78- 81, 80.

43 See Harry Belafonte, *My Song: A Memoir* (New York, 2011); Joan Baez, *And a Voice to Sing with* (Summit Books, 1987); David Dunaway, *How Can I Keep from Singing: The Ballad of Pete Seeger* (London, 1985); Robert Shelton, *No Direction Home: The Life and Music of Bob Dylan* (New York, 1986).

44 In an official commemoration of Martin Luther King Jr. on April 10, 1968, the president of the East »

icon of the American civil rights movement in both German states, was permitted to enter East Berlin although he had no passport with him, but his appearances in two East Berlin churches, in St. Mary's Church and in Sophia Church right in the center of Berlin, were not publicly announced.[46] In his speech on the occasion of the Tag der Kirche (Day of the Church) in front of more than 20,000 citizens at the Waldbühne, an amphitheater in West Berlin, and in his sermons in East Berlin in overcrowded churches, King presented an overview of the civil rights struggle in the United States and emphasized the necessity of nonviolent protest to bring about social change.

It is not easy to assess the impact of King's only visit to Germany on East Germans. I agree with Britta Waldschmidt-Nelson: "The event may not have had any immediate visible effect in 1964, but it certainly had a long-term impact. King's visit and message gave the Christian minority in the GDR new hope. His theology and the method of nonviolent resistance doubtlessly inspired the GDR opposition in the following decades and thus — at least to some degree — contributed to the eventual downfall of the communist regime there."[47] As the East German government tried to keep tight control over all citizens, large social movements were not able to develop. Nevertheless, small dissident, "alternative groups" arose at the end of the 1960s. In an authoritarian state, they demanded basic civil rights (free elections, freedom of opinion, freedom of speech, freedom of assembly) and protested the militarization of education, especially the so-called *Wehrunterricht* (teaching defense politics to children), as well as the arms race in East and West and growing ecological grievances in the GDR.

The churches in East Germany were the only organizations that had a certain degree of independence from state control, so they became more significant as pockets of resistance in the 1970s and 1980s. This was especially true of the Protestant churches, where more freedom of expression was allowed than in the Roman Catholic Church, which followed a policy of "political abstinence" secured

46 For King's visit to West and East Berlin on Sept. 12-14, 1964, see the excellent documentation and analysis by Maria Höhn and Martin Klimke in *A Breath of Freedom*, chapter 5: "Bringing Civil Rights to East and West: Dr. Martin Luther King Jr. in Cold War Berlin," 89-105, where they assert: "King's visit to the East is particularly striking in two respects: First, apart from his adventurous border crossing, he did not encounter East German government representatives, and second, his visit generated relatively little coverage in the East German media" (102). See also Britta Waldschmidt-Nelson, "'We Shall Overcome': The Impact of the African American Freedom Struggle on Race Relations and Social Protest in Germany after World War II," in *The Transatlantic Sixties: Europe and the United States in the Counterculture Decade*, ed. Grzegorz Kosc, Clara Juncker, Sharon Monteith, and Britta Waldschmidt-Nelson, 66-97 (Bielefeld, 2013).

47 Waldschmidt-Nelson, "'We Shall Overcome'," 77. Höhn and Klimke state: "King's visit to Berlin in the fall of 1964, only a month before winning the Nobel Peace Prize, stands out as an important point in the reception of the African American civil rights movement in Germany. ... In the shorter term, the repercussions of King's visit were felt primarily in the religious sphere. East German publishing houses thus considered it politically safe to extensively publish texts by and about him in the following years. In this way, these publishers helped to incorporate King into the official doctrine by insisting that 'Christianity and the humanistic goals of socialism' were not opposed to one another. This ideological usurpation notwithstanding, King's writings and actions, as well as his theology, did undoubtedly serve as an inspiration for the East German opposition movement in the long run" (*A Breath of Freedom*, 89 and 104). Bishop Markus Dröge (of the Protestant Church of Berlin-Brandenburg-schlesische Oberlausitz) wrote to the author on Nov. 6, 2013: "The visit of Martin Luther King in Berlin sowed a seed that 25 years later resulted in the 'peaceful revolution.' His call for freedom later encouraged many Christians in the GDR to stand up to the lack of freedom and the injustice in the GDR."

by its hierarchical structure. About 27 percent of the population of East Germany, the "motherland of the Reformation," belonged to the Protestant churches compared to about 6 percent in the Roman Catholic Church. In them, nonconformist thoughts and opposition could be expressed "under the umbrella" of local and regional churches. In church-owned rooms small dissident groups openly discussed issues of political participation and human rights and — like their West German counterparts — questions about peace, justice, and the environment.[48] This does not mean that there were no conflicts or tensions between politically alternative groups, on the one hand, and leading representatives of the churches or members of local congregations, on the other.[49] Besides, like the majority of the population of the GDR, many of the dissidents and courageous activists were not church members.

In the 1970s and 1980s such dissident groups came into being not only in larger cities like Berlin, Dresden, and Leipzig, but also in smaller towns and rural areas. An impressive example is the Christliches Friedensseminar (Christian Peace Seminar) in the small village of Königswalde near Chemnitz (known as Karl-Marx-Stadt from 1953 to 1990).[50] The peace seminar was founded in 1973 by electrician Hans-Jörg Weigel (b. 1943) and other Christians who were critical of the militarization of their society and the world nuclear arms situation. Nearly all of them were former "construction soldiers"(conscripts who did construction work in lieu of military service).[51] Personal testimonials from these courageous dissidents show that many of them were inspired by the civil rights movement in the United States, and especially by King.[52] In religious devotions, presentations, musical compositions, artworks and in an exhibition on King,[53] they commemorated this legacy of nonviolent action as alternative to war and violence and of the mobilizing power of the "dream."

With admirable perseverance and creativity, Georg Meusel (b. 1942), another electrician, from the small town of Werdau in Saxony, who

» (Conciliar process for peace, justice and the integrity of creation). See Gerhard Lindemann, "Kirche und friedliche Revolution im Bereich der Ev.-Luth. Landeskirche Sachsens," in *Durch die Ritzen der Mauer. Kontinuitäten, Brüche, Neuanfänge in kirchlichen Partnerschaften seit 1949*, ed. Martin Cordes, 161-79 (Hanover, 2011).

49 See Neubert, *Geschichte*, esp. 539-50; Pollack, *Politischer Protest*, 197-200; and Thomas Mayer, *Der nicht aufgibt. Christoph Wonneberger — eine Biographie* (Leipzig, 2014).

50 Martin-Luther-King-Zentrum für Gewaltfreiheit und Zivilcourage — Archiv der Bürgerrechtsbewegung Südwestsachsens, ed., *Raum für Güte und Gewissen. Das christliche Friedensseminar Königswalde im damaligen Bezirk Karl-Marx-Stadt/DDR 1973-1990* (Werdau, 2004).

51 The activists of the peace seminar established contacts to the peace movement in West Germany and in the Netherlands. See *Raum für Güte und Gewissen*, 13. "The groups of construction soldiers and conscientious objectors ... were the germ of the developing independent 'peace movement' in the GDR." (Pollack, *Politischer Protest*, 68).

52 One such testimonial was a presentation in May 1979 by Georg Meusel in Königswalde entitled "Nonviolent Action — Alternative to War and Violence, to Indifference and Resignation" (Pollack, *Politischer Protest*, 59).

53 This was an exhibition in St. Jacob's Church of Königswalde from Oct. 7 to Nov. 10, 1989.

48 See Ehrhart Neubert, *Geschichte der Opposition in der DDR 1949-1989* (Berlin, 1997, 2nd ed., 1998); Detlef Pollack, *Politischer Protest. Politisch alternative Gruppen in der DDR* (Opladen, 2002); Gerhard Rein, *Die protestantische Revolution 1987-1990. Ein deutsches Lesebuch* (Berlin,

1990); Michael Haspel, *Politischer Protestantismus und gesellschaftliche Transformation. Ein Vergleich der Rolle der evangelischen Kirchen in der DDR und der schwarzen Kirchen in der Bürgerrechtsbewegung in den USA* (Tübingen, 1997), 186-231; Marianne Birthler, *Halbes Land.*

Ganzes Land. Ganzes Leben. Erinnerungen (Berlin, 2014). In the 1980s, in the context of partnerships between parishes, East and West German Christians engaged and cooperated in the so-called *Konziliarer Prozess für Frieden, Gerechtigkeit und Bewahrung der Schöpfung* »

was a founding member of the Christian Peace Seminar in Königswalde, spread the ideas of nonviolent social change in the GDR. A pacifist who was strongly opposed to the militarization of education in the GDR, he was very impressed by a presentation about the Montgomery bus boycott as well as by King's book "Why We Can't Wait."[54] Meusel was fascinated by King's adherence to nonviolence and "the way in which he related the biblical message to societal problems."[55] After King's assassination, Meusel used stamp exhibitions to promote pacifist ideas. It took him four years (to 1987) to raise enough money and obtain permission to show Landau's documentary film about King in the GDR.[56] The state security service of the GDR, the Stasi, wrote about Meusel in 1977: "There is reason to believe that M. intends to transfer the fighting method of nonviolent resistance, which has been developed for capitalistic conditions, to the socialist conditions in the GDR and to initiate a civil rights movement."[57] Although the communist regime was eager to celebrate the civil rights movement to indict the capitalist enemy, it feared its very methods might be used against its own regime.

In 1980, the youth pastor of the Lutheran Church of Saxony, Harald Bretschneider (b. 1942), initiated the first so-called decade of peace in the GDR. He had the creative idea of producing bookmarks and cloth badges with the words "swords into plowshares" and "Micah 4" alongside a stylized version of the famous sculpture by the Russian artist Evgeniy Vuchetich, thus openly challenging the militaristic ideology of the GDR.[58] Highly impressed by two of King's texts, "Why We Can't Wait" and his Nobel Peace Prize acceptance speech, which had been published in the GDR in 1965 and 1966, Bretschneider became a conscientious objector and later a "construction soldier." He passed these texts on to his companions.[59] As a parish minister and youth pastor he had many occasions to share the ideas and methods of the civil rights movement. Bretschneider regularly brought together state-independent peace groups, human rights groups, and environmental groups in Saxony.

Pastor Christoph Wonneberger (b. 1944), who was inspired by the "Prague Spring," Solidarnosc in Poland, and Theodor Ebert's publications about the concept of civil as opposed to military defense, publicly demanded in the early 1980s the installation of a *Sozialer Friedensdienst* (SoFD, social peace service) in the GDR. He founded the Gruppe Menschenrechte (group for human rights) and organized peace prayers in Dresden. In 1985 he became a pastor at St. Luke's

54 Meusel makes this claim himself in his still unpublished autobiography, "Die Marder sind unter uns — eine politische Autobiografie aus der DDR." He even named his second son "King" to honor this inspiration.

55 Meusel, "Die Marder."

56 The title of the German version of this film is *Dann war mein Leben nicht umsonst* (Then I have not lived in vain).

57 BStU Chemnitz, XIV/951/79.

58 See Neubert, *Geschichte*, 398-404; and Zander, *Die Christen*, 259-62.

59 Information by Harald Bretschneider in a telephone interview with the author on March 14, 2014. In 1966/67, Bretschneider, a construction soldier at the time, shared a tent with Hans-Jörg Weigel, who later initiated the Peace Seminar in Königswalde, and with Rudolf Albrecht, who initiated the Peace Seminar of Meißen (in 1974). From tent to tent they passed on texts written by Martin Luther King Jr.

Church in Leipzig and was soon coordinating the peace prayers in Leipzig in which opposition groups, including human rights, peace, and environmental groups, expressed their grievances and visions.[60] The weekly Monday Prayers in St. Nicholas Church became the starting point for mass demonstrations for change in the GDR. This connection between religious worship, political information, and peaceful demonstrations is strongly reminiscent of the mass meetings and demonstrations of the black freedom struggle in the South. Many activists and historians see Wonneberger's sermon in the peace prayer on September 25, 1989, as a decisive call for the "peaceful revolution" in the GDR in October 1989.[61] This peace prayer ended with the singing of the "Internationale" and "We Shall Overcome." Wonneberger later reflected on the figures who had most influenced him: "I learned back then in India from Gandhi how nonviolent action functions. I learned back then in the USA from King the ten commandments for the civil rights movement."[62]

The parish pastor of St. Nicholas Church in Leipzig, Christian Führer (1943-2014), also played a key role in the Monday Prayers. He praised King as one of the few Christians who took the Sermon on the Mount seriously and had training in and exercised nonviolent resistance. He reminded his listeners of King's vision. In his autobiography he states: "The 'Peaceful Revolution' ... belongs to the real experiences with the Sermon on the Mount, with the power of nonviolence. It was expressed in the mighty call: 'No violence!' "[63]

On many occasions, GDR opposition groups sang "We Shall Overcome." This hymn had special meaning for the GDR activists as an allusion to King and the influence of his nonviolent protests, as Uwe Koch explained: "The civil rights movement and the peace movement in the GDR referred to the experienced transformative power of nonviolence that had emerged from King. [The] hymn 'We Shall Overcome' was in the hearts and on the lips of many who went into the streets in the fall of 1989 in the GDR."[64] One Monday Prayer participant in 1989 described the effect that singing this hymn communally had on him and many others: "When I sang ... the American civil rights song, tears came to my eyes. I didn't feel left alone. We learned to walk upright."[65] Interestingly, this song was also incorporated into the songbook of the official youth organization of the GDR, the Free German Youth, which provides an example of the ideological usurpation of the civil rights movement by the East German regime.

60 For a more detailed discussion of Wonneberger's activism, see Mayer, *Der nicht aufgibt.*

61 Transcript of Wonneberger's sermon in Rein, *Die protestantische Revolution,* 224-25.

62 Mayer, *Der nicht aufgibt,* 163.

63 Christian Führer, *Und wir sind dabei gewesen. Die Revolution, die aus der Kirche kam* (Berlin, 2008), 321.

64 Uwe Koch, "Ein bescheidener Botschafter mit weltweiter Wirkung," *Der Sonntag* (weekly newspaper of the state church of Saxony), Jan. 10, 1999, 3.

65 This statement was made by a 56-year-old man in Leipzig, quoted in Mayer, *Der nicht aufgibt,* 100. The former bishop of Thuringia, Werner Leich, wrote in his memoirs *Du aber bleibst — im Wechsel der Horizonte* (Weimar, 2002), 127: "Often tears came to my eyes, when we were holding hands and sang the song of the blacks with which they, guided by Martin Luther King, had demanded freedom and equal rights in nonviolent resistance: 'We shall overcome ...'."

On the 9th of October 1989 in Leipzig, the crucial *Tag der Angst* (day of fear), it was not clear whether the expected mass demonstration after the Monday Prayer would be violently suppressed by the army and the police and end in bloodshed. In the Monday Prayer of that day, the pastor of the Reformed Church, Hans-Jürgen Sievers (b. 1943), who had heard King preach in St. Mary's Church of Berlin in 1964, purposely referred to a famous passage of Paul's First Letter to the Corinthians.[66] It was the same one Reverend Bob Graetz had chosen for his sermon when the Montgomery bus boycott had successfully ended.[67] Sievers reminded his listeners of how the protesters in Montgomery had won new human dignity and assured them that they, too, would gain dignity and respect as long as they stuck to nonviolent methods: "we will not allow ourselves to be treated like children either. … As we have a good goal, the way toward it and the means we apply must be good."[68] A month later, November 9, on the very day when the Berlin Wall was torn down, the pastor of an East German congregation near Leipzig, which had a partnership with our congregation in Wolfsburg (West Germany), wrote me a postcard in which he explicitly addressed King's influence as a model for the movement: "Since Oct. 2, my son Tobias has taken part in every Monday Prayer in Leipzig. I think Martin Luther King accompanied many of them as a role model."[69] In April 1990, after the collapse of the GDR, Horst Sindermann, who had been one of the most powerful functionaries of East Germany's ruling Socialist Unity Party, confessed that it was the nonviolence that had been most effective in disarming the state: "We were prepared for anything, but not for candles and prayers."[70]

The Legacy of the American Civil Rights Movement in Unified Germany

After the so-called *Wende* (turnaround/change) in the GDR, the unification of Germany, and the end of the Cold War, economic and resource problems caused by unemployment, low wages, deficits in the social systems, and cuts in social services became more important to many citizens, especially in East Germany, than environmental or peace or human rights questions.[71] These problems were caused or exacerbated by global economic and ideological neoliberalism. At the same time, an unprecedented number of migrants and asylum-seeking refugees, mainly from eastern European and African countries, entered Germany. Right-wing extremists and xenophobic groups reacted to this situation with street marches carrying racist symbols and with violent, sometimes fatal, attacks

66 "When I was a child, I spoke as a child, I felt as a child, I thought as a child. Now that I have become a man, I have put away childish things" (1 Cor. 13:11).

67 See Martin Luther King Jr., *Stride Toward Freedom* (New York, 1964), 141.

68 Hans-Jürgen Sievers, *Stundenbuch einer deutschen Revolution. Die Leipziger Kirchen im Oktober 1989* (Zollikon, 1990), 76-79; Wolf-Jürgen Grabner, Christiane Heinze, and Detlef Pollack, eds., *Leipzig im Oktober. Kirchen und alternative Gruppen im Umbruch der DDR* (Berlin, 1990), 129.

69 Postcard in author's possession.

70 Horst Sindermann in an interview with the political magazine *Der Spiegel* on April 20, 1990, qtd. in Martin-Luther-King-Zentrum, ed., *Raum für Güte und Gewissen*, 26. In 2003 about 150 persons who had been active in opposition groups in the GDR were interviewed about their role models in the 1980s. The name most often mentioned as "very important" was Martin Luther King Jr. See Christof Geisel, *Auf der Suche nach einem dritten Weg* (Berlin, 2005), 253.

71 See Roth and Rucht, eds., *Die sozialen Bewegungen*, 29-34.

on members of these unwanted minorities. For the first time since the end of World War II, the German population was confronted with widespread and violent manifestations of racism in its own country.[72] The quantitative and qualitative growth of social injustices and of open racism was a new challenge for protest movements in unified Germany.

In recent times, there seem to have been fewer initiatives for social justice influenced by the American civil rights movement. I know of two examples: The "Workshop for Nonviolent Action" in Baden initiated a campaign against cuts in social services inspired by "the campaign concept of the American civil rights movement."[73] Secondly, the Monday Prayers and demonstrations in Leipzig, so clearly influenced by the civil rights movement, did continue after the *Wende* as well, focusing their attention on economic questions, especially the problems of the unemployed, the working poor, and welfare recipients.

Initiatives and groups opposing the growing racism in unified Germany in most cases do not explicitly refer to or recognize the legacy of the American civil rights movement or Martin Luther King Jr. as a source of their inspiration.[74] But their strategies and methods — nonviolent demonstrations and direct or symbolic actions, such as *Lichterketten* (lines of demonstrators carrying lights) against xenophobia or prayer vigils for asylum-seekers in pre-deportation detention, acts of civil disobedience in sanctuary work — are probably often indirectly influenced by that legacy.

Moreover, there are other examples of how the American civil rights movement has inspired actions against xenophobia and racism in Germany. In 1998 the "Martin Luther King Center for Nonviolence and Civil Courage" was founded in Werdau, Saxony, with the following mission: "In an increasingly violent world, the center promotes the legacy of Martin Luther King, Jr., and other pioneers of nonviolence. Drawing on the experience of the 1989 peaceful revolution in the German Democratic Republic (GDR), we aim to apply lessons from history to present-day conflicts, particularly in the field of right-wing extremism."[75] At the biannual Protestant Church congress in Munich in 1993, one day was dedicated to the theme of "Walking on with Martin Luther King" and involved the presentation of examples

» the first order in unified Germany" (28). For a discussion about the use of the terms *Rasse* and *Rassismus* in Germany, see Christine Morgenstern, *Rassismus macht Fremde. Begriffsklärung und Gegenstrategien* (Düsseldorf, 2001).

73 See Ulrich Wohland, "Soziale Rechte gewaltfrei verteidigen," *epd-Dokumentation* 15 (1999): 15-28.

74 Anne Broden of the Informations- und Dokumentationszentrum für Antirassismusarbeit (IDA, Information and Documentation Center for Anti-racism Work, founded in 1990) stated: "The movement against racism in Germany is a very young movement, existing perhaps twenty or even fewer years. During this time, the civil rights movement of the USA was not as much in the focus as in the 1960s" (e-mail to the author, Aug.7, 2013). Tahir Della, chairman of the Initiative Schwarze Menschen in Deutschland — ISD (Initiative of Black People in Germany), who is active against racial profiling by the police and other manifestations of racism, states that the methods of the ISD "cannot necessarily be compared to those used in the 1960s in the USA," but that some of the initiative's demands, e.g., education free of racism, "can be compared to those of the civil rights movement of the 1960s" (e-mail to the author, Aug. 8, 2013).

72 See Kirchenamt der EKD and Sekretariat der Deutschen Bischofskonferenz, eds., *Gemeinsames Wort der Kirchen zu den Herausforderungen durch Migration und Flucht* (Bonn, 1997), esp. 9-13, which states: "In the early 1990s, fear of and hostility to foreigners became societal problems of »

75 Flyer of the Martin Luther King Jr. Center in Werdau (in English).

76 There are examples of streets named after Martin Luther King Jr. in Berlin, Hanau, Mainz, Munich, Münster; of schools in Aachen, Düsseldorf, Göttingen, Hanover, Münster, Velbert; of churches and congregations, e.g., in Berlin, Hamburg, Hürth, and Stuttgart. Some schools in Germany are named after Rosa Parks. In the GDR, there were hospitals and other state-run institutions named after Martin Luther King Jr. as an expression of "anti-imperialist solidarity."

77 Martin Luther King, Jr., "A Time to Break Silence," in *A Testament of Hope: The Essential Writings of Martin Luther King, Jr.*, ed. James M. Washington (San Francisco, 1986), 242.

of nonviolent action and civil disobedience against racism and manifestations of social injustice in Germany.

In Germany today, there are a number of streets, as well as about two dozen institutions and edifices, mainly church-owned buildings and state schools, named after Martin Luther King Jr.[76] Curricula and books for high school students deal with the civil rights movement and King's life and work. "We Shall Overcome" has even found its way into the Lutheran hymnal. Since November 2013 an exhibition "Hewing out of the Mountain of Despair a Stone of Hope — Martin Luther King and the GDR" has been circulating throughout Germany, and in September 2014 the fiftieth anniversary of King's visit to West and East Berlin was commemorated with a variety of events. Still the question remains: Will the various ways in which Martin Luther King Jr. and the American civil rights movement are commemorated in Germany end up being just an excuse for not really taking more decisive action against racism, xenophobia, and social injustice? Or will their legacy further inspire Germans to actively "go out into a sometimes hostile world declaring eternal hostility to poverty, racism and militarism"?[77]

At any rate, in a time when many concerned citizens all over the world are critical of many aspects of U.S. politics, it is encouraging and challenging to keep "the other America" in mind, the United States of the March on Washington and the civil rights movement, which has helped Germany overcome its authoritarian heritage and has shaped its social protest movements and groups over the past five decades and continues to do so today.

Heinrich W. Grosse was a professor at the Institute of Pastoral Sociology/Social Sciences in Hanover until retiring in 2007. He has worked on Martin Luther King Jr.'s legacy and questions of social justice throughout his career, from his dissertation *Macht der Armen. Martin Luther King und der Kampf für soziale Gerechtigkeit* and participation in civil rights organizations in Mississippi and Washington, DC, in 1968 to German translations of many of MLK's speeches. His publications also focus on practical theology, the role of the Protestant churches during the Nazi era, and Dietrich Bonhoeffer.

THE MARCH ON LONDON: BRITISH-AMERICAN CONNECTIONS DURING THE CIVIL RIGHTS MOVEMENT

Stephen Tuck

At the March on Washington, a couple of hours before Martin Luther King Jr. famously spoke of his dream "deeply rooted in the American dream," the actor Ossie Davis encouraged the crowd to recognize "the international character of the struggle of which we are currently engaged." Davis was introducing Josephine Baker, the Missouri-born African American entertainer who had long been based in France, "far ... from these shores." Suitably dressed in French Resistance uniform, Baker urged the crowd to believe that they were "on the eve of complete victory." Baker exhorted them: "Continue on. You can't go wrong. The world is behind you."[1] Davis and Baker were right. This was an international moment, and the world did seem right behind them. There were demonstrations in support of the March on Washington outside the American embassies in Egypt, Jamaica, Paris, Ghana, Israel, and Norway. Three days after King spoke in Washington, there was a march in London, too. Some 750 people gathered at Ladbroke Grove Tube Station in central London, and they marched three miles to the American embassy.[2]

This march in London demonstrated that there was British backing for the American movement. The marchers delivered a petition to the American embassy calling for the U.S. government to act on behalf of the civil rights movement. The organizer of the march, the Trinidad-born communist activist cum journalist, Claudia Jones, had spent most of her adult life working in the black section of New York City — Harlem — and retained close ties with American activists. Marchers prepared banners with slogans that declared their solidarity with, and knowledge of, the American civil rights movement: "Support the Negro People's Struggle in the U.S.A," "America's Negroes Fight World Imperialism!," and, referring to the recently murdered Mississippi activist and local president of the state's National Association for the Advancement of Colored People, "Medgar Evers' Blood Reddens the Thirst for Freedom!" Outside the American embassy, the demonstrators sang the American civil rights anthem, "We Shall Overcome."[3]

Despite the many references to the struggle in the states, the London demonstration in support of the March on Washington was also about race matters in Britain. The London march commenced close to the site of anti-immigrant riots in Notting Hill in 1958 and near the scene of

1   "Celebrity Participation in the March on Washington," WGBH online archives www.openvault.wgbh.org/catalog/march-bc109d-celebrity-participation-in-the-march-on-washington.

2   On Jamaica, see "Kingston Marchers Support Negro Rights Struggle," *West Indian Gazette and Afro-Asian-Caribbean News*, October 1963, 2. For more details on solidarity marches, see Mary Dudziak, *Cold War Civil Rights: Race and the Image of American Democracy* (Princeton, 2011), 191.

3   "Londoners Demonstrate against U.S. Racial Discrimination," *West Indian Gazette and Afro-Asian-Caribbean News*, September 1963, 16; "UK Supporters Visit US Embassy," *West Indies Observer*, June 15, 1963, 1. For an excellent analysis of the march, see Kenyetta Perry, "'U.S. Negroes, Your Fight Is Our Fight': Black Britons and the 1963 March on Washington," in *The Other Special Relationship: Race, Rights, and Riots in Britain and the United States,* ed. Robin D. G. Kelley and Stephen Tuck (New York, 2015).

the unprovoked attack upon, and murder of, an Antiguan immigrant, Kelso Cochrane, by a gang of young white men the following year. In her report in Britain's main black newspaper, *The West Indian Gazette,* Jones explained that the march was held to signal that discrimination and anti-immigration sentiments were prevalent in Britain, too. Amid the signs calling for change in the U.S. were slogans that spoke directly to black British concerns: "End the Colour Bar in Britain!," "Repeal the Immigration Act!" (of 1962), and, referring to the deportation of immigrants, "End Mccarthyite Witch Hunt." One marcher held up a picture of Kelso Cochrane.[4] This, then, was a march for equality in Britain as well as a march in solidarity with those demanding civil rights in America. Or, as one banner put it, "Your Fight Is Our Fight."

In many ways, the march in London, or rather the March on London, encapsulated the relationship between Britain and America during the civil rights era. In the first place, it pointed to a close connection between Britons and Americans over the issue of civil rights — with a widespread belief, especially among Britons, that issues of race in Britain were inextricably intertwined with those in the U.S. Yet historians have devoted little attention to the broader issue of British-American links during the civil rights era.[5] This lacuna in the literature stands in stark contrast to the extensive historical scholarship on antebellum British-American connections over slavery and persists despite the fact that black studies scholars have been in the vanguard of the transnational turn.[6] There is an emerging interest

4   For details on the banners, also see Nicholas Juravich, "Your Fight Is Our Fight," (MPhil. Thesis, University of Oxford, 2008).

5   For example, Gerald Horne's call for a transnational research agenda discusses links between African Americans and most parts of the world during the civil rights era but does not mention Britain and Europe. Horne, "Toward a Transnational Research Agenda for African American History in the 21st Century," *Journal of African American History* 91, no. 3 (2006): 288-303. Notable exceptions, which have tended to focus on the impact of high-profile African American visitors on Britain, include Joe Street, "Malcolm X, Smethwick, and the Influence of the African American Freedom Struggle," *Journal of Black Studies* 38, no. 6 (2008): 932-50; Brian Ward, "A King in Newcastle: Martin Luther King, Jr. and British Race Relations, 1967-1968," *Georgia Historical Quarterly* 79, no. 3 (1995): 599-632; and Mike Sewell, "British Responses to Martin Luther King, Jr., and the Civil Rights Movement," in *Martin Luther King and the Making of the Civil Rights Movement,* ed. Anthony Badger and Brian Ward (Basingstoke, 1996), 194-212. Recent, mostly unpublished research on connections or comparisons between African Americans and black Britons heralds the emergence of a new field in the near future. See, for example, Joshua Bruce Guild, "You Can't Go Home Again: Migration, Citizenship, and Black Community in Postwar New York and London" (Ph.D. dissertation, Yale University, 2007); Kennetta Perry, "Black Migrants, Citizenship and the Transnational Politics of Race in Postwar Britain"

(Ph.D. diss., Michigan State University, 2007); Rosalind Eleanor Wild, "'Black Was the Colour of Our Fight': Black Power in Britain, 1955-1976" (Ph.D. diss., University of Sheffield, 2008); and Anne-Marie Angelo, "The Black Panthers in London, 1967-1972: A Diasporic Struggle Navigates the Black Atlantic," *Radical History Review* 103 (Winter 2009): 17-35. See too Stephen Tuck, "Malcolm X's Visit to Oxford University: U.S. Civil Rights, Black Britain, and the Special Relationship on Race," *American Historical Review* 118 (Spring 2013): 76-103, from which

many of the points in this article about British-American connections on race are taken.

6   As the historian of African American and global black history Robin D. G. Kelley observed, "black studies ... were diasporic from their inception." Precisely because of this diasporic framework, however, the first African American historians "always began in Africa" rather than Europe. Robin D. G. Kelley, "'But a Local Phase of a World Problem': Black History's Global Vision, 1883-1950," *Journal of American History* 86, no. 3 (1999): 1045-77,

here 1045, 1051. Among numerous works on the African American diaspora, see *Becoming African Americans: Black Public Life in Harlem, 1919-1939* (Cambridge, MA, 2009); and Winston James, *Holding Aloft the Banner of Ethiopia: Caribbean Radicalism in Early Twentieth-Century America* (London, 1998). On antebellum connections, see Van Gosse, "'As a Nation, the English Are Our Friends': The Emergence of African American Politics in the British Atlantic World, 1772-1861," *American Historical Review* 113, no. 4 (October 2008): 1003-28.

in the international context of both the British and particularly the U.S. struggles over racial equality in the mid-twentieth century. But historians of black Britain have mostly looked to the important connections with the British Commonwealth. For their part, scholars of the U.S. civil rights movement have focused on the Cold War context and links with postcolonial nations or the communist bloc — yet they have tended to center the United States in their analysis of the so-called American century.[7]

The relationship between the British and American movements was asymmetrical. The march in London was in solidarity with the March on Washington, not vice versa. After all, the mid-twentieth century was, as transnational historian Ian Tyrrell aptly put it, the "high noon of American hegemony."[8] More generally, the U.S. movement was a point of inspiration for British activism. But it was not a simple one-way relationship. British activists also made use of the march — and other iconic American demonstrations — for their own purposes. In return, American activists, like Ossie Davis, used the international dimensions of the struggle for their own benefit — the following year, Davis would support Malcolm X's call to bring the issue of American racism before the United Nations. Although American activists were inspired by news of colonial states in Africa gaining independence, many looked to Britain, and in some cases visited Britain, too. And as they did so, American activists — even Martin Luther King Jr. — had their views challenged by what they saw.

Britons and the American Civil Rights Movement

By the time of the March on Washington in 1963, Britain and America had strong connections on race matters. Such connections built on a long tradition, from the anti-slavery (and, indeed, pro-slavery) movement to the nexus of Asian, African and African American activists during World War II. But by the 1960s, far-reaching changes in international relations, media, and transportation had made those connections closer still. In the Cold War, the British and American governments forged a close alliance through their famous special relationship. Politicians shared ideas across the Atlantic — British politicians concerned about race matters traveled to the United States, first and foremost, on fact-finding tours. As postwar Britain increasingly imported American news and popular culture, the U.S. civil rights movement — with its set piece demonstrations staged for dramatic effect — appeared in the headlines and front pages in

7   On Britain see, for example, Winston James, "The Black Experience in Twentieth-Century Britain," in *Black Experience and the Empire*, ed. Philip D. Morgan and Sean Hawkins (Oxford, 2004), 347-86. On connections between black Britons and the anti-apartheid movement, see the articles in Hilary Sapire, ed., "Liberation Struggles, Exile and International Solidarity," Special Issue, *Journal of Southern African Studies* 35, no. 2 (2009); Elizabeth Williams, "We Shall Not Be Free until South Africa Is Free! The Anti-Apartheid Activity of Black Britons" (Ph.D. diss., Birkbeck College, 2009). By contrast, cultural studies scholarship has extensively explored the connection with the United States, notably Paul Gilroy, *The Black Atlantic: Modernity and Double Consciousness* (London, 1993). On the U.S. see, for example, Mary L. Dudziak, *Cold War Civil Rights: Race and the Image of American Democracy* (Princeton, 2000); Glenda Elizabeth Gilmore, *Defying Dixie: The Radical Roots of Civil Rights, 1919-1950* (New York, 2008); and James H. Meriwether, *Proudly We Can Be Africans: Black Americans and Africa, 1935-1961* (Chapel Hill, 2002).

8   Ian Tyrrell, *Transnational Nation: United States History in Global Perspective since 1789* (Basingstoke, 2007), 171.

the UK. Thanks to the newly launched Telstar satellite, Britons were able to watch live coverage of major civil rights events, such as the March on Washington, on television. With the increasing availability and decreasing cost of transatlantic travel, some Britons, particularly white students, flew to America to experience the civil rights movement firsthand. One group from the University of Oxford joined the Freedom Riders in Mississippi; a Durham University student wound up in jail after joining demonstrations in Monroe, North Carolina, while Cambridge (UK) University's Jonathan Steele, a journalism intern on a Yale scholarship, found himself close to Martin Luther King Jr. during the speech in Washington. (Steele would later become the lead foreign affairs editor for the *Guardian*.)[9]

The closest connections, though, were between African Americans and African and Caribbean immigrants to Britain. For all the inspiration that black Britons and African Americans may have drawn from anticolonial movements in the Caribbean, Africa, and South Asia, their own situations were much more analogous with each other. Both black Britons and African Americans belonged to non-white, minority groups demanding equality in Western capitalist democracies that prided themselves on their liberal creeds.

As a result, many Americans and Britons came to perceive their racial situations as comparable. When preaching at St. Paul's Cathedral in London in December of 1964, Martin Luther King Jr. compared the "festering sores" of inner city British housing to American ghettos. The situations were sufficiently similar, and King thought that "lessons had been learnt in the United States which had some relevance" for Britain.[10] When Malcolm X came to Britain that same winter, he was struck by the common portrayals of African Americans and black Britons in the media. "Press calls us racists, imagery bad, crime stats fed, white communities actually high crime, false image, justify police state," he wrote in his notebook, "leads to vandalism, hoodlumism, same in Britain, colored communities, divide and conquer."[11]

On the British side, the title of a lead editorial in 1963 in the black London weekly the *West Indies Observer* described British racial discrimination as "Mr James Crow, Esq."[12] British sociologists of race tested their nation's development against the American example. Dr. Kenneth Little, founding father of the discipline in the UK, popularized the concept of a "British dilemma" (imperial creed of equal citizenship but discrimination in practice) akin to Swedish sociologist Gunnar Myrdal's influential 1944 study *An American*

9 See Stephen Tuck, *The Night Malcolm X Spoke at the Oxford Union* (Oakland, 2014).

10 "Dr King's Racial Warning to Britain," *Times* (London), December 7, 1964, 6.

11 Notes, Outlines for Speeches, 1964-1965, box 9, folder 8, Malcolm X Collection, Schomburg Library, New York.

12 "Editorially Speaking: Mr James Crow, Esq.," *West Indies Observer* 1, no. 16 (March 23, 1963), 4.

Dilemma (national creed of all men created equal but segregation in many states).[13] Politicians and journalists — on the political Left and Right — frequently spoke of the "American-style" situation that Britain found itself in, and they assumed that the countries were on the same path. Commonwealth leaders of newly independent former British colonies drew the comparison between the British and U.S. situations, too.[14]

Those making the comparison had a compelling narrative to tell. Some of the landmark moments of racial strife in the two countries did seem to be uncannily similar. The anti-black riots in Nottingham and London followed hot on the heels of white mobs defending school segregation in Little Rock, Arkansas, and all-white neighborhoods defending integrated housing in Levittown, Pennsylvania. The outrage that followed the murder of Cochrane in London in 1959 paralleled that surrounding Emmett Till's murder in Mississippi in 1955 — in both cases the obvious perpetrators were not brought to justice. Southern U.S. politicians who played the "nigra" card had their counterparts in conservative British anti-immigrant politicians who warned, "If you want a nigger for your neighbour, vote Labour."

Legislative responses to discrimination also grew simultaneously across the Atlantic. The British Race Relations Act of 1965 followed the American Civil Rights Act of 1964. Striking, too, were the similar justifications for racial discrimination. British landladies who put up "No blacks, no dogs" signs in their front windows justified their stance by inadvertently invoking the American shibboleths of home-owners' rights and anti-communism. And like U.S. segregationists, they raised the specter of black women's sexual promiscuity and black men's sexual aggression.[15]

It was because of these contemporary assumptions about the comparability of the British and American situations that the two stories became deeply entwined. In everyday British language, some black neighborhoods were called Little Harlems, and the word "coloured" to describe non-white peoples was a U.S. import. British Black Power activists used Malcolm X's slogan "by any means necessary" even though they had no intention of pursuing an armed struggle. Political decisions about civil rights and immigration legislation — particularly those made by British politicians — were often made in the light of perceptions about the other side of the Atlantic. During an interview in 2010, Godfrey Hodgson, the *Times* (London) correspondent on racial conditions in the 1950s, chuckled when he recalled the "rush

13 K. L. Little, *Negroes in Britain: A Study of Racial Relations in English Society* (London, 1947).

14 "Coloured Audience Shouts Down M.P.," *Guardian*, September 8, 1958.

15 On landladies' language, see Tuck, "Malcolm X's Visit."

to bring inappropriate remedies across from America."[16] He had good reason. For example, when the British prime minister appointed the archbishop of Canterbury to chair a committee on racial conditions, the prelate declared that he was "anxious to learn of similar problems in America first hand." So when the Motown musical group the Temptations came to London in 1970 to promote their new album, he was quick to invite them to Lambeth Palace to learn about how to tackle racial tensions — before blessing them ahead of their upcoming tour.[17]

As news and people crossed the Atlantic, it is little surprise that strategies did too. In headline terms, it seemed that British activists took instructions from their counterparts in the United States. Many of the major British protest organizations of the 1960s were formed in response to American visitors. Most notably, Martin Luther King Jr.'s visit to London in 1964 was the catalyst for a meeting of a dozen or so leaders of civil and immigrant rights groups. Accompanied by Bayard Rustin, the March on Washington organizer, King shared lessons from home and asked questions about Britain. Both men then encouraged the assembled leaders to join together to put pressure on the British government. The Campaign Against Racial Discrimination (later known as C.A.R.D.), the highest profile British campaign organization of the decade, was born, sharing many of the same principles as King's Southern Christian Leadership Conference. The following year, after a meeting with Malcolm X, Trinidad-born Michael de Freitas changed his name to Michael X and created the Racial Adjustment Action Society — its acronym, RAAS, was a Jamaican obscenity. In 1967, Black Power leader Stokely Carmichael's visit to London coincided with the formation of the United Coloured People's Association, a British Black Power organization.[18]

Tactics associated with American protest also regularly turned up in Britain. The Montgomery bus boycott of 1955 was followed by the 1963 bus boycott in Bristol; it was led by local activist Paul Stephenson, who had recently visited the American South at the invitation of civil rights leaders there. Stephenson cited King as his hero. The student sit-ins in American restaurants had their counterparts in the unsurprisingly popular freedom drink-ins in British pubs: Operation Guinness in Lewisham was a particular hit.[19] There was also a London Black Panther group. And there were plenty on the American side who presumed that it was their job to teach. "The Grand Experiment which we now conduct in America," King explained to a gathering in

16 Author interview with Godfrey Hodgson, May 20, 2010.

17 "The Archbishop of Canterbury Talks with the Temptations," *Chicago Defender*, February 3, 1970, 11; "The Archbishop of Canterbury Receives Motown's Temptations," *Philadelphia Tribune*, February 3, 1970, 18.

18 Benjamin W. Heineman, Jr., *The Politics of the Powerless: A Study of the Campaign against Racial Discrimination* (London, 1972), 19–21; John L. Williams, *Michael X: A Life in Black and White* (London, 2008). For the UCPA's founding statement, see clipping from *Aframerican News Service*, January 3, 1968, Student Nonviolent Coordinating Committee Papers (microfilm) [hereafter SNCC Papers], Subgroup B: New York Office, 1960–1969, Series II: International Affairs Commission, 1964–1969, 19, reel 51. See also Obi Egbuna, *Destroy This Temple: The Voice of Black Power in Britain* (London, 1971), 18.

19 John Ross, "Operation Guinness," *Flamingo*, February 1965, 9–11; letter, *Flamingo*, April 1965, 2. See also "West Indians Stage an American Style Sit-In," *Chicago Defender*, July 9, 1963, 4; "Strikers Protest Firing," *Chicago Defender*, July 16, 1963, 16; "Shabby Protest," *Chicago Defender*, June 22, 1963, 14; "Watch to Be Kept on Colour Bar Premises," *Irish Times*, April 9, 1965, 10.

London, "is of tremendous relevance to the rest of the world and you, by your support of the nonviolent movement in America and your concern for social justice in America, contribute to the dawn of a new day of brotherhood." As for the American Ku Klux Klan, a spokesman boasted to British reporters, "We have told them how to organise."[20]

Contemporary commentators invariably portrayed the transfer of ideas and tactics for protesting (or defending) racial hierarchies as one-way traffic from the United States to Britain. In this line, British activism was merely a somewhat quaint version of the story proper. Atlanta-based civil rights journalist Calvin Trillin wrote of Britain in the *New Yorker* in 1965. He described "watching an old familiar play performed by an inexperienced road company." Even a death threat sent to a black activist by a "Deputy Wizard" of the British Klan, mocked Trillin, ended in impeccably polite British terms: "Faithfully yours."[21]

Yet as the March on London suggests, the British movement was not simply the overspill from its American counterpart. British activists could, and did, draw on examples from other parts of the world where they had close connections, and they had a protest tradition of their own. Moreover, for all the seeming similarities, there were important differences between the two contexts. The U.S. had a domestic history of removing, enslaving, and subjugating its non-white population, but in the British imperial imagination, "coloured people were subjects to nurture, even a source of pride." (This imagination, of course, ignored Britain's historical role in the slave trade and was rudely exposed when immigrants from former colonies took up British citizenship in large numbers. The government swiftly passed an act restricting non-white immigration in 1962.) Segregation was formalized under the Jim Crow laws in the American South but was never on the statute books in Britain. In the United States, African Americans had a highly developed institutional structure, including long-standing protest organizations, while mass protest and litigation had won important victories before the civil rights movement. The British non-white population, by contrast, began to increase significantly only in the 1950s, with immigration from the Caribbean, South Asia, and Africa. As a result, non-white people from a wide variety of national backgrounds were lumped together (and self-identified) as black, whereas in the United States Asian, Hispanic, and African American groups often asserted their differences. One Indian immigrant complained to a British interviewer, "When I was in U.S.A. I was not considered as a coloured man."[22]

20 "The Lunatic Fringe," *Flamingo*, September 1961, 41; W. J. Weatherby, "A Guest of the Ku-Klux-Klan," *Guardian*, December 3, 1960, 6.

21 Calvin Trillin, "A Reporter at Large: Color in the Mother Country," *New Yorker*, December 4, 1965, 115–65.

22 W. W. Daniel, *Racial Discrimination in England: Based on the P.E.P. Report* (London, 1968), 48.

Rather than import the American movement wholesale, activists in Britain often used the British-American connections on race for their own purposes. Even the March on Washington was protean and pliable once it crossed the Atlantic. Therein lay its power. British campaigners took advantage of the publicity surrounding the March on Washington to denounce anti-immigration legislation. Indeed, when British activists used American civil rights or Black Power–style tactics, they were able to be selective in their choices and use them at their own timing. The Bristol bus boycott occurred eight years after its counterpart in Montgomery, and the issue was the color line in employment rather than passenger segregation. The first British sit-ins began three years after their American counterparts and were few and far between. Meanwhile, Black Power groups used Malcolm X's image and words on their mastheads even though his slogans did not, in fact, easily translate to British contexts. The British Black Panther Party formed before the American Panthers had begun to establish international affiliates, and most likely without their knowledge.

In other words, American styling was a strategic choice by British activists. They were well aware that British discrimination was not Mr. James Crow esq., but they chose to portray it as such. The reason was simple. British campaigners sought to ride the coattails of the American movement to legitimize their complaints. Sympathy for the U.S. civil rights movement was widespread across Britain. After the bombing of an African American church soon after Martin Luther King Jr. led demonstrations in Birmingham, Alabama, in 1963, for example, residents of Llanstephan, Wales, raised funds to replace the main stained-glass window. But British support for the U.S. civil rights movement was not matched by support for British civil rights campaigners. Indeed, British commentators routinely contrasted American horrors with British decency. The Welsh stained-glass artist sent to Alabama, for example, was "entirely dismayed by what I discovered" over there.[23]

23 A plaque with the inscription "Donated by the people of Wales" is still positioned beneath the stained-glass window with an imposing black messiah on a cross. Bill Patterson, "Alabama Window," *Flamingo*, December 1964, 9-12.

Hence, black British civil rights activists asserted connections with the American civil rights movement to show their dismay with the reality of immigrant life "over here." During the Bristol bus boycott, Stephenson took the comparison with the U.S. civil rights movement further, telling reporters, "People are saying that it is worse [here] than it is in the deep south of America" because of restrictions on immigration and the British denial of discrimination. Such complaints found their way into the mainstream British press. In an exquisite piece of timing, the Bristol Bus Company agreed to Stephenson's demands on the very day of the March on Washington. (As for Michael de Freitas, a man on the make, by taking the surname X, he briefly gained outsized media interest.)[24]

In any case, because Britain did not have *de jure* Jim Crow-style segregation, the classic tactics of the civil rights movement were not applicable. Members of the Operation Guinness group met no opposition in the first ten or so pubs they visited because black customers were not formally excluded. Indeed, reports are not entirely clear on whether members of the group were eventually barred because of their color or because they had already drunk almost a dozen pints of beer by that stage. The Race Relations Act of 1965, which was modeled on far-reaching U.S. federal and state legislation against *de jure* discrimination, made little impact on *de facto* employment and housing discrimination in Britain (this critique of the limitations of the original American legislation was, in fact, already being made by many African American leaders with regard to race relations in Northern and Western U.S. cities).

Ultimately, it was Black Power, with its explicit international vision, confrontational rhetoric, and emphasis on community control over resources, that was the best fit for black Britons angered by immigration restrictions and frustrated by the moderate response of major black equality organizations. Black Power's Islamist connections (because of Malcolm X) appealed to London's East End Bengali community, too. Indeed, black British activists borrowed directly from American Black Power more than any other aspect of the American struggle. London became a meeting ground for any number of Black Power conferences, and Black Britons consciously adopted Black Power tactics, rhetoric, and dress codes, and welcomed Black Power visitors like Stokeley Carmichael. Even so, U.S. Black Power's calls for black political empowerment, cultural nationalism, and armed self-defense were lost in translation because non-white Britons represented less than 3 percent of the population, half were from Asia with long-established cultural traditions, and virtually none owned guns.[25] British Black Power activists adapted the American credo to their own situation — in Britain, Indian and Pakistani immigrants joined West Indian immigrants as equal partners in Black Power activity, thus broadening the range of those involved in this new phase of protest beyond the American version.

24 "Busmen Heckle Marchers," *Evening Post* (Bristol), May 2, 1963, 12, IRR, folder 01/04/04/01/04/01/01–05. See too Edward Scobie, "Black Englishman," *Flamingo*, November 1962, 32; and letters to the editor, *Guardian*, December 8, 1960, 10.

25 For discussions of Black Power's (lack of) transferability, see Wild, "'Black Was the Colour of Our Fight'"; Angelo, "The Black Panthers in London"; and Leila Kamali, "The Sweet Part and the Sad Part: Black Power and the Memory of Africa in African American and Black British Literature," *Atlantic Studies* 6, no. 2 (2009): 207–21.

If British civil rights activists invoked the American movement to influence British authorities, the small cadre of British Black Power activists stressed connections with the U.S. to gain legitimacy with black Britons — by importing the Black Power aesthetic, they allied themselves with a powerful brand. Meanwhile, liberal British politicians and so-called race relations lobbyists openly borrowed ideas directly from their American counterparts not simply to develop their proposals but to increase the likelihood of getting them accepted. As for anti-immigration campaigners, they used news of American violence in ghettos during the late 1960s for their own propaganda. The British government passed a more restrictive immigration act in March 1968. Conservative MP Enoch Powell was not satisfied. The following month, after his first visit to the United States, he delivered his infamous anti-immigration "Rivers of Blood" speech, warning of the "horror on the other side of the Atlantic ... coming upon us here by our own volition and our own neglect."[25] An even more restrictive immigration act was passed in 1971.

What was true in Britain was true in countries across Europe and beyond. Communist governments in Eastern Europe celebrated King as the champion of the "other America," the America that had been subjugated by capitalist tyranny. In Italy, the Catholic Left portrayed King as a political activist and ignored the fact that he was also a Protestant preacher. And in white-majority countries with racial minorities, from New Zealand to Western Europe, commentators lauded King's role in the turmoil "over there," while taking comfort that any problems at home, by comparison, could not be too bad. In Britain, conservative politicians hailed King as a nonviolent role model for immigrants who were threatening to fight for their rights (and much better than another popular black American icon and visitor to Britain, Malcolm X).[26]

Americans and the British Struggle for Equality

For their part, African American leaders used news from Britain to put pressure on the State Department to stand up to southern segregationists. Malcolm X publicly denounced American racism as "a cancer spreading all over the world" that was manifesting itself in Britain.[27] During the 1950s, virtually all African American press coverage of the black experience in Britain had actually been negative. This framing reflected anti-imperial sentiment and seems to have been part of the broader Cold War rebuttal of the claim by overseas

26 See, for example, Martin Klimke, "Bringing Civil Rights to East and West: Dr. Martin Luther King Jr. in Cold War Berlin," in *A Breath of Freedom: The Civil Rights Struggle, African American GIs, and Germany*, by Maria Höhn and Martin Klimke, 89-105 (New York, 2010).

27 See Malcolm X, personal notebook, Malcolm X Collection, Schomburg Library, and Malcolm X, "The Fight against Racism from South Africa to Australia to the U.S.A.," interview with the *Sunday Express* (Johannesburg), February 12, 1965, in Malcolm X, *The Final Speeches: February 1965* (New York, 1992), 69.

black radicals that discrimination against African Americans in the U.S. was akin to colonial-style oppression. The rise of the American civil rights movement — and particularly the massive resistance to it — marked an about-turn in reportage. "Race relations in England, in the past, have been on a higher plane of conviviality," reported the influential African American newspaper the *Chicago Defender* after the anti-immigrant riots of 1958 — thereby changing its stance and ignoring virtually all of its own past reports from the previous decade. "Nevertheless, America's brazen, vulgar display of racial hatred has assumed the virulence of a communicative disease which is infecting the mind and soul of the stolid Englishman."[28]

Mainstream white American commentators, by contrast — to the exasperation of African American journalists — used anti-immigrant news from Britain to debunk U.S. exceptionalism in the matter of racist mob violence. "Radio station announcers," a West Indian visitor to New York noted ruefully, would "interrupt a programme to splash — not without satisfaction — the news of Britain's race riots." White supremacist groups in the American South followed Enoch Powell's career with admiration and invited him to lecture. As for Governor Orval Faubus of Arkansas, orchestrator of the Little Rock crisis, he enjoyed telling British reporters to shove it. "What about that shindy in Nottingham?" he asked the *Daily Express*. "We have sympathy for you." Hence the African American press fought back. The *Afro-American* warned Faubus not "to chortle too much over Notting Hill." There were no police officers and mobs there blocking children from going to school, no need for federal troops to protect children attending school, and even the worst offenders in the crisis received only four-year sentences from the courts. The *Defender* noted how few votes were cast for Britain's own Faubus figure, Sir Oswald Mosley, in an election in Notting Hill the following year. "Even a metropolitan dogcatcher would have done better. London, of course, is not Little Rock."[29]

Meanwhile, the high-profile visits of African American leaders to Britain enhanced the prestige of both the hosts and the guests. King, by speaking at St. Paul's Cathedral, enhanced his status as an international religious statesman at a time when southern opponents were denouncing him as a communist. He also met with the Lord Chancellor at the House of Lords, and he breakfasted with the visiting Indian premier — securing a promise that India would stay out of the nuclear arms race.[30] In December of 1964, Malcolm X accepted

28 Tuck, "Malcolm X's Visit," 96.

29 Ibid.

30 "Dr. King's Racial Warning," *Times* (London), December 7, 1964, 6.

an invitation to speak at the prestigious Oxford Union to bolster his demands to be heard in the United States — at rallies before leaving for England, he talked about his invitation to the University of Oxford to the exclusion of all other parts of his itinerary. The self-promotional purpose of such visits by U.S. leaders is underscored by the amount of time they devoted to publicity while in England. Malcolm X spent much of his visits to England meeting with black journalists or with BBC reporters. Benefiting from a Church of England public relations officer, King's two-day London visit in 1964 included seven media interviews.[31] Speaking abroad also provided American leaders with a platform to espouse their philosophies to a wider audience. Malcolm X tried to go to Paris to connect with black French and Francophone anticolonial activists. King's speechwriter, Clarence Jones, recalled that "they accepted the invitations to England to get their message out." By preaching that "the doctrine of black superiority is just as dangerous as the doctrine of white superiority," noted the *New York Times*, King also sought to counter the "activities of Malcolm X ... who [was] also in London."[32]

Time in Britain allowed African American leaders to build up their international networks, too. Malcolm X visited the Council of African Organisations while in London, King met with delegations of international students and immigrant leaders, while Stokely Carmichael, who had overseen the main U.S. student protest organization's adoption of Black Power in 1966, came to London in 1967 to participate in an international congress to explore "new forms of action" to challenge violent social systems. There was also the question of financing the movement. As a Protestant minister, King was particularly well placed to harness support from British churches. "In the dark hours," King wrote to one donor, "we will always remember the many people in England who encouraged our work ... by their very tangible expressions by which our movement is continued." British students supported their American counterparts financially, too — hosting a fundraising exhibition of photographs of student civil rights work in Mississippi. There was even talk of the Beatles playing a fundraising concert.[33]

Yet even as they used connections with Britain for their own purposes, activists in the United States were changed by those connections — particularly those American leaders who visited Britain, and none more so than King. He traveled to London in 1964 en route to receive the Nobel Peace Prize in Oslo. King's Nobel lecture, however,

31 "London Programme for Dr Martin Luther King," *Washington Post*, December 7, 1964, 1; *New York Times*, December 7, 1964, 1.

32 Author interview with Clarence Jones, January 18, 2011; "Dr. King Preaches Negro Restraint," *New York Times*, December 7, 1964, 1.

33 "Christians in Action gave $561.25," Payment Order, January 5, 1962, Records of the Southern Christian Leadership Conference, 1954–1970 (microfilm), Schomburg Library, Part 2: Records of the Executive Director and Treasurer, reel 14, box 51:12, frame no. 0359. See also Wyatt Tee Walker to Canon Collins, January 24, 1962, ibid.

one of his first speeches to address global concerns — but written before he made his stop in London — did not even mention black Europeans. King only referred, optimistically, to the "black brothers of Africa and brown and yellow brothers in Asia, South America, and the Caribbean." King's speechwriter recalled that the subject of race in Britain never came up in it.[34] Moreover, King's prepared speech for London was set to be an update on American affairs. Yet after meeting British activists, King hastily edited — on hotel stationery — the version of the speech he would deliver in London, denouncing the "segregation and discrimination that is emerging [and] that you have quite rightly deplored in others."[35] Further visits to Britain, and travels abroad more generally, would hasten King's transformation from an advocate of the American dream into a critic of unfettered capitalism and militarism worldwide.[36]

Unlike Martin Luther King Jr., Malcolm X came to Britain at the end of 1964 and in early 1965 with a well-developed global vision — he had spent almost half of the year 1964 in the Middle East and Africa, calling on the leaders of newly independent nations to protest to the United Nations about American racism. Yet his time in England refined that vision because of his experience of racial discrimination and his time with British and European activists — those he met were surprised that the great orator spent most of his time asking questions rather than trying to teach. During a visit to Birmingham (UK), the scene of a particularly vicious election campaign that focused on immigration, Malcolm X warned that unless politicians took action, it would be (Holocaust-style) "gas ovens" next. He was particularly shocked to be turned away from France, a country with a reputation for transcending the color line, when attempting to visit early in 1965.[37]

Before his visit, Malcolm X had spoken of two categories of black people: those fighting colonial rule and those under quasi-colonial rule in the United States, with no mention of black Europeans. "Only Americanism is more hypocritical than colonialism." After spending time with black Britons and (via the telephone) Parisian activists, he began to speak in terms of "4 types of blacks in [the] West, under Spanish, British, French or U.S. influence," all facing common problems. By adding new categories to his list of the non-white oppressed, he sharpened his thinking about discrimination and anti-racist possibilities. There were "over 100 million Afros in [the] West," he noted while in Britain, "*inside* the Western Power Structure."[38]

34 *Nobel Lecture by the Reverend Dr. Martin Luther King, Jr., Recipient of the 1964 Nobel Peace Prize, Oslo, Norway, December 11, 1964* (New York, 1964); author interview with Clarence Jones.

35 "Rough Notes," Southern Christian Leadership Conference Papers, Schomburg Library, Bayard Rustin Papers, reel 3, no. 0258.

36 On King's emerging human rights vision, see Thomas F. Jackson, *From Civil Rights to Human Rights: Martin Luther King, Jr., and the Struggle for Economic Justice* (Philadelphia, 2006), and Ward, "A King in Newcastle."

37 See Street, "Malcolm X." Malcolm X believed that U.S. intelligence might have been behind the incident and complained to the State Department (though he was still dismayed by French complicity). In fact, French intelligence may have been motivated out of fear of an assassination plot, wanting to avoid an incident on French soil, rather than out of a desire to keep out Malcolm X on account of his radical views.

38 Tuck, "Malcolm X's Visit," 99-100.

This observation hastened Malcolm X's shift from an anticolonial framework to a more nuanced international and somewhat socialist position, dovetailing with lessons he learned in the Middle East and Africa. From 1965, his speeches optimistically addressed internal resistance within America *and* Europe working in harmony with external resistance to the Western power structure. "During 1965," he wrote in his notebook, "we shall see the longest, hottest and bloodiest summer yet witnessed, by ... the Black Revolution." "It's trouble for old John Bull," he mused. Malcolm X looked forward to seeing that trouble in person on return visits. (He did not get the chance. In February, one week after his return to the United States, he was shot dead.)[39]

For African Americans who couldn't make the journey, news from Britain came to them through a black press that paid close attention to race matters overseas. The spread of global news mattered. In the U.S., the sense of a shared race-relations trajectory with Europe heightened the salience of Black Power, as it would come to be known, at the earliest stages of the modern civil rights movement. As is well known, it was good news of anticolonialist movements abroad, especially Ghanaian independence in 1957, that helped to galvanize the mass nonviolent protest against segregation that erupted across the southern states of America in 1960. Or as the leading African American novelist and civil rights advocate James Baldwin put it, "all of Africa will be free before we can get a lousy cup of coffee." But bad news of anti-immigrant campaigns — especially of the London riots of 1958, which student activists in the sit-ins that swept the South in 1960 knew about[40] — and racial discrimination in Britain, a country without formal segregation or disfranchisement, served as a bleak counterpoint.

Thus, even at the optimistic start of the modern civil rights movement, bad news from Britain counterbalanced good news from Africa and portended trouble for African Americans living in a nation with a liberal credo. No doubt, it would have added to the increasing unease of many volunteers in the early 1960s about the limits of nonviolent direct-action protest for integration and strengthened the arguments of those, such as Malcolm X, who advocated self-defense and rejected integration from the outset.

News of Malcolm X being turned away from France reinforced his argument — a year before the Black Power slogan first came to prominence in Mississippi — that black Americans, and their allies around

39 Ibid.

40 This is based on interviews with former SNCC activists. To be sure, they may have learned of these riots in later life, but given the limited coverage of British race history in the U.S., this is unlikely.

the world, should not seek to integrate with white, supposed liberals. Or rather, Malcolm X reinforced his argument with characteristically punchy one-liners: "I have never been prevented from entering Mississippi," he told reporters. "General de Gaulle has too much gall."[41]

When Black Power did come to dominate American discourse, news of discrimination from Britain, and the testimony of black immigrants in Britain, confirmed the diagnosis of American Black Power leaders who condemned the international system of exploitation rather than individuals or southern segregation. Stokeley Carmichael accepted an invitation to speak in London in 1967 precisely because he hoped to meet, and learn from, "Black Power formations [that] had begun to emerge in the African/Caribbean immigrant communities in Britain."[42] After meeting them, he told reporters, "it is institutionalized racism that keeps the black people locked in dilapidated slums, tenements, where they must live out their daily lives subject to ... exploitative slum landlords, merchants, loan sharks and the restrictive practices of real estate agents." "We're talking now about the U.S." Carmichael continued, but "you can apply a little of it to London."[43]

Remembering the March on Washington in Britain

Fifty years after the March on Washington, Martin Luther King Jr.'s dream is still widely remembered in Britain. Indeed, it is remembered better now than it was known at the time, since contemporary British press coverage focused more on the peaceable nature of the Washington march. The American civil rights movement more generally is well known, too. In Britain, King's statue stands above the west entrance to Westminster Abbey, while the American civil rights movement is among the top five most popular history subjects in high schools. Some thirty university history lecturers in in the United Kingdom specialize in the American civil rights movement (out of roughly one hundred and eighty tenured faculty who study American history) — by far the most popular of any modern U.S. history topic.

Absent from Westminster Abbey, though, is a statue of a black British figure, and — despite pioneering work by black academics and campaigners — black British history remains on the sidelines at schools and universities. Malcolm X and Martin Luther King Jr. are studied in depth, while Claudia Jones and Paul Stephenson are largely unknown. Interest in the American story and disinterest in the British version arise, in part, because of the readily available resources on African American history: compilation video packages of civil

41 "Aid to Malcolm X by B.B.C. Assailed," *New York Times*, February 14, 1965, 24.

42 Stokely Carmichael with Ekwueme Michael Thelwell, *Ready for Revolution: The Life and Struggles of Stokely Carmichael (Kwame Ture)* (New York, 2003), 572.

43 Stokely Carmichael and Mumia Abu-Jabal, *Stokely Speaks: From Black Power to Pan-Africanism* (Chicago, 1971), 78-91.

rights demonstrations, YouTube clips of speeches and freely available web resources, digitized African American newspaper reports, and American civil rights organization papers in British university libraries. But the focus on the American movement at the expense of its British counterpart is also a legacy of mainstream support for American protest and the sidelining of British campaigns against racial discrimination during the 1960s. Thus, while remembering Martin Luther King Jr. and his dream may help young Britons to consider the question of racial justice, it can be used to forget about the British dimensions of that question, too.

Using and abusing Martin Luther King Jr. is perhaps inevitable abroad, where he was and is so well publicized but little understood. Yet it has echoes in the United States, where Dr. King should be known best. The preacher who spoke at a march in Washington for jobs and freedom fifty years ago is frequently invoked by activists on both sides of the political spectrum. Some African American activists on the Left seek to honor his legacy by calling for race-based remedies to combat stubborn racial inequality. Similarly, some conservatives invoke his call for racial peace to support color-blind ideology and to remove those same race-based remedies. At the dedication of the Martin Luther King Jr. Memorial on the National Mall in Washington in 2011, President Barack Obama even used King's teachings to challenge the polarization of contemporary American politics: "He calls on us to stand in the other person's shoes, to see through their eyes, to understand their pain."

As King calls on America and the world through the memory of his famous speech in Washington, everyone, it seems, can call on him.

Stephen Tuck is Director of TORCH | The Oxford Research Centre in the Humanities and Professor of Modern History at Oxford University. His most recent books are *The Night Malcolm X Spoke at the Oxford Union: A Story of Global Human Rights* (Oakland, 2014) and, edited with Robin D. G. Kelley, *The Other Special Relationship: Race, Rights, and Riots in Britain and the United States* (New York, 2015).

Different Views and Voices

JOACHIM PRINZ, THE SOUTH, AND THE ANALOGY OF NAZISM

Stephen J. Whitfield

Posterity has been unfair to Joachim Prinz (1902–1988). As president of the American Jewish Congress, he was assigned a slot on the program of the March on Washington in 1963. An electrifying orator, he was considered so suitable for prime time that he was granted the penultimate speaking slot on the program, which meant that to top his effect upon an audience required the thundering eloquence of Martin Luther King Jr., who gave the speech of his life. It might also have seemed mischievous (though hardly intentional) for the program committee to have scheduled Prinz immediately *after* the equally dazzling gospel singer Mahalia Jackson. Such arrangements may help to explain why few remember or know the name of the speaker who immediately preceded King. Typical of such exclusion is the "I Have a Dream" anniversary issue of *Time*. It emphasized how "integrated" the gathering was and stressed that "speaker after speaker — the young John Lewis, the aged A. Philip Randolph — made the case for racial justice."[1] Yet the only white orator in the lineup was Prinz, whom *Time* did not mention in its retrospective account of the August 28, 1963, event. Not even the Smithsonian Institution website, which provides an excellent, brief oral history of the march and its program, refers to Prinz.

Obscurity has dogged him in other ways as well, consigning to near-oblivion the German-born rabbi who escaped Nazi Germany to find a home in the United States. He was an icon of embattled liberal Judaism under the Third Reich, an exemplar, based in Berlin, of the compatibility of a historic religion with the advances of modernization. But in this respect Leo Baeck, who chaired the Reichsvertretung der Juden in Deutschland in the 1930s, continues to eclipse him. He officiated at the wedding of Prinz's parents in 1901, and it is Rabbi Baeck's name that adorns the cultural institution that remains dedicated to preserving the legacy of surely the most scrutinized of the modern Diaspora communities devastated in the Holocaust. That Baeck had also survived the concentration camp of Theresienstadt fortified his status as the personification of German Jewry in all its tragic grandeur. In 1958 Prinz became president of the American Jewish Congress, and at its annual meeting that year he insisted that Reverend King be the keynote speaker. Because the convention was

1 Jon Meacham, "One Man," *Time* 182 (Aug. 26-Sept. 2, 2013): 42.

held in Miami, the arrangement was unprecedented; never before had King spoken to a predominantly white audience in the South.[2] Yet in public memory the refugee rabbi most associated with the civil rights movement is not Joachim Prinz but Abraham Joshua Heschel. In 1965 Heschel famously marched in the front line from Selma to Montgomery and is sprinkled with the stardust of a close personal connection with King himself. Both Baeck and Heschel exhibited the dignity of erudition as well as an aura of self-abnegating saintliness.

Prinz also suffers in another way when compared to Heschel, who was celebrated for his skill in portraying the condition of souls on fire, with the injection of divine mysteries into the mundane texture of experience. Prinz's vocation was also religious. But he could not convincingly convey the intensity of the interior life; nor does a posthumously published memoir report whether Prinz waged any struggle with the inner demons that test the authority of faith itself. The rational features of liberal Judaism had dominated his approach to the demands of faith. The most profound religious experience that Prinz claimed to have ever felt was a civic rather than a sacred occasion, and it was the March on Washington.[3]

Prinz served for nearly four decades in the pulpit of Temple B'nai Abraham in Newark and then in nearby Livingston. But did that make him the most prominent Jewish clergyman in New Jersey? That distinction belonged to another foreign-born rabbi, Arthur Hertzberg, of Temple Emanu-El in Englewood. Like Prinz, Hertzberg served as president of the American Jewish Congress and also as vice-president of the World Jewish Congress. A more prolific writer and scholar, Hertzberg was a public intellectual, an academic, and a controversialist who contributed to the *New York Review of Books*. His works, especially on Zionism, are still cited and assigned.

Yet Prinz did lead a remarkable public life, and Philip Roth rendered it in a fictional guise in rewriting Sinclair Lewis's *It Can't Happen Here* (1935) in the form of a chilling counterfactual history. *The Plot against America* (2004) is a novel in which Prinz makes a cameo appearance as a fierce and gallant opponent of homegrown fascism. He is depicted as confronting Rabbi Lionel Bengelsdorf, a figure so sordidly submissive to fictional President Charles A. Lindbergh that the beleaguered Jewish minority is betrayed. "Before Rabbi Bengelsdorf's rise to national prominence, Rabbi Prinz's authority among Jews throughout the city, in the wider Jewish community, and among scholars and theologians of every religion had far exceeded his elder

2 Allan Nadler, "The Plot for America," *Tablet*, Feb. 25, 2011, 4 (at http://www.tabletmag.com/jewish-news-and-politics/59863/the-plot-for-america?print=1 (accessed Aug. 11, 2013).

3 Michael Meyer, "Editor's Introduction" to Joachim Prinz, *Rebellious Rabbi: An Autobiography — The German and Early American Years* (Bloomington, 2008), xxxvi.

colleague's," Roth wrote, "and it was he alone of the Conservative rabbis leading the city's three wealthiest congregations who had never flinched in his opposition to Lindbergh." At least the novelist got Prinz's political consciousness right, for he had indeed publicly opposed the shortsighted isolationism of the America First Committee, which had opposed efforts to intervene in a global war that the United States was presumably unprepared to win against the Axis.[4]

Prinz's own Judaism was charmingly heterodox. He cared much less for personal observance than for democratic commitment. He doubted the efficacy of prayer, and he promoted education in the Jewish heritage more energetically than he championed the primacy of religious law. He sought to instill an appreciation of peoplehood, but he did not articulate a notion of the chosenness of any particular nation. His religion was temperate and rational instead of romantic or pietistic. Temple B'nai Abraham was formally unaffiliated with any denomination, although in ritual the synagogue was generally Conservative; and there even the observance of the Sabbath tended to bleed rather seamlessly into the rest of the week. The laws of kosher food were a way of separating Jews from their neighbors. Despite the dietary prohibition that historically classifies shellfish as unclean, Prinz loved eating lobsters.[5]

That delicacy, it is safe to speculate, was unavailable in the tiny Upper Silesian village of Burkhardsdorf (now Bierdzan), where he was born. His was the only Jewish family. Although his parents were thoroughly assimilated, Prinz was somehow inspired while still an adolescent to become a rabbi. As he grew to manhood, his resistance to an obtuse patriarchy, to bourgeois smugness, and to the bellicose patriotism of his native land activated an impassioned commitment to emancipatory modernism. Formally ordained in 1929, he had already begun his career preaching and teaching three years earlier at the Friedenstempel in Berlin. But as early as 1915, Max Weber had devised a term applicable to Prinz's talent: charisma. Thousands flocked to hear him speak; the synagogue was usually packed. Yet while imbibing Weimar culture, he was fascinated with the United States and became "Americanized" long before he could have seriously imagined becoming an American. In the 1920s he had already learned English. Without apparently having read the works of John Dewey, Prinz became a champion of experiential learning. As a teacher (which is, of course, what "rabbi" means), he inserted within the Jewish cultural history that he taught figures who were usually

4 Nadler, "Plot for America," *Tablet*, Feb. 25, 2011, 8; Meyer, "Editor's Introduction" to Prinz, *Rebellious Rabbi*, xxxi; Philip Roth, *The Plot against America* (Boston, 2004), 247.

5 Meyer, "Editor's Introduction" to Prinz, *Rebellious Rabbi*, xxxii-xxxiii.

considered to be on the margins of the community, like Jesus and Spinoza. Prinz was also clean-shaven when all of Berlin's other rabbis wore beards.[6] To sum up the persona of this dashing and informal young rabbi, Weber may have devised a word. But postwar America would have termed Prinz, a rabbi born in the twentieth century, *hip*. He was a man of faith, a man of the cloth, but he was also — to put it bluntly — a man. Despite the moral clarity of the Seventh Commandment, he persuaded his wife, the former Lucie Horovitz, to agree to an open marriage. The couple scorned bourgeois sexual hypocrisy. After all, they lived in a city that, among all the European capitals of the 1920s, ranked second only to Paris in celebrating such freedom. His memoirs include a fond reminiscence about one bout of sex in an open field, during which he claims to have recalled a key passage in Kant's *Kritik der praktischen Vernunft*. Such philosophical influences, it might be added, were not unique to Prinz, who was hardly alone in feeling the immense authority of German learning. For instance, even former *Obersturmbannführer* Adolf Eichmann, when he was put on trial in Jerusalem in 1961, though a high school dropout was able to give a reasonably accurate definition of the categorical imperative.[7]

The patrimony of Germany included a dense and formidable high culture, and Prinz therefore exalted in it. He loved his native language too. But his rebellious nature exempted him from delusions that, for so many other German Jews, would prove deadly. He refused to sing the German national anthem. Something about the Fatherland antagonized him — perhaps its history of an excessive appreciation of authority. Resisting that political legacy, Prinz became an early and lifelong Zionist and regarded Jewish nationalism as indispensable to Jewish resilience and resistance. Yet he did not consider settling in Palestine, possibly because of the cosmopolitanism that animated his own religious sensibility as well.[8]

His private life underwent transformation even as democracy was emitting its death-rattle. Prinz's wife died in 1931, and he married Hilde Goldschmidt the following year. They had five children.[9] Prinz also foresaw, even as many of his fellow Jews were luxuriating in the anything-goes aura of the Weimar Republic, that their existence on German soil was doomed. They could flourish only temporarily under conditions that Martin Heidegger pejoratively described in 1929 as an injection of Jewishness (*Verjudung*), an atmosphere that upended the rigidities as well as the verities of prewar Germany.[10] But Prinz foresaw that the republic was dancing on the edge of a volcano. After

6   Meyer, "Editor's Introduction" to Prinz, *Rebellious Rabbi*, xix, xviii, xxiv; Prinz, *Rebellious Rabbi*, 71-75, 81, 96, 97.

7   Prinz, *Rebellious Rabbi*, 54-55, 97; Hannah Arendt, *Eichmann in Jerusalem: A Report on the Banality of Evil* (New York, 1964), 135-36.

8   Meyer, "Editor's Introduction" to Prinz, *Rebellious Rabbi*, xxvii, xxix-xxx; Prinz, *Rebellious Rabbi*, 38.

9   Glenn Fowler, "Joachim Prinz, Leader in Protests for Civil-Rights Causes, Dies at 86," *New York Times*, Oct. 1, 1988, I, 33.

10   Quoted in Richard Wolin, "Hannah and the Magician," *New Republic* 213 (Oct. 9, 1995): 30.

it erupted in 1933, he was taken several times to the offices of the Gestapo and was twice taken into custody and jailed. In 1937, when together with his second wife and their children he bade farewell to the Jewish community in Berlin, Eichmann sat in the audience to monitor him.[11]

The nation that granted Prinz and his family refuge elicited ambivalence, however. His feelings did not consist only of gratitude and admiration. He was aware that the United States was considerably east of Eden, and he dismissed the culture of his new asylum as philistine. Formed in the crucible of Weimar modernism and avant-garde art, Prinz found disappointing even the furniture in the homes he visited. He considered it unfortunate that the chairs and tables showed no evidence of the influence of Bauhaus. He found "hardly any knowledge of art in architecture, sculpture, and painting." Newark itself was "very ugly," and the search for beauty was easily frustrated. Prinz's dispirited reaction to the "very empty" character of the United States could not be disguised, and his new neighbors "resented the fact that we did not admire America more openly and profoundly than we did."[12] But he did enjoy the support of Rabbi Stephen S. Wise, who was the de facto leader of American Jewry. Wise impressed Prinz with his sonorous oratorical power, his ardent Zionism, and his political astuteness, as well as his attentiveness to desperate refugee families such as Prinz's own. Wise helped Prinz to obtain a job at Temple B'nai Abraham when he was so destitute that he had to borrow the railroad fare to Newark and back to New York City. But he often scorned other Jews whom he met as uncultivated, vulgar, and even bigoted. Too few were curious about the outside world, in his view. Prinz thought they were ignorant of Hebrew, and shockingly devoid of the trappings of *Bildung*, the ideal of self-cultivation and refined breeding that had bewitched Germany Jewry for a century.[13]

Perhaps the most demoralizing encounter occurred in 1937 in Atlanta, long before its business and political leaders boasted that it was a "city too busy to hate." There Prinz was invited to speak to Zionist groups. Before the event, he had wanted to meet Willis Jefferson King, an African American specialist on the poetry of the Hebrew Bible and a former student at the American School for Oriental Research in Palestine. King was a Methodist bishop who was serving as president of Atlanta's Gammon Theological Seminary, and Prinz suggested that they dine together at his hotel. "He hesitated," Prinz recalled, "saying that it would be more advisable if we would

11 Prinz, *Rebellious Rabbi*, 86, 92, 168-69.

12 Prinz, *Rebellious Rabbi*, 161, 191, 192, 214.

13 Prinz, *Rebellious Rabbi*, 190-96, 211-14.

take dinner in my room rather than in the hotel dining room. I did not quite understand the meaning of his words." Prinz was too naïve to grasp how systematically segregation was enforced. But when he met afterwards with his Jewish hosts, one of them made that code clear to their German-born guest: "I understand that you visited that nigger in the black seminary, and somebody told me that you invited him to have dinner with you tonight." Prinz was stunned. But he was not entirely speechless, and he told his hosts how appalled he was that Jews, who were "the classic victims of racial persecution," could be racist. He also compared the fate of southern blacks to what the Jewish people were then experiencing in Europe. Embarrassment and silence followed, an atmosphere that one member of the Jewish group tried to remedy by offering Prinz a drink. He accepted the gesture, and under the circumstances expected — and needed — a very strong beverage. Instead, he was rather ungenerously given a glass of Coca-Cola. Prinz's memoir claims that he never again sipped a Coke.[14]

One year later, the Wehrmacht marched into Austria, and then into the Sudetenland, and then conquered the rest of Czechoslovakia. During that period Prinz promoted U.S. interventionism, from the pulpit and through the American Jewish Congress. But he sensed that too few American Jews shared his sense of urgency, and his appeals could gain little traction. And the war came. The account in Prinz's memoir of the impact of the global conflict is surprisingly brief. That he had managed to survive while so many of his own relatives and millions of his co-religionists were exterminated was a horror that haunted him. His warnings had been unheeded, his worst nightmares realized. But like even the most astute and best-informed American Jews of his time, Prinz did not devise any means to try to decelerate the slaughter; and on the home front he devoted himself to ministering to his congregants in Newark and increasingly to the organizational agenda of the American Jewish Congress, the most progressive of the Jewish defense agencies. In the postwar era, even after decades of living in New Jersey, Prinz and his wife continued to speak German to one another; and their summer vacations were spent in Europe.[15]

Weimar culture had promoted a spirit of forbearance and a rejection of rigid moralism, and such stances were evident in Prinz's attitude toward the best-known member of his synagogue. That congregant was also Newark's most notorious Jew: Abner Zwillman, the 6'2" mobster who had been a charter member of Murder,

14 Prinz, *Rebellious Rabbi*, 193-95.

15 Meyer, "Editor's Introduction" to Prinz, *Rebellious Rabbi*, xxxvi; Prinz, *Rebellious Rabbi*, 223-27.

Inc., the loosely organized syndicate that specialized in bootlegging, drug-peddling, numbers-running, vice, and other crimes. Murder, Inc., emerged during Prohibition and included enforcers whose tasks were homicidal — usually against other gangsters. Zwillman's boyhood nickname, "Longy," may have been derived from Jewish pushcart peddlers, whose vulnerability to marauding Irish toughs compelled these merchants to yell for help from the tall one and his gang ("*Ruf dem Langn!*" in Yiddish). Zwillman "was one of the most interesting men I ever met," Rabbi Prinz recalled. "Soft-spoken, well read, very hospitable, and charitable, he governed city and state and many others affairs with some degree of dignity, and certainly no signs of violence." For virtually every immigrant group, crime had offered the prospect of upward mobility; and Jews like Zwillman were sometimes seen as protectors of the community when legal processes were dubious or corrupt. In 1959, when the king of the New Jersey underworld was found hanged under very mysterious circumstances, Prinz felt obliged to perform the funeral. Whatever Longy Zwillman's crimes, Prinz believed he merited Jewish rites. The deceased had been born and had died a Jew and had been generous when financial help was needed. Prinz did skip the eulogy, which he said would have required "mentioning facts ... that were not flattering."[16]

Four years later Prinz stood before the Lincoln Memorial, as the personification of the connection between the recent German past and southern race relations. He began by announcing to the crowd of at least two hundred thousand: "I speak to you as an American Jew." But he was not only that; and he claimed to have learned that, while serving as a rabbi under the Nazis, silence "in the face of brutality" was "shameful" and "disgraceful." Prinz therefore urged America not to repeat the sin of indifference and neutrality.[17] His remarks were pithy and salient, a harbinger of increased attention that scholars and ethicists would give to the problem of the bystander. Prinz thus suggested an affinity, a symbolic link that can be understood as lending special poignancy to his speech in Washington in 1963. He exemplified an enduring progressivism that the nation's First Lady had recognized when Rabbi Wise's daughter, Justine Wise Polier, stayed overnight as a guest in the White House. "When people are in trouble," Eleanor Roosevelt remarked to her in the fall of 1941, "whether it's the Dust Bowl or the miners — whoever it is, and I see the need for help, the first people who come forward and try to offer help are the Jews."[18]

16 Prinz, *Rebellious Rabbi*, 215-20; Robert A. Rockaway, *But He Was Good to His Mother: The Lives and Crimes of Jewish Gangsters* (New York, 2000), 31-37, 170-75.

17 Appendix B: "Prinz's Speech at the Lincoln Memorial, August 28, 1963," in Prinz, *Rebellious Rabbi*, ed. Meyer, 261; Eric J. Sundquist, *King's Dream* (New Haven, 2009), 54; Jonathan Prinz in "The Jews Who Were Present at a Moment That Changed American History," *Forward*, Aug. 30, 2013, 6.

18 Monty Noam Penkower interview with Justine Wise Polier, May 17, 1976, quoted in Penkower, "Eleanor Roosevelt and the Plight of World Jewry," *Jewish Social Studies* 49 (Spring 1987): 125.

By 1963 the momentum of that liberalism, which Prinz had first enunciated in Germany, was not depleted; and younger Jews in particular were conspicuous in the struggle for racial equality. During Freedom Summer in 1964, about half of the volunteers who worked on voting rights and similar causes in Mississippi are estimated to have been Jews.[19] The decade of the March on Washington would end in turmoil, however, with heightened Jewish fears of the implications of black radicalism and black anti-Semitism, as well as the rising threat of black crime. In a letter to King in the aftermath of rioting in Newark, Prinz reasserted his commitment to civil rights. But he urged King to join others in "the responsible Negro leadership ... to speak up clearly and unequivocally on the tragic crime of Negro anti-Semitism." At the National Mall four years earlier, Prinz reminded King, "I condemned silence of the American white community. I now condemn silence on the part of the Negro leadership." But with regret Prinz reported that Temple B'nai Abraham would be moving away from Newark, the home of the synagogue for over a century.[20]

Prinz's congregation could scarcely have remained immune to pressures that were affecting so many other synagogues and to the larger pattern of white flight. But Temple B'nai Abraham managed to persist as the most resistant of Newark's major synagogues to the process of suburbanization, which marked not only the growing affluence of congregants but also offered them a measure of security. The social problems associated with the inner city, which had been building for generations, stood no chance of being immediately solved; nor was there sufficient political will to do so. Thus, the relocation to the suburb of Livingston took on a glum air of inevitability, well before Prinz died. That move occurred a decade after the March on Washington. While still in Newark, on his way to the synagogue, Prinz himself had become the victim of a holdup. He tried to placate the mugger by telling him, "I'll have you know I marched with Dr. King." The response was (and here I must paraphrase): "I really don't care who your physician is; just hand over the money."[21] He did.

The March on Washington deserves its place as a milestone in the progression toward greater democratic inclusion. In the decades immediately after the Second World War, grisly evidence had been accumulating about the policies of the Third Reich; and the implications for the United States could not be entirely suppressed. Postwar racism came with a warning label, which Rabbi Prinz had incarnated in 1963. By coincidence the only other Jew who participated in the

19 Marc Fisher, "When Freedom Summer Came to Town," *Moment* 39 (July-Aug., 2014): 32.

20 Joachim Prinz to Martin Luther King, Jr., September 8, 1967, in Joachim Prinz Papers, MS-673, Box 3, Folder 7, Jacob Rader Marcus Center of the American Jewish Archives, Cincinnati, Ohio.

21 Nadler, "Plot for America," *Tablet*, Feb. 25, 2011, 5.

program that day, troubadour Bob Dylan, also invoked the recent German past, though much more indirectly. That same month he had composed a song that he (and Joan Baez) sang at the Lincoln Memorial, "When the Ship Comes In," a song almost certainly indebted to the vengeful fantasy that "*Die Seeräuberjenny*" reveals in Bertolt Brecht and Kurt Weill's cynical conflation of respectability and criminality, *Die Dreigroschenoper* (1928).[22] Whatever the Weimar antecedents of Dylan's verses, with its warnings of retribution and apocalypse, new questions were posed about the implications of the evil indigenous to the Third Reich. Would its history also affect consciousness of the evil of Jim Crow? How could the persecution of one minority in Europe provoke outrage while discrimination against another minority at home could induce passivity, silence, and rationalization?

Segregation was once believed to be impregnable, and southern white attitudes were presumed to be immutable. Hadn't Alabama Governor George C. Wallace warned in 1963 that, if the civil rights bill that Congress was contemplating were passed, American troops would have to be withdrawn from West Berlin and from Indochina to keep order among his fellow southerners?[23]

***

But soon what was once deemed impervious to political, legal, and social change became unacceptable. In the dichotomy of the sociologist William Graham Sumner, the "folkways" of the region yielded to the "state-ways" irradiating from Washington. The impossibility of reconciling the value of equality with the practice of Jim Crow instigated the crisis of civil rights that erupted in the 1960s. In that decade the federal government demanded that the region live according to the American Creed and conform more closely to the civic patterns of the rest of the republic. Because the spokesmen for the South — as well as those who claimed to know its habits so intimately — had commonly anticipated the most violent sort of resistance, the mystery that historians must solve is how such expectations were invalidated. Several reasons can be given. But perhaps awareness of the genocide that had been perpetrated against European Jewry must be factored in. The influence of the Shoah cannot be conclusively proven. No single figure or institution pushing hard for racial justice was decisively shaped by the knowledge or the memory of the Final Solution. Scrupulous scholars may well conclude that the evidentiary base of

22 Jason Zinoman, "When Bobby Met Bertolt, Times Changed," *New York Times*, Oct. 8, 2006, 7.

23 J. Hoberman, *The Dream Life* (New York, 2003), 84.

the argument is thin. Indeed, it is more a matter of atmospherics, of inference rather than induction. But a case is tenable.

That is the symbolic importance of Joachim Prinz. At the National Mall he alone cited and represented the parallel that was becoming expressed, the link between Nazi Germany and Jim Crow. He alone specified the danger, based on his background in the Third Reich, of inaction in the face of racial injustice. He alone issued the reminder that systemic prejudice and discrimination had a lethal precedent. The speech that Prinz delivered at the Lincoln Memorial was therefore symptomatic of the growing realization that the consequences of passivity were not unimaginable; historic evidence could be marshaled.

In making such connections, the date that constitutes the most decisive year in the argument presented here is 1960. That was when Israeli agents captured Eichmann in Argentina, and the process by which he was forced to stand trial inaugurated the genuine emergence of Holocaust consciousness. It has become a fundamental feature of the sensibility of Western nations, including the United States as well as Israel. Unlike the war criminals who were prosecuted and convicted in Nuremberg, this particular defendant was associated specifically with the Final Solution — and *only* with the Final Solution. He therefore embodied the genocide that has never vanished from public memory. The year 1960 is noteworthy for other reasons as well. Elie Wiesel's memoir of Auschwitz and Buchenwald, *Night*, was also published then (translated from the French). Living mostly in New York, and writing mostly in French, Wiesel happened to have visited the South as a tourist in 1957. The future Nobel laureate wrote of being "struck by its citizens' courtesy, and the unforgivable humiliation of its blacks. Looking at the 'Whites Only' signs," Wiesel recalled, "I felt ashamed of being white."[24] The first of the sit-ins to attract genuine national attention also began in 1960; what happened in Greensboro became a movement. The civil rights organization that flirted with the greatest danger in the struggle against racial segregation was also founded in 1960: the Student Nonviolent Coordinating Committee (SNCC).

Something was happening to establish a kind of synchrony, a sort of symmetry. The civil rights revolution revealed the truth of what William Faulkner's village lawyer asserts: "The past is never dead. It's not even past." The memory of the Holocaust could not be entirely expelled from the consciousness of those who struggled for racial justice in the South.

24 Elie Wiesel, *All Rivers Run to the Sea: Memoirs, 1928-1969* (London, 1997), 302.

It was also no accident that *Life*, the most popular mass magazine of the era, commissioned Harry Golden to cover the trial of Eichmann in Jerusalem. The Charlotte journalist lacked any expertise on the history of the Third Reich (unlike Hannah Arendt, the *New Yorker*'s correspondent in Jerusalem); and in his autobiography Golden admitted that his consciousness of his own ethnicity was thin until the rise of Nazism. Hitler had, in effect, jolted Golden into becoming a Jew. His three best-selling collections of feuilletons, *Only in America* (1958), *For Two Cents Plain* (1959), and *Enjoy, Enjoy!* (1960), address the phenomenon of anti-Semitism; but he barely mentioned the Nazi version. In 1956, his newspaper, the *Carolina Israelite*, had indirectly anticipated the sit-ins by observing that white southerners had no objection to standing next to blacks. Sitting down was an offense to proper race relations, however. Famous for his satirical moral criticism of racial segregation in the region where he lived,[25] Golden was assigned to tell the readers of *Life* how lethal (and not merely how amusing) bigotry could be. He portrayed a defendant who — "despite his ordinary appearance," indeed the "drabness" of his persona — was "really a stranger, a stranger to the human race."[26] The trial that Golden covered was bound to raise questions about the commonplace character of evil and to raise doubt that it was a phenomenon confined to the contours of German history.

1960 was significant for yet another reason, because the juxtaposition of the Third Reich and the American South that Prinz would enunciate at the Lincoln Memorial was made explicit in a Pulitzer Prize-winning novel. Harper Lee's *To Kill a Mockingbird* has sold more than 30 million copies since its publication in 1960, and even in the new century continues to sell about 750,000 copies annually. By 1988, according to the National Council of Teachers of English, this novel had been taught in three out of every four public schools in the United States. *To Kill a Mockingbird* has been translated into more than forty languages and was named the best American novel of the twentieth century by the nation's librarians.[27]

In setting her first published book in small-town Alabama in the depths of the Great Depression, Lee did not intend for the evidence of racial injustice to be peripheral. The narrator, Scout Finch, is a motherless 8-year-old girl who realizes the cruelty and sadness that pervade the world that the adults will bequeath to her. One instance is Nazi anti-Semitism, which one of Scout's teachers, Miss Gates, denounces. The German policy of discrimination against the Jews

25 Harry Golden, *The Right Time: An Autobiography* (New York, 1969), 116, 193, 210, 226; Stephen J. Whitfield, "The 'Golden' Era of Civil Rights," *Southern Cultures* 14 (Fall 2008): 31-32, 35-39; Leonard Rogoff, "Harry Golden, New Yorker: I ♥ NC," *Southern Jewish History* 11 (2008): 44-57.

26 Quoted in Golden, *Right Time*, 406.

27 See www.tokillamockingbird50year.com, Thomas Mallon, "Big Bird," *New Yorker* 82 (May 29, 2006): 81; Mark Seal, "To Steal a Mockingbird?," *Vanity Fair*, no. 636 (Aug. 2013): 110.

makes no sense, Miss Gates explains, because they "contribute to every society they live in, and most of all, they are a deeply religious people. Hitler's trying to do away with religion," she adds, "so maybe he doesn't like them for that reason."[28] The teacher cannot acknowledge that the motive behind Nazi policy might not be anti-religious but "racial" prejudice instead, and tells the children, with heavy authorial irony, that the Third Reich differs from the United States because "over here we don't believe in persecuting anybody." The sensitive daughter of Atticus Finch, an attorney and honorable man, realizes, however tentatively, that Miss Gates, like other respectable whites in the town of Maycomb, is a hypocrite. Scout has overheard her teacher expressing concern that local blacks are getting uppity, "an' the next thing they think they can do is marry us."[29] Such self-delusion, passing for conventional wisdom, was certainly ripe for exposure. Samuel Johnson had done so as early as 1775. Ever since Virginians had led the demand for national independence during the American Revolution, the South had, after all, lived in an active state of hypocrisy. "How is it," Johnson famously wondered, "that we hear the loudest yelps for liberty among the drivers of Negroes?"[30] Such paradoxes can often be found in the mind of the South, and *To Kill a Mockingbird* deftly exposes the effort to distinguish racial from religious prejudice.

Scout's father cannot even bear to listen to Hitler on the radio and dismisses him as "a maniac." The town's one Jewish family, named Levy, qualifies as "fine folks," and has no reason to any fright in Maycomb akin to the horror that their German coreligionists know. Sam Levy even stands down the Klan with impunity.[31] But no white adult in the town seems able or willing to connect the Nazi cult of "race" to the plight of the black citizens there. The subtle recognition of that cognitive short-circuiting makes *To Kill a Mockingbird* the canonical text for the argument of this essay, especially because the actual chasm was wider than in this work of fiction. The model for Atticus Finch was the author's father, a Monroeville lawyer and Methodist elder named A. C. Lee. For most of his life, he regarded segregation as the most congenial way to manage race relations. Sermons that he listened to in church were not so certain; and in 1952 A. C. Lee was urging his own minister to "get off the [preaching of] 'social justice' and get back on the Gospel."[32] But by the time that *To Kill a Mockingbird* was published, he could not help becoming more aware of the racial injustice surrounding him, and that his daughter's novel was revealing.[33]

28 Harper Lee, *To Kill a Mock-ingbird* (New York, 1962), 247-48.

29 Lee, *To Kill a Mockingbird*, 248, 249-50.

30 Quoted in Peter Martin, *Samuel Johnson: A Biography* (Cambridge, MA, 2008), 447.

31 Lee, *To Kill a Mockingbird*, 149, 248.

32 Quoted in Charles J. Shields, *Mockingbird: A Portrait of Harper Lee* (New York, 2006), 123, and in Mallon, "Big Bird," *New Yorker*, 80.

33 Shields, *Mockingbird*, 121.

The film adaptation nevertheless makes no reference whatsoever to Nazism. Robert Mulligan's 1962 movie also muffles the issue of the double standards of Alabama's whites when the topic of persecution is raised. The cinematic version nevertheless widens even further the distance from historical actuality, because the local attorney whom Gregory Peck played is so idealized. When the American Film Institute ranked the greatest cinematic heroes, Atticus Finch came out #1, ahead of Indiana Jones, for example. Even Harrison Ford, the actor who played Indiana Jones, named *To Kill a Mockingbird* his all-time favorite film.[34]

Curiously enough, the autobiography of David Duke, the most prominent of recent leaders of the Ku Klux Klan, also cites the impact that Harper Lee's novel exerted upon him. Duke absorbed its spirit as an eighth grader in New Orleans and claims to have become "a racial egalitarian" who "sympathized with the plight of the Negro." However, Duke confides that later in adolescence he "saw the light" and achieved notoriety by redefining himself as a Nazi (and still later as a Grand Wizard of the Klan). In 1991, when Duke became a gubernatorial candidate on the Republican ticket, the Louisiana Coalition Against Racism and Nazism was formed to help torpedo his political ambitions. The explicit coupling of those two ideological targets of racism and Nazism might be understood as a replay of the Double-V campaign that civil rights advocates promoted during the Second World War in demanding that the defeat of the Axis could not be separated from the dismantling of Jim Crow. The cofounder of the Louisiana Coalition (and David Duke's chief adversary within the Republican Party) was a white conservative named Elizabeth Rickey. She happened to be the niece of the Brooklyn Dodgers' general manager Branch Rickey, who brought an army veteran named Jackie Robinson into major league baseball. They desegregated the national pastime in the very era when the wartime struggle against fascism had raised significant doubts about the acceptability of white supremacy.[35] In the 2013 film about Robinson, Harrison Ford plays Branch Rickey.

The astonishing popularity of *To Kill a Mockingbird* reinforced such episodes as the speech that Joachim Prinz delivered in Washington. They pointed to the realization, by the early 1960s, that if the ideology of the Third Reich was wrong, then racial discrimination — especially in the South — was wrong. The explosive decade that began with the sit-ins in Greensboro consolidated that deepening awareness. In 1961, in the same year that Adolf Eichmann was put on trial in

34 Deborah Friedell, "Austen in Alabama," *New Republic* 232 (Aug. 28, 2006): 33; "Harrison Ford Will Now Take Your Questions," *Time* 175 (Jan. 25, 2010): 8.

35 David Duke, *My Awakening: A Path to Racial Understanding* (Covington, LA, 2000), 30; Lawrence N. Powell, *Troubled Memory: Anne Levy, the Holocaust, and David Duke's Louisiana* (Chapel Hill, NC, 2000), 440-51, 462, 463; Kenneth Stern, "Obituary: Elizabeth Rickey, Derailed David Duke," *Forward*, Sept. 25, 2009, 9.

Jerusalem, political scientist Raul Hilberg's monumental study, *The Destruction of the European Jews*, was published. 1961 also marked the release of Stanley Kramer's *Judgment at Nuremberg*. Kramer was Hollywood's most staunchly liberal Jewish filmmaker, and he interpreted the moral of his didactic but compelling movie as follows: "An individual is responsible" for what his government does, or fails to do.[36] To be sure, no Jewish characters appear in *Judgment at Nuremberg*. Instead, it explores the failure of conventional society to mount an effective resistance to barbarism. Whether apolitical domestics or well-educated judges, German citizens are shown to be so eerily passive as to be virtually paralyzed when the Nazi juggernaut menaces them. Instead of offering resistance, they were bystanders.

Early in 1965 *Judgment at Nuremberg* was shown as ABC's Sunday Night Movie. But at 9:30 p.m., the telecast was interrupted, as fifteen minutes of shocking footage from Selma, Alabama, was injected into the nation's living rooms. There Sheriff Jim Clark and his men were shown attacking peaceful civil rights demonstrators. Clark was, according to SNCC chairman John Lewis, "basically no different from a Gestapo officer during the Fascist slaughter of the Jews." Clark could be heard shouting to the posse: "Get those goddamned niggers. And get those goddamned white niggers."[37] In an era when some Jews were formulating the slogan "Never Again" as the lesson of the Holocaust, Sheriff Clark wore a button on his uniform proclaiming: "Never." To underscore the need for civil rights legislation, Kramer's film could not have come at a more fortuitous moment. About 450 clergymen soon descended upon Selma; and Charles Morgan Jr., the southern director of the American Civil Liberties Union, overheard many of the ministers making statements like "*Judgment at Nuremberg* was on for the first time on television," and "I was watching *Judgment at Nuremberg*, and I just couldn't stay away. I just had to come." Among the clergymen who had seen the film on ABC and came to Selma from Boston was the Reverend James Reeb, a Unitarian Universalist minister whom white thugs in the Alabama town beat to death outside an integrated restaurant. They were acquitted,[38] as was usually the case when southern whites committed crimes intended to maintain the racial hierarchy.

If the accusation John Lewis made against the constabulary of Selma was overstated, the climate of intimidation and fear was hardly a figment of Lewis's imagination. Nor was he alone in drawing such a link, which extended from the actualities of the movement to the

36 Stanley Kramer, with Thomas M. Coffey, *It's a Mad, Mad, Mad, Mad World: A Life in Hollywood* (New York, 1997), 178-79, 186.

37 Quoted in David Remnick, *The Bridge: The Life and Rise of Barack Obama* (New York, 2010), 8, and in Gene Roberts and Hank Klibanoff, *The Race Beat: The Press, the Civil Rights Struggle, and the Awakening of a Nation* (New York, 2006), 386.

38 Quoted in Roberts and Klibanoff, *Race Beat*, 388; Rick Perlstein, *Nixonland: The Rise of a President and the Fracturing of America* (New York, 2008), 8.

precincts of popular culture. In the 1960s the connection between the ideologies of Jim Crow and German Nazism was made even more explicit and was extended to the musical stage. In 1966 *Cabaret* opened on Broadway and would win eight Tony Awards, including the prize for Best Musical. Its connection to the battle for civil rights went beyond the shared initials of Berlin's tawdry (and fictitious) Kit Kat Klub and the Ku Klux Klan. Producer Harold Prince had initially wanted to end a musical about the collapse of the Weimar Republic with a film clip that showed the demonstrations in Selma, an idea that he scrapped as too obvious. But set designer Boris Aronson came up with something much more imaginative, an immense tilted mirror that reflected the audience itself. Theatergoers were thus forced to stare at themselves as they contemplated the contemporary parallels with the systematic hatred that had triumphed in interwar Germany. In *Cabaret* the realization of one of the inhabitants of the recreated atmosphere of Berlin ("If you're not against all this, you're for it — or you might as well be") echoes the warning against the price of neutrality that Prinz had issued three years earlier from the steps of the Lincoln Memorial.[39]

Another indictment of the indifference that Prinz had underscored as ethically repellent came from the University of Mississippi. There historian James W. Silver was operating on the same track of making an analogy between past and present. Silver concluded his book on the stifling orthodoxy of segregationist belief and practice with a plea for awareness; other Americans needed to know the extent of the injustice to which Mississippi was expecting its black citizens to submit. "When present-day German children ask their parents about the Jews, the concentration camps, and the most awful atrocities of this or any century," he wrote in 1966, "the answer is always the same: 'We didn't know these things were going on.'" Silver was dubious, because the violent Judeophobia of Hitler and his National Socialist Party was not disguised. And by recording how wretchedly white Mississippians mistreated the blacks who lived among them, Silver's book was designed to make that rationale implausible in the rest of the United States. If his state were to confront its past honestly, history textbooks had to be drastically revised to counter the bias that was hardwired into the public memory of white residents. One response to Silver's plea was *Mississippi: Conflicts and Change* (1974), a high school text written by historians at Tougaloo College and elsewhere. This volume constituted an early effort to correct the myths that comforted generations of whites in the state. The battle

39 John Bush Jones, *Our Musicals, Ourselves: A Social History of the American Musical Theatre* (Hanover, NH, 2003), 241-44.

was uphill, and the NAACP Legal Defense and Education Fund had to file a lawsuit to ensure that the text would be considered for adoption. A dozen publishers rejected the work. But André Schiffrin, a French-born Jew whose family had escaped German occupation in 1940, was hospitable; and he served as the managing director of Pantheon Books, based in New York. *Mississippi: Conflicts and Change* thus became a key text in the regional imperative of *Vergangenheitsbewältigung*, the struggle to master the past. This volume happened to be the only textbook that Schiffrin ever published, and the following year *Mississippi: Conflicts and Change* won the Lillian Smith Award from the Southern Educational Conference for the best work of nonfiction.[40]

The award was aptly named. During the Depression decade and during the Second World War, Lillian Smith was quite exceptional among white southerners in her willingness to highlight resemblances between the tyranny of the Third Reich and the oppression that was very much closer to home. Her most famous polemic against Jim Crow, *Killers of the Dream* (1949), mixed "concentration camps" like Dachau with "burning crosses and the KKK" to demonstrate "man's broken faith with himself."[41] Smith did not merely equate, in a casual way, the Klan and the Brown Shirts, as other white southerners — including editorial writers — occasionally did. She experienced a shock of recognition with what the Nazis were doing to crush dissent and to demonize the enemy within, even though Smith later conceded that she had greatly underestimated the unprecedented turpitude of National Socialism. No jackbooted secret police had come to power in America, after all, as she acknowledged in a 1944 essay. Nevertheless, Smith added, "We make a Gestapo of our fears and become cowards at the sound of our own heart-beat."[42]

Her sense of foreboding was more forceful than what Wilbur J. Cash, for example, could muster. In *The Mind of the South*, a classic work published in 1941, he called the Klan "an authentic folk movement" that displayed some "kinship" with the German Nazis. But with much of Europe under German rule (or about to be), his gnawing fear was the military threat posed to Western civilization. Cash, who wrote editorials for the Charlotte *News*, did not care to construct parallels, as Smith did, with the *Herrenvolk* philosophy at home. Her sense of dread would be echoed by the North Carolina-born Edward R. Murrow, who had achieved fame at CBS Radio by covering the advance of the Third Reich. By 1961 Murrow had become director of the U.S.

40 James W. Silver, *Mississippi: The Closed Society*, enlarged ed. (New York, 1966), 363-64; Herbert Mitgang, "Mississippi Textbook Dispute Revived," *New York Times*, Mar. 29, 1981, I, 36.

41 Lillian Smith, *Killers of the Dream* (Garden City, NY, 1963), 206.

42 Lillian Smith, "Humans in Bondage" (1944), in *The Winner Names the Age: A Collection of Writings*, ed. Michelle Cliff (New York, 1978), 45; Johnpeter Horst Grill and Robert L. Jenkins, "The Nazis and the American South in the 1930s," *Journal of Southern History* 58 (November 1992): 685-86; W. J. Cash, *The Mind of the South* (New York, 1941), 344; Richard H. King, "Cash and the Crisis of Political Modernity," in *W. J. Cash and the Minds of the South*, ed. Paul D. Escott (Baton Rouge, LA, 1992), 69, 78-80.

Information Agency and thus an official propagandist for the Kennedy administration. And yet that year he acknowledged that the climate of intimidation and prejudice in Birmingham reminded him of Nazi Germany.[43]

Certainly the rise of the Third Reich was not required to expose the problem of how to reconcile white behavior with the ideals of equality and liberty. Yet as early as 1944, with the publication of Gunnar Myrdal's canonical work on race relations, *An American Dilemma*, doubt had been cast on the prospect that the South could continue to violate the American Creed. Just as Robert Penn Warren would foresee the end of segregation when white southerners realized that they "cannot live with themselves anymore,"[44] Myrdal had suspected that the South could not continue indefinitely to violate the American Creed. It therefore does seem reasonable to surmise that the shadow of the Holocaust quickened an awareness of what was wrong and made it easier to attach a stigma to racial segregation in the South.

Of course demagogues and other politicians continued to express defiance. From Virginia, where public officials toyed with the discredited antebellum doctrine of interposition, through the hoisting in the Deep South of the tattered battle flag of "nullification," down to the truculent motto emblazoned on license plates in the Lone Star State ("Don't Mess with Texas"), the former Confederacy certainly did not yield easily or gracefully to the Constitutional requirement of desegregation. Admittedly, white supremacists showed no inclination to die for the principle of state sovereignty. But some of them were willing to kill to preserve the privileges of white skin. Time had run out, however. The racial policies of the South had become so indefensible that bipartisan federal legislation was enacted to prevent the region from continuing to pursue its *Sonderweg*. The United States could no longer countenance a distinctive set of racial mores; and these domestic disgraces had to be eliminated, or at least moderated.

A paradox nevertheless needs to be noted. By the end of the 1960s, the deepening distaste for the escalating war in Vietnam dramatically undercut the prestige of the military; and its virtues no longer seemed as attractive as in the past. Yet the following historical curiosity needs to be recorded: the region that was being increasingly compared to elements of Nazism had also produced many of the very soldiers who were decisive in crushing the Third Reich. To be sure, few of the troops who had landed in North Africa and Italy and France

43 Roger K. Newman, *Hugo Black: A Biography* (New York, 1994), 539.

44 Robert Penn Warren, *Segregation: The Inner Conflict in the South* (New York, 1956), 113; Alan Brinkley, *Liberalism and Its Discontents* (Cambridge, MA, 1998), 98-102.

presumably did so in order to extirpate racism, which Allied leaders had not declared to be an official war aim. Very few of the GIs who marched through Germany had read about Nazi racial doctrine in *Mein Kampf* (which had not been fully translated into English until 1939). American military commanders generally took for granted the durability of the structure of white supremacy. At least they declined to champion the cause of desegregation, whether in the armed services or in civilian life. The architect of victory in the Second World War was a Virginian, George C. Marshall; and to lead the crusade in Europe, he picked a Texan, Dwight D. Eisenhower. Neither of these commanders could be considered an advocate of racial equality. As Army Chief of Staff, Marshall had at first resisted the reorientation of the military to solve "a social problem" that civilians had failed to redress. "Experiments" like desegregation of military units, Marshall added, would endanger "efficiency, discipline, and morale." Eisenhower would also testify against the policy that President Harry Truman initiated to desegregate the armed forces, and neither in nor out of uniform did "Ike" demonstrate any sympathy for black Americans in their efforts to end discrimination.[45]

The paradox merits emphasis. One of the acquitted murderers of Emmett Till, who had reportedly whistled at a white woman in Mississippi in 1955, was J. W. Milam. He was a much-decorated combat veteran of the European theater of operations. "For heroic achievement in action" during the week that began on D-Day, Strom Thurmond of South Carolina was awarded a Bronze Star; he also fought in the Battle of the Bulge. Thurmond also entered the concentration camp of Buchenwald not long after it was liberated,[46] and three years later he would become the Dixiecrats' candidate for the presidency. George Wallace had served in the Pacific theater. But at least privately he took a revisionist stance toward the Second World War that makes his role equivocal: "I'm sorry it was necessary for us to fight against those anti-Communist nations. I thought that back then. Hell, we should have been in those trenches with the Germans ... fightin' them Bolsheviks." Perhaps any American who would have preferred his fellow combatants to join on the side of the Third Reich in the no-holds-barred bloodbath of Operation Barbarossa deserved no less than the swastika that caricaturist David Levine drew on Wallace's chin.[47] But the role of white southerners in liberating Europe from Axis occupation should nevertheless be credited, even though they stemmed from a region that would find its racial policies increasingly difficult to justify.

45 Quoted in Richard M. Dalfiume, *Desegregation of the U.S. Armed Forces: Fighting on Two Fronts, 1939-1953* (Columbia, MO, 1969), 46-47, 61; Ed Cray, *General of the Army: George C. Marshall, Soldier and Statesman* (New York, 1990), 661; Michael J. Klarman, *From Jim Crow to Civil Rights: The Supreme Court and the Struggle for Racial Equality* (New York, 2004), 192.

46 Jack Bass and Marilyn W. Thompson, *Ol' Strom: An Unauthorized Biography of Strom Thurmond* (Atlanta, 1998), 75-76.

47 Quoted in Marshall Frady, *Wallace* (New York, 1968), 245; David Levine, *No Known Survivors: David Levine's Political Plank* (Boston, 1970), 35, 36.

The Second World War must be understood as, in part, a propaganda battle that pitted the ideals of Western democracy against the twisted malice of Aryan doctrine. The repugnance generated by what the Nazis did should not be identified as the single most important pressure point in corroding the defense of racial segregation, but the rules of engagement between blacks and whites would thereafter be altered. The connection that Joachim Prinz adumbrated at the March on Washington in August 1963 constituted only one factor in that shift in attitudes, and it was not decisive. But the shadow of Nazism did help ensure that the once-solid South — cohesive and defiant in its opposition to desegregation — became more receptive to change than had earlier been imagined.

Stephen J. Whitfield holds the Max Richter Chair in American Civilization at Brandeis University, where he has taught since 1972. He has served as Fulbright Visiting Professor of American Studies at the Hebrew University of Jerusalem and as Allianz Visiting Professor of Jewish Studies at the Ludwig-Maximilians University in Munich. He is the author of eight books, including *A Death in the Delta: The Story of Emmett Till* (1988) and *In Search of American Jewish Culture* (1999). Professor Whitfield is especially interested in the intersection of politics and ideas in the United States in the twentieth century.

IN DEFENSE OF LAW AND ORDER: THE MARCH ON WASHINGTON AND ITS BLACK CONSERVATIVE CRITICS

Angela Dillard

Although nearly universally embraced and celebrated today, in 1963 the March on Washington was divisive not only among Americans in general but also within African American communities. Because historians have focused much more attention on the former than the latter, I use this commemorative occasion to excavate lost, buried, and forgotten moments of opposition to the march and critiques issued by African American figures who stood against it in principle and practice. We are much more conversant with critiques of the mass gathering from the *Left*, as encapsulated in Malcolm X's famous "farce on Washington" quip. But what about lesser-known patterns of opposition emanating from the *Right* of the mainstream of the civil rights movement, including those black conservatives of the era who would lay the foundation for the African American presence within the New Right of the late 1970s and early 1980s?

This essay is part of a larger project that considers moments of conflict and collusion between the civil rights movement, on the one hand, and the conservative movement, on the other. Both the book I am currently preparing (tentatively titled *Civil Rights Conservatism* and forthcoming from the University of California Press) and this present article attempt to delve into figures, such as James H. Meredith, who occupy positions within both of these major movements, which, in their post-World War II iterations, literally "grew up" together and remained intertwined in ways that are sometimes surprising and unexpected. Meredith is an ideal figure for this kind of analysis. Although a well-recognized symbol of the movement from the moment he successfully desegregated the University of Mississippi in 1962, he was never a willing movement operative. He belonged to none of its constituent organizations, and he rejected many of the movement's goals and tactics. Meredith's post-1960s drift toward the political Right, his denunciation of integration as "a con job," his work on the staff of North Carolina Senator Jesse Helms in the late 1980s, and his support for David Duke's 1991 Louisiana gubernatorial campaign are treated (when noted at all) as iconoclastic (at best) and simply crazy (at worst), but are never fully taken seriously.[1]

1 Meredith quoted in Juan Williams, "Integration Is a 'Con Job,'" *Washington Post*, February 23, 1985, C1. Examples of attempts to assess Meredith's career include Lois Romano, "The Long, Long Journey of James Meredith," *Washington Post*, November 3, 1989; and Arturo Gonzales and Sandra Salinas, "The Long, Lonely Road of Rights Hero James Meredith," *People*, October 16, 1989.

In a recent assessment of Meredith, University of Mississippi historian David Sansing correctly observes that Meredith was never "in the mainstream of the civil rights movement," and that he was "often critical of the leadership." Sansing goes on to say, by way of explanation, that "He has always been a loner. He really does march to the sound of a different drummer."[2] Sansing is not entirely wrong, but his interpretation renders Meredith not only safe but also inconsequential, like a strange uncle to be tolerated and not heeded. Such assessments also flatten out our view of the movement overall by branding certain kinds of uncomfortable critiques as wholly exceptional. An engagement with Meredith, and others like him, reminds us of the rich stew of arguments and debates that characterized black political culture in and around the movement. Critical voices, from the Left and from the Right, call attention to the fact that the movement involved protest not only against an oppressive and often indifferent white society. It also involved, and was structured by, arguments inside of black communities. Acknowledging that is a crucial part of the history of the movement and should be an equally important part of how it is remembered and represented. This essay is offered in that spirit.

Meredith was hardly the only prominent black spokesperson to question the efficacy of the March on Washington. The Reverend J. H. Jackson of Mt. Olivet Baptist Church in Chicago and head of the National Baptist Convention characterized the idea as a dangerous rejection of law and order; and the increasingly cantankerous journalist George Schuyler denounced the march — and the movement — as communist dominated. But that Meredith did so as a persistent symbol of the movement makes him especially provocative. His 1962 victory over the University of Mississippi officially desegregated that institution and firmly fixed his place in the "pantheon" of civil rights "heroes"; none of his criticisms of the movement seemed to matter or shake his hold on a reputation he deserved but didn't want. His criticisms didn't quite register in the press; nor did they deter the movement spokespersons from publicly claiming Meredith and his victory at Ole Miss as their own. Most dramatically, in his famous 1963 "Letter from Birmingham Jail," Martin Luther King Jr. expressed the hope that one day the nation would recognize its real heroes: "They will be the James Merediths, courageously and with a majestic sense of purpose, facing the jeering and hostile mobs and the agonizing loneliness that characterizes the life of a pioneer." [3]

2   Sansing quoted in William Doyle, *An American Insurrection: James Meredith and the Battle of Oxford, Mississippi, 1962* (New York, 2001), 299.

3   The full letter is at http://www.thekingcenter.org/archive/document/letter-birmingham-city-jail-0#

James Meredith had other ideas and saw himself as a different kind of pioneer. "Concerning the proposed march on Washington," Meredith opined, "I will say that in my opinion the march would not be in the best interest of our cause." The cause, he insisted, was best served by pursuing black advancement through alternative means — specifically, economic development, education, and proper leadership. Indeed, it was to Meredith's mind the "very low quality of leadership present among our young Negroes and the childish nature of their activities" that constituted his great "dissatisfaction" with the movement in general — or so he told the audience at the Youth Freedom Banquet at the NAACP annual convention in July 1963.[4] It was classic Meredith: to be an honored guest who can't resist the temptation to insult the host.

Convened just weeks before the scheduled march, the NAACP's proceedings were rife with tensions over tone and tactics. The convention, therefore, supplies a way to explore some of eddies and rip tides that lay beneath the historic gathering in the nation's capital in 1963, and which continue to shape American and African American political culture today. Fifty years later, it seems to be getting harder to recall that there were *white* critics of the march and the movement — apart from full-fledged segregationists like Bull Connor, the notorious sheriff of Birmingham, Alabama. How much more challenging, then, to recall and to credit — and to fully explicate — African American ones, including a prominent minister (Jackson), an influential journalist (Schuyler), and an icon of the movement itself (Meredith). This brief overview of the 1963 convention helps to set the stage for and to conceptualize these three distinctive critics.

For the NAACP, rolling into Chicago that early July meant setting up shop in territory dominated by the Reverend J. H. Jackson — no relation, either biologically or ideologically, to the better-known Reverend Jesse Jackson. Pastor of Olivet Baptist Church, the largest black Baptist church in the nation, since 1941 and head of the five-million-plus strong National Baptist Convention (NBC) since 1953, Jackson was formidable then even though he is not widely remembered now. He was also perhaps the most influential black critic of the movement in general and of Martin Luther King Jr. in particular. He had publicly denounced King as a "hoodlum" and a "power-keg philosopher" and pointedly refused to endorse any of King's initiatives.[5] Although King had known Jackson since childhood, the two came to blows, almost literally, as King conspired to oust Jackson

4   Meredith's speech is reprinted in his memoir, *Three Years in Mississippi* (Bloomington, 1966), 312-18.

5   Wallace Best's "'The Right Achieved and the Wrong Way Conquered': J. H. Jackson, Martin Luther King, Jr., and the Conflict over Civil Rights," *Religion and American Culture: A Journal of Interpretation* 16, no. 2 (Summer 2006): 195-226, gives a good overview of the nature of the conflicts between King and Jackson, as does Taylor Branch, *Parting the Waters: America in the King Years, 1954-63* (New York, 1988).

from the NBC's leadership through the latter part of the 1950s, hoping to use the powerful organization as the main institutional basis for the civil rights movement. If movement people had controlled the National Baptist Convention, a Southern Christian Leadership Council (SCLC) might not have been necessary.

But Jackson thwarted King at every turn and ruled over the NBC with an increasingly iron hand until 1982. In 1968, when the Chicago city council decided to rename South Parkway in honor of the recently assassinated King, Jackson went so far as to change the official address of his church from Parkway to Thirty-First Street to avoid having King's name on the letterhead. He also changed the orientation of the church's front door to 31st so that congregants would not have to enter from a street named after King. This longstanding feud was more than mere petty jealous and rivalry among men of the cloth but a reflection, at least in part, of real philosophical, religious, and strategy-driven differences between the two men and the communities they represented.

The 1963 NAACP convention in Chicago embodied some of these differences. Much like the organization's national convention in 1937 in Detroit, during which the question of industrial unionization was hotly debated, the Chicago convention provided a forum for disputation around the appropriate strategies for civil rights activism and included debate about the upcoming March on Washington for Jobs and Freedom. Reverend Jackson had already lit the first match by issuing a statement in the days before the convention denouncing the march as a "dangerous, unwarranted" form of protest.[6] Chicago Mayor Richard J. Daley, who welcomed the organization to town by declaring, with a perfectly straight face, "there are no ghettos in Chicago," exacerbated the situation.[7] Even though Daley participated in leading an estimated ten thousand convention delegates and others on the July 4th "Freedom March" down State Street that culminated in a rally at Grant Park, he was booed for ten to twenty minutes (accounts vary) before leaving the platform, unable to deliver his speech.

Jackson's reception by the angry and agitated crowd was little better than Daley's. The reverend did not deny the existence of segregation either nationally or locally, but he did attempt to call a halt to demonstrations for a six-day mourning period in honor of slain civil rights activist Medgar Evers. It was a resolution that Jackson, who had previously offered his very public support to President Kennedy's plea for a temporary cessation of civil rights demonstrations, never

6 Branch, *Parting the Waters*, 848-49.

7 Ibid, 848.

got to put before the convention. He, too, was booed off the stage, and the following Sunday his church was picketed.[8]

A critique of the upcoming march and a call to halt demonstrations was entirely consistent with Jackson's political theology and his understanding of good and proper strategy. Back in 1957 he had issued a sharp critique of the NAACP for staging demonstrations against the Little Rock, Arkansas, school board's decision to place no more than six black children in schools that were previously all white but had endorsed the association's filing of a lawsuit. While the lawsuit was, he believed, a "step in the right direction, which should be encouraged by all who have worked for the preservation of free public schools," demonstrations were unwarranted. "The struggle for democracy in education is not only a legal question," he wrote at the time, "but a question of achieving constructive human relations and good will … We must not sacrifice the latter in a meticulous contention for the letter of the law." [9]

A richer articulation of Jackson's views can be found in his 1964 address to the Eighty-Fourth Annual Session of the National Baptist Convention held that year in Detroit, Michigan. Therein, he framed the civil rights struggle not as "a struggle to negate the high and lofty philosophy of American freedom. It is not," he continued, "an attempt to convert the nation into an armed camp or to substitute panic and anarchy in the place of law and order."[10] It was, instead, the very fulfillment of the promise of American freedom, and he argued that it should therefore remain in what he called the "mainstream" of American democracy. He allowed that this might feel like an uphill battle. "But we as a people," he insisted, "must keep ever the true meaning of our struggle so that we will never be used as tools in the hands of those who love not the nation's cause but seek the nation's hurt and not our help." He advocated that all "stick to law and order" and to a "commitment to the highest laws of our land and in obedience to the American philosophy and way of life."

For Jackson, this meant resisting the temptation to place the struggle in open opposition to the law. "In some cases," he asserted, "the technique of direct action and demonstrations have led to mob violence and to vandalism. At least some who have desired to practice these negative methods have used the technique of so-called direct action." In the speech's climax, he intoned:

8   Ibid.; "4th of July Crowd Boos Rev. J. J. Jackson Off Platform," *Philadelphia Tribune*, July 6, 1963, 1; "NAACP Convention Called the 'Boldest,'" *Los Angeles Sentinel*, July 11, 1963, A1.

9   "Dr. Jackson Raps NAACP," *Daily Defender*, August 13, 1959.

10 The full text of Jackson's address can be accessed via TeachingAmerican-History.org: http://teachingamericanhistory.org/library/joseph-h-jackson/. The following quotations are all taken from this source.

Today, I call for another type of direct action; this is, direct action in the positive which is oriented towards the Negro's ability, talent, genius, and capacity: Let us take our economic resources, however insignificant and small, and organize and harness them, not to stop the economic growth of others, but to develop our own and to help our own community ... In the act of boycotting, our best economic talents are not called into play, and we ourselves are less productive and seek to render others the same. Why not build for ourselves instead of boycotting others?

And, finally:

The progress of the race lies not in continued street demonstrations, and the liberation of an oppressed people shall not come by acts of revenge and retaliation but by the constructive use of all available opportunities and a creative expansion of the circumstances of the past into stepping stones to higher things.

The substance of Jackson's views was not terribly different from James Meredith's, who also encountered some problems during the 1963 NAACP convention in Chicago. In his Youth Fund dinner speech, Meredith raised critical questions about the proposed March on Washington for suggesting the entire business of civil rights legislation be left in the hands of the six "Negro congressmen." He also dressed down the Youth Council members for their lack of discipline, their lack of attention to the virtues of thrift, economic self-reliance, and saving, ultimately losing his temper and denouncing the crowd as immature "burr-heads."[11] Yet Meredith's point, much like Reverend Jackson's, was that the march was wrong, strategically, from a law-and-order point of view, and that it encouraged, ideologically, an insufficient focus on legislative action as opposed to economic and community development.

Reverend Jackson was not a full-fledged conservative. His views reflect a fairly characteristic 1950s' "vital center" preoccupation with national consensus, political moderation, and religious unity. And part of what lay beneath the disputes between King and Jackson, as Wallace Best, a contemporary professor of African American religious history at Princeton argues, was a struggle over the nature and the role of black religion in the public realm.[12] Yet both Meredith and

11 Meredith tactfully omits the "burr-heads" reference in the text and discussion of his remarks reprinted in his *Three Years in Mississippi*, but they are captured in Frank L. Spencer, "Meredith Bemoans 'Bigotry' in NAACP," *Atlanta Daily World*, July 7, 1963, among other contemporary newspaper sources.

12 Best, "'The Right Achieved and the Wrong Way Conquered,'" 197-98, 205-209.

Jackson do embody a set of ideas that would be seen as a hallmark of *black* conservatism. This is especially true when these ideas are read back in time through the lens of Booker T. Washington with the stress on economic self-help and respect for law and order as opposed to faith in overt political activism. Although both were chastised in Chicago in 1963 for their critical views of the march and the movement, it is equally important to note that they were both there, on the ground, and part of a significant dialogue and debate that was taking place within African American communities.

George Schuyler was not present in Chicago in 1963, but he, too, was part of a series of debates about the efficacy of the civil rights movement and its strategies. Unlike Meredith and Jackson, he issued what looks like a much more recognizably mainstream conservative critique and aligned himself directly and increasingly with the American Right — which Meredith would not do until almost two decades later. Once a member of the post-World War I Socialist Party, this expressive Harlem-based writer was one of the most prolific black journalists of the twentieth century. By the late 1950s, he had embraced the Cold War and moved decisively rightward.[13] He tended to believe that all mass protests and marches — not only the 1963 March on Washington but also the 1957 Prayer Pilgrimage — were essentially useless. "The great illusion of the civil rights strategists," he wrote in a *Pittsburgh Courier* column in 1965, "is that by provoking and inciting inconvenience and nuisance, leading inevitably to law violations and force to suppress them, the prejudices of whites in the Deep South will be minimized to the point where whites will love and respect blacks" and that the federal government would protect them.[14]

Schuyler articulated a classic law-and-order position that was similar to Reverend Jackson's but far more overtly conservative, especially because of Schuyler's virulent anti-communism. In November 1963, he lectured on why Congress should not pass civil rights legislation. He argued that the law should not be used as a weapon to compel social change and that the full achievement of African American civil rights depended on the tolerance and will of the majority — something that would only come about gradually. "Changes have been slow since 1865, but there have been marked changes; and civil rights laws, state or federal, have had little to do with it," he insisted. "They have been enforced and accepted only when the dominant majority acquiesced and have generally lain dormant in the law books. In short, custom has dictated the pace of change."[15] His views were not dissimilar to

13 For a good overview, see Oscar R. Williams, *George S. Schuyler: Portrait of a Black Conservative* (Knoxville, 2007).

14 Schuyler, "Views and Reviews" Column, *Pittsburgh Courier*, April 3, 1965, 10.

15 Schuyler quoted in Williams, *George S. Schuyler*, 141-42.

those penned by William F. Buckley in the pages of the *National Review* at the time. What is particularly interesting is that Schulyer's pieces appeared on a regular basis in his column in the *Courier*, then one of the most popular and widely read black newspapers. Not all of his views were embraced by all of his readers, and the paper's editor did indeed ask him on several occasions to stop sniping at King, but Schuyler's commitment to gradualism, patriotism, and economic empowerment surely resonated with many people inside black communities across the country.

Schuyler's was not really a lone voice on the margins of black political culture. He was howling but not in the wilderness. While he mostly parted ways with the pro-civil rights movement paper by the end of 1964, his writing appeared in the *Courier* until 1966. As far as I know, there is only one recorded instance of his views being deemed too extreme — his 1964 editorial insisting that King had made no contribution to the world or to the cause of peace and that instead of a Nobel Prize, the "Lenin Prize" would be more appropriate. Not only did he describe King as being part of an international communist movement; Schuyler also characterized him as a "sable Typhoid Mary, infecting the mentally disturbed with perversions of Christian doctrine." It was just too much for *Courier* editor Robert L. Vann. He refused to run that particular piece, and William Loeb in his far-right *Manchester Union Leader* ultimately published it instead.[16] It was a pivotal moment for Schuyler. From there it was but a short hop to the John Birch Society — one of the key organizations of the far or "radical" Right of the 1950s and 1960s.

Schuyler became a Bircher. James Meredith went on to campaign for ex-Klansman David Duke on the grounds of their shared opposition to affirmative action, welfare, and "forced busing." That both Schuyler and Meredith became increasingly marginal within mainstream black political culture should not allow us to ignore the fact that in the early 1960s they represented and voiced opinions and critiques that were part of the fabric of black political thought. Examining the lives and views of difficult figures like Schuyler, Meredith, and Reverend Jackson, who were in positions that allowed them to function as thought leaders and provocateurs, should remind us that African Americans responded to the civil rights movement in myriad ways. Some resisted the movement out of fear of violent reprisals while others thought the time and energy would be better spent attacking problems of drunkenness, extramarital sex, and other manifestations

16 Schuyler, "King No Help to Peace," *Manchester (N.H.) Union Leader*, November 10, 1964, 25.

of moral decay. Still others were gradualists made uncomfortable by direct-action tactics, and some were, for various reasons, supportive of segregation. A 1966 study by Donald Matthews and James Prothro revealed that one in three "Negroes is not committed to the goal of racial integration," with 16 percent favoring "strict segregation," and 15 percent favoring "something in between" strict segregation and integration.[17] This snapshot study calls our attention to the idea that the civil rights movement, and the Black Freedom struggle overall, was not simply a series of confrontations between (white) segregationists and (black) integrationists. Rather, at every step and throughout each era there was a certain degree of ambivalence and uncertainty as people were forced to choose among competing values and strategies.

The fiftieth anniversary of the March on Washington is a good reminder of how one-dimensional and sanitized "commemorative history" can become. At the same time, it can signal the need for better, more complicated stories about figures like Meredith, Schuyler, and the Reverend J. H. Jackson, and for a more expansive narrative about the movement overall. Taken in isolation, each of these examples can be written off as merely iconoclastic or opportunistic — the product of political sour grapes and personal disappointments. Viewed together, however, they start to appear not only to be the product of individual choices but also to be part of broader political and historical trends that are reshaping how we think — and argue about — race and rights in twenty-first-century America.

17 Donald R. Matthews and James W. Prothro, *Negroes and the New Southern Politics* (New York, 1967), 128-40, cited in Lauren F. Winner, "Doubtless Sincere: New Characters in the Civil Rights Cast," *The Role of Ideas in the Civil Rights South*, ed. Ted Ownby (Jackson, 2002), 158.

Angela D. Dillard is the Earl Lewis Collegiate Professor of Afroamerican and African Studies at the University of Michigan. Her most recent book is *Faith in the City: Preaching Radical Social Change in Detroit* (2007). Her first book, *Guess Who's Coming to Dinner Now?: Multicultural Conservatism in America* (2001), was among the first critical studies of the rise of political conservatism among African Americans, Latinos, women, and homosexuals. Her current book project, *Civil Rights Conservatism*, examines unexpected "alliances" and "intersections" between the post-WWII civil rights movement and the rise of a New Right.

Visual Histories and Cultural Memories

HOLLYWOOD ACTIVISM, DAYTIME VERITÉ, AND THE MARCH ON WASHINGTON

Allison Graham

Several hours after the conclusion of the 1963 March on Washington for Jobs and Freedom, six participants in the march gathered in a television studio to discuss the day's events. Sponsored and taped by the U.S. Information Agency for distribution to international broadcast stations, schools, and consulates, the 30-minute dialogue was intended to counter negative foreign perceptions of U.S. race relations by showcasing a collegial exchange of ideas between black and white Americans. With live satellite coverage of the march picked up by six countries, and recorded coverage scheduled by many more in the coming week, the conversation would serve as a coda to those images, reinforcing the day's spectacle of peaceful protest by offering a more personal glimpse of "unrehearsed discussion" among people with "deeply held personal views" (according to the program's voiceover narrator).[1] To represent American discourse in action, the USIA chose "a small group from Hollywood, California": James Baldwin, Harry Belafonte, Marlon Brando, Charlton Heston, director and screenwriter Joseph Mankiewicz, and Sidney Poitier. To ensure that few would confuse the production with a sampling of just any American discourse, however, the USIA called it *Hollywood Roundtable*.

While the propaganda value of this group of literary and film stars was openly acknowledged in the grave intonation of each participant's name and repeated references to the men's fame and status, a subtler, and perhaps more effective, rhetorical aspect of "Hollywood Roundtable" was its deceptively simple mise-en-scène. Arrayed in a semi-circle around the program host, veteran reporter David Schoenbrun, the six celebrities embodied nothing so much as mid-century American "cool": dark suits and thin ties on bodies alternately sprawling and sitting at attention, serious recitation punctuated by easy laughter, chumminess interrupted by sudden intensity, chain-smoked cigarettes tapped out of packs and dangled from fingers. Decades before it was stylized by the hit series *Mad Men*, this was the look of cosmopolitan American masculinity in the early 1960s, and it was the look of live television.

Hollywood Roundtable may have been "unrehearsed," but its first minutes echoed a script that had been heard earlier that day when

1 https://www.youtube.com/watch?v=1u27coFlGXg. Subsequent quotations from the program are taken from this site.

Martin Luther King Jr. had compellingly described "the fierce urgency of now." In choral fashion, Mankiewicz announced that the "urgency of civil rights" had brought him to Washington, Schoenbrun confessed that he had "felt this sense of urgency myself," Poitier divulged that "the urgency that was evident today has been bubbling in me, personally, for most of these years," and Heston, completing the tribute, declared that he "could no longer pay only lip service to a cause that was so urgently right and in a time that is so urgently now."

After its epigraphic beginning, though, the program quickly strayed from the USIA's tacit script. Hoping to move attention from the cause of the march to the fact of its success, Schoenbrun turned to American exceptionalism: "Demonstrations of this kind could not easily be held elsewhere, and when we talk about oppression and repression I haven't seen any march on Moscow or march on Peking." Mankiewicz allowed that although the U.S. is almost the only Western country in which this could happen, it is "also the only country in which it is necessary." When Heston disagreed, Belafonte put an emphatic end to the comparisons: "It is long since past the time when we can measure our own conscience and our own sense of morality based on what some decayed society refuses to give its own."

With the program veering dangerously from its intended purpose, Schoenbrun issued a warning to Mankiewicz and Belafonte: "Remember, the entire world watches this sort of thing. The world doesn't have a correct measuring stick.... Here, we are talking to the world. More than a hundred countries will be listening to the discussion today." Shifting to a seemingly safer topic, Schoenbrun asked Poitier how he had faced the "problem" of Negro rights. "My country has to successfully negotiate the Negro question," Poitier replied. "It is to me not a *problem*. It's the question." When Heston voiced agreement with "the vital importance of this question not only for Negro Americans but for all Americans," Mankiewicz once again cut against the grain: "That's why I think, for a starter, why don't we sometimes refer to it as the 'white' question?"

"It's an *American* question," Heston responded.

"No, I think it is the *white* question."

"It's a *human* question," Brando interjected.

Introduction and
Prologue / Music and
the March / Transatlantic
Legacies / Different Views
and Voices / **Visual Histories and
Cultural Memories**

"I think you're both right," Heston offered in an attempt to end the debate, but Brando, warming to the subject, continued his historical ramblings.

"There's always an ebb and flow in history. One country's up, one country's down...."

"No, it's been cozy to think of it, Marlon, as the 'Negro question'," Mankiewicz interrupted, stepping in to educate the actor he had directed in *Julius Caesar*.

"I don't disagree with that," Brando conceded, hanging his head.

"The responsibility has shifted to the white people of America," Mankiewicz concluded, at which point Schoenbrun rushed to ease the rising tension in the studio by suggesting that they all seemed to agree that "words often get in the way of what we mean to say." After all, he noted with some relief, even Poitier had felt moved to correct himself earlier when he had changed "Negro problem" to "Negro question."

"Implied in 'Negro problem' is a suggestion that I represent a problem. I do *not* represent a problem," Poitier fired back, and Mankiewicz interrupted again to emphasize the point: "The Negroes are not a problem for us. *We're* a problem to the Negroes!"

"It's the same thing," Brando suggested, trying again to argue for universal equivalence.

"No, it's not the same thing, at all!"

"Yes, it is, Joe," Heston asserted with authority.

Belafonte interceded to say that Mankiewicz was right, "because the person who holds the power in his hands to fulfill the American Dream ... happens to be a person who is *white*." Still not understanding the issue, Heston tried to restore the illusion of group harmony. "To imply that it's solely a white problem is to deny the burning interest of every fellow Negro citizen," he said, before turning to the others to plead for agreement. "Really, we all feel the same!"

Realizing that he had lost control of the intended narrative, Schoenbrun moved to shut down the free-for-all, but not before reproaching his unruly guests. "Gentlemen, the crosstalk is such that what you're saying, which I think everybody wants to hear, is being lost over your words of wisdom."

For all of Schoenbrun's (and no doubt the USIA's) exasperation with the trajectory of this star-studded propaganda experiment, *Hollywood Roundtable* was a showcase of American-styled democratic discourse. This was live television, with its risks exposed and its rewards coming unexpectedly. Because it was not edited for distribution (all cutting being done through camera-switching on the set), the program revealed moment-by-moment shifts in personal and political alliances within the group, as each man tried and (except for Heston) failed to stay "on message," supported and then took issue with others, and ultimately threw out the script altogether.

Although Brando never brandished the cattle prod stowed under his chair (a memento from a demonstration in Gadsden, Alabama, that he had attended a week earlier), a more serious breach of TV etiquette had threatened the proceedings from the moment Heston had seconded Schoenbrun's case for American exceptionalism. With the march concluded and already being lauded as a triumph, the Hollywood contingent's tolerance for Heston's conservatism was quickly disintegrating. Having reluctantly acceded to Martin Luther King Jr.'s wish to allow Heston, an actor whose politics usually situated him "across the divide" from Hollywood liberals,[2] to serve with Brando as co-chair of the coalition, the others now began to break rank, exposing the fault lines that had run beneath the group for months.

Schoenbrun's frustrated description of what he saw as the discussion's chaos illuminates how central television had become to American politics. Contrary to his assertion, the men's "crosstalk" did not obscure the substance of their dialogue; if anything, it *was* the substance of the dialogue. Urbane "crosstalk" was a form of political discourse that Americans had grown used to seeing on television by 1963 (as opposed to the witless "crossfire" of political shouting matches made popular by CNN and Fox News forty years later). Improvisation, spontaneity, impatience, anger, embarrassment, fatigue, furtive asides — in short, going "off script" — were the hallmarks of live television itself, and were far more credible expressions of U.S. "freedom" than well-rehearsed and edited testimonials.

One might wonder how Schoenbrun would have managed an even larger group of celebrities. Whether misreading or sticking too closely to the USIA's script, he introduced the roundtable as "seven men," though only six were present.[3] The missing guest might have been on the "celebrity plane" that had left Los Angeles that morning carrying not only Brando, Heston, Belafonte, Mankiewicz, and Poitier,

2 Harry Belafonte, *My Song: A Memoir of Art, Race, and Defiance* (New York, 2011), 277.

3 As of this writing, the identity of the possibly missing seventh member hasn't been found.

Introduction and
Prologue

Music and
the March

Transatlantic
Legacies

Different Views
and Voices

**Visual Histories and
Cultural Memories**

but also Paul Newman, Diahann Carroll, James Garner, Sammy Davis Jr., Joanne Woodward, Gregory Peck, Lena Horne, Tony Franciosa, and Tony Bennett. On the other hand, he (and it was assuredly a "he") might have been Ossie Davis, who served as an emcee at the Lincoln Memorial, or Burt Lancaster, who had come from Europe to read a petition in support of the march signed by 1500 Americans living in Paris.

Although most of the celebrities who attended the march had been supporting the cause of civil rights in additional ways, Belafonte, Brando, Lancaster, and Newman were the most visible faces of Hollywood activism. Early in 1963, the group had organized a rally and fundraiser in support of the SCLC at Dodger Stadium in Los Angeles, and Brando and Newman had later joined a sit-in organized by CORE at the Georgia state capitol. In the month leading up to the march, Brando had been particularly active, joining Newman, Lancaster, Heston, Anthony Franciosa, and James Whitmore to press for greater representation of African Americans in the film and television industries; participating (with actor Pernell Roberts, star of *Bonanza*) in a housing discrimination protest in Torrance, south of Los Angeles; and, along with Newman, Tony Franciosa, and actor Virgil Frye, lending support to protesters against hiring discrimination in Gadsden, Alabama (where he encountered the notorious cattle prods used by police, one of which he would take to Washington as evidence of police brutality in the South).

Against the backdrop of popular films that had been made in and about the postwar South starring Brando, Newman, Woodward, Franciosa, and Peck, the stars' public support of civil rights generated associations that, for the most part, enhanced Hollywood's value to the movement. Brando had most famously played New Orleans factory worker Stanley Kowalski in *A Streetcar Named Desire* (1951), a film that co-starred *Gone With the Wind*'s Vivien Leigh, but he had also played a southern Air Force officer who struggled to overcome his racism in *Sayonara* (1957) and, more recently, a Mississippi Delta drifter in Tennessee Williams's *The Fugitive Kind* (1959). By 1963, Paul Newman had risen to stardom in adaptations of works by William Faulkner and Tennessee Williams (*The Long, Hot Summer* and *Cat on a Hot Tin Roof* [both 1958]), and had maintained his familiar southern persona in both Williams's *Sweet Bird of Youth* (1962) and *Hud*, a widely acclaimed movie that was showing in theaters across the country in August 1963. Newman's wife Joanne Woodward, a southerner herself, had won an Academy Award for her 1957 performance as a Georgia housewife in *The Three Faces of Eve*, and had co-starred with her husband in *The Long, Hot Summer*. Like Newman, she had often starred in Faulkner and Williams adaptations (*The Sound and the Fury* [1959] and, with Brando, *The Fugitive Kind*). Anthony Franciosa's roles in *A Face in the Crowd* (1957); *The Long, Hot Summer* (1958); and Tennessee Williams's *Period of Adjustment* (1962) had established him as a recognizable southern sidekick to stars like Newman and Andy Griffith. The regional character types represented by these roles were familiar and almost predictable installations in mainstream Hollywood films by 1963. Regardless of the kinds of characters they played, it was the fact of the actors' entrenched celluloid "southernness" that offered justification of a kind for their highlighted attendance at the march.

Gregory Peck's presence, however, did more than simply conjure associations with the Deep South. *To Kill a Mockingbird* had opened across the nation just five months earlier, and in April Peck had won the Best Actor Oscar for his portrayal of Atticus Finch. Standing apart from the contemporary and blatantly regional characters played by Brando, Newman, and Franciosa, Atticus had been played by Peck as a timeless, universally appealing patriarch, white America's emblem of enlightened racial tolerance. For much of the movie-going population, Gregory Peck *was* Atticus Finch. The sight of his tall frame and composed face among the marchers and dignitaries must no doubt have collapsed the distance between fact and fiction for many television viewers, as if Atticus himself had simply walked off one screen and onto another.

As useful as such stars were to the public appeal of the march, however, their media compatibility proved especially valuable. In its first event staged for a global audience, the civil rights movement could not claim expertise in television aesthetics. Industry professionals behind the cameras and in network control booths could ensure broadcast-quality coverage of the day's events, but whether or not those events would "work" on television was a different matter. As it turned out, the occasional organizational stumbles, inelegant orations, or redundant monologues that threatened to curb dramatic momentum on the steps of the Lincoln Memorial did little to diminish the day's inherent "televisuality." In fact, they ensured it.

Perhaps easy to forget is that what most people experienced as the March on Washington in 1963 was not the parade of colliding sensory pleasures later recalled by those who marched, sang, and sat on the National Mall. For many, the march was a purely auditory experience, a live monaural soundtrack heard on transistor and car radios, while for others, who only glimpsed the front pages of afternoon newspapers, it was an already registered historical event, devoid of sound and motion. For most, however, the march took shape as a two-dimensional electronic canvas of black, gray, and off-white images, a "special" broadcasting event that interrupted scheduled programs throughout the day (on ABC and NBC) but was in fact visually indistinguishable from the rest of daytime TV.

Unlike news coverage of critical events in the movement's history, which had often seemed profoundly discordant with the sensibility of network programming (never more so than in the footage of Birmingham police turning high-powered water hoses and attack dogs on peaceful protesters just months earlier, on May 3 and 4), the August 28th broadcast settled comfortably into the unhurried pace of non-prime-time television, especially on CBS, where it unfolded in real time from 1:30 to 4:30 Eastern Time. Like the live serial dramas and game shows it displaced for the day, coverage of the march's schedule of events was restricted to a location that had to accommodate an astounding amount of equipment: tripods, cherry pickers, unwieldy wiring, bulky sound recorders, and bulkier static cameras. Turning confinement on sound stages to an advantage by using extensive close-ups and dialogue, afternoon programming had become the domain of faces, emotion, and continuous talk. If in addition to songs and speeches, participants in the march heard revving motors, walkie-talkies, twittering birds, crying babies, airplane engines, radios, and even occasional silence, television viewers heard continuous talk — not just from dignitaries on the podium, but from network anchors, field reporters, celebrities, politicians, random marchers, and, of course, commercial sponsors. Introduced early in the day, the march eased into the community of daytime TV conversation in brief but predictable appearances, becoming a familiar constituent by afternoon. Considered within its original context, a crucial aspect of the broadcast's historical significance is apparent in every frame — in its unremarkable formal features, its nearly seamless embeddedness in the TV schedules of a late-summer Wednesday afternoon, its stealth integration of the national airwaves.

In late August of 1963, black and white news was within two years of its demise. CBS would broadcast the first all-color evening news report on August 19, 1965, eight days after the beginning of the Watts eruption, bringing an end to a particular way of perceiving American race relations. From the film clips of the 1955 Emmett Till murder trial, which had been rushed by car through the Mississippi Delta to New York-bound planes at the Memphis airport, to the videotaped Selma marches in 1965, "civil rights" was framed, transmitted, and received as a literal black and white narrative, an elemental story of contrasts — racial, regional, and moral. The splintering of black unity would be told in color against a background of urban flames, and journalism would struggle to fashion a revision of the old story from unconventional characters and unfamiliar settings.

Color programming had appeared sporadically during prime time in the late 1950s and early 1960s (the NBC series *Bonanza*, the Rose Bowl parades, special broadcasts of *The Wizard of Oz*), but black and white was the lingua franca of the quotidian and the familiar — soap operas, talk shows, game shows, and children's programs. It was, in effect, the language of "reality," and by 1963, it had attained a cultural cachet unimaginable in 1961, when newly installed FCC Chairman Newton Minow had called television a "vast wasteland." Monochromatic images and monaural sound transmitted electronically within fractions of seconds from studio sound stages to less than finely tuned living-room receivers were simply what TV was in its first decade. What TV was by 1963, however, appeared to be less the unavoidable product of its limitations than the skillful exploitation of its uniqueness, to the point that a televisual aesthetic was now recognizable. At the heart of this aesthetic was simply the fact of visual immediacy. Crossing generic boundaries and blurring distinctions between fiction and nonfiction, television — and live television especially — signified authenticity in a way that was unavailable to other media. Even at its most banal, TV could convey an authenticity of space, time, and character.

Thanks in large part to Newton Minow's unrelenting pressure on the broadcast industry to elevate the quality of its offerings, networks in the early 1960s had made an unprecedented investment in a type of literate, adult programming that began to sensitize audiences to the social value and rhetorical meanings of electronic authenticity.[4] The unprecedented outpouring of television documentaries between 1961 and 1963 coincided fortuitously with the development of cinéma verité, a style of filming that used lightweight cameras and make-shift synchronized sound to capture the private conversations

4 Newton Minow's crucial role in shaping U.S. television programming in the early 1960s is examined by Mary Ann Watson in the first chapter of *The Expanding Vision: American Television in the Kennedy Years* (New York, 1990).

and unrehearsed actions of people in a way that had never been seen before — and in a way that made viewers feel as if they were hearing and seeing how those figures "really" talked and behaved. Shaky hand-held cameras and inadequate lighting often erased the past tense, creating the impression that what was in the frame not only was happening here and now but was also slightly illicit and immensely personal.

This kind of documentary sensibility had already begun to retune the look and sound of prime time programming in series like *Naked City* (1958-63), *Route 66* (1960-64), and *The Twilight Zone* (1959-64). *Naked City* and *Route 66* were shot on location (in New York and on back roads throughout the U.S., respectively), while *The Twilight Zone* attempted to render realistically "a dimension of mind," but all three were written and performed by artists intent on examining, often relentlessly, the emotional depth and psychological complexity of "ordinary" people in stressful situations. The immense popularity of Alan Funt's *Candid Camera* (1960-67), a "reality" comedy show that used hidden cameras and microphones to record anonymous people's reactions to practical jokes, indicates the widespread fascination with observing (seemingly) unstaged behavior at close range (a fascination that was fueling the demand for spy movies and novels, notably the James Bond series).

The verité era of television was also the Kennedy era, to the benefit of both. As a presidential candidate, Kennedy had allowed the pioneers of the style, Robert Drew and Ricky Leacock, to shadow him on the campaign trail, and had appeared cooly televisual during his live debates with Nixon; as president, he allowed documentary makers ample access to his office and began holding live televised press conferences within five days of his inauguration. He also hired TV and film director Franklin Shaffner to be his production advisor for live broadcasts from the White House. So important was Shaffner to the administration that on October 22, 1962, he was called in to direct the lighting, makeup, and videography of Kennedy's Cuban Missile Crisis announcement.[5]

Shaffner's central qualification for this role was his experience directing live dramas during TV's "golden age," that period in New York from the mid-1950s to the early 1960s in which acting studios, theaters, and television studios shared an interest in what might be called dramatized verité. Stanislavski's "Method," as the style was loosely called, had been employed by artists for decades, but by the

5 Mary Ann Watson, *The Expanding Vista: American Television in the Kennedy Years* (New York, 1990), 78.

1950s it had become a cultural style (to many, *the* cultural style) for communicating postwar angst, anger, and love on stage and on the screen. For several decades, Lee Strasberg, Sanford Meisner, and Stella Adler had been training aspiring actors to approach their art as an unstinting revelation of emotional truth. Improvisation, word play, and (in Strasberg's case) memory recovery were tools for achieving one overarching goal on stage: being present.

Marlon Brando, Paul Newman, Joanne Woodward, Gregory Peck, and Anthony Franciosa had studied under one or more of these mentors, and James Baldwin would soon develop and stage *Blues for Mister Charlie*, a thinly disguised study of the Emmett Till murder, at Strasberg's Actors Studio. Countless actors (Sidney Poitier, for example) had learned Method techniques informally, often on the job (in Poitier's case, through tutoring by Joe Mankiewicz during the filming of *No Way Out* in 1950). Method-inspired acting pervaded screens and stages and had come to define contemporary American self-expression. The era's anxieties would find their most convincing and powerful representation through unwavering focus on being "in the moment."

If ever a dramatic style were suited to the "fierce urgency of now," it was the Method, and if ever a medium were suited to the Method, it was live television. Theater may have been the most prestigious showcase for the style, but live television was its laboratory. In the hands of writers like Rod Serling, Paddy Chayefsky, and Gore Vidal and directors like Arthur Penn and Delbert Mann, teleplays that premiered on *Kraft Television Playhouse* (1947-58), *The Philco Television Playhouse* (1948-56), *Playhouse 90* (1956-61), or *The United States Steel Hour* (1953-63) showcased the talents of actors, directors, and writers who understood the unique demands of the medium.

"Sets had to be improvised and tucked into each other, together with the commercials, which were done live in the same studio," Mann later recalled.[6] Vidal remembered it more vividly: the studio was "concentrated hell," rehearsal was "the time of distinct disaster," and going live was "terrifying and exhilarating."[7] Performers who worked best under live television's constraints turned out to be theater actors, especially those who were skilled in dramatic spontaneity and improvisation. According to Penn, "These were theatre actors, not actors who needed four takes or five takes.... They had the flexibility, the training, the sense that once they began performing the play, there was no stopping it, and that is what was consistent with

6 Gordon F. Sander, *Serling: The Rise and Twilight of Television's Last Angry Man* (New York, 1992), 84.

7 Ibid., 86.

live TV. There was no going back. We'd go on at nine and off at ten, and it was a complete living experience."[8]

The danger of this kind of immediacy was felt by viewers, but in a way that was strangely new. "It had that highly personal feeling about it," Mosel would remember: "Because it was live, when you sat in your living room and looked at a live play, you really honestly had the feeling that Paul Newman was performing for you. Just for me, sitting here … and you saw he was nervous and you said, 'Oh, I hope he's going to get through it all right'."[9] Rather than being depleted by the weekly ritual of anticipation and relief, viewers were invigorated. According to *Playhouse 90* director Buzz Kulik, "The audience was so excited about this new thing, that they brought a kind of energy and vitality to it also."[10]

Enduring both the "terrifying and exhilarating" process of making the production and the tension-ridden intimacy of watching that production created a bond among the survivors. Gore Vidal recalled thirty years later, "Sunday nights we had the country. Monday morning you would be walking down First Avenue and every other group of people would be discussing your play."[11] Undergirding this bond was a shared understanding of what had been attempted: With the clock ticking, anything could have happened. For that hour, they all had been "in the moment."

Actors weren't the only artists at the march who understood the urgency of live performance. As increasing numbers of stand-up comedians became recording stars in the late 1950s and early 1960s, they too had begun to move between the worlds of theater and television. Nightclub stages were the stand-ups' traditional venue, but younger comics (such as Mike Nichols and Elaine May) had begun gravitating to improvisational theaters. In contrast to an older generation of apolitical, Borscht Belt comedians, performers like Lenny Bruce, Godfrey Cambridge, Mort Sahl, and Tom Lehrer embraced satire as the most effective weapon against political and social hypocrisy. During this era, even the most controversial popular comics appeared on television, and often live. Among them was Dick Gregory, the only comedian who spoke on the steps of the Lincoln Memorial on August 28.

Ossie Davis introduced Gregory to the marchers as a "comedian fresh from the jail," a reference to Gregory's arrest and four-day imprisonment during the Birmingham protests three months earlier.

8   Ibid., 83.

9   Ibid., 85.

10 Ibid., 87.

11 Ibid., 88.

"I can't tell you how elated I am over looking out at so many of our smiling faces," Gregory said in his brief remarks. "And to be honest with you, the last time I've seen this many of us, Bull Conner was doing all the talking!"[12] The press had covered the Birmingham protests extensively, largely because of the brutality exercised by police commissioner Bull Conner and the arrest of Martin Luther King Jr., and most people in the audience were undoubtedly familiar with Gregory's outspoken support for the campaign. What many in the audience were probably less familiar with was Gregory's activism on other fronts. Ironically, his blink-of-an-eye appearance on the Lincoln Memorial steps gave no indication of the role he had played in the transformation of popular American discourse — a transformation that in no small measure had ensured the success of the march as a broadcasting phenomenon.

In January 1961, Hugh Hefner, founder and editor of *Playboy* magazine and owner of the Playboy Club in Chicago (the sole club in what would soon become an international franchise), had asked Dick Gregory to fill in at the club for a white comic who had canceled his spot. When Hefner's staff later discovered that the audience would be a group of white southern businessmen, they decided to cancel Gregory's performance but to honor their contract to pay him. The club manager tried to prevent the comedian from walking on stage, but Gregory, running late, rushed past the manager to arrive in front of the audience at 8:00, right on time. Taking his measure of the audience, Gregory loaded his routine with southern race jokes and was a hit. He stayed on stage for three hours, and Hefner himself came to the club after midnight to offer Gregory a six-week engagement at the club.

"Never before had white America let a black person stand flat-footed and talk to white folks," Gregory said in 2006. "You could dance, and you could stop in between the dance — Pearl Bailey could talk about her tired feet or Sammy [Davis] could tell a joke — but you could not walk out and talk with white America."[13] The courage of the stand-up comic is estimable to begin with, but Gregory evokes a stark picture of the black comedian's dangerous position in that era: one person isolated on a stage, armed with nothing except words, a clearly lit target surrounded by half-hidden strangers. Talking first, talking back — talking at all — had for centuries been reason enough for white men to kill black men with impunity. As Gregory would repeatedly say of that night in 1961, "Blacks were allowed to sing and dance, but not talk."[14]

12 Davis and Gregory quoted in The Educational Radio Network's coverage of the March on Washington for Jobs and Freedom, http://openvault. wgbh.org/catalog/march-bc109d-celebrity-participation-in-the-march-on-washington.

13 https://www.youtube.com/watch?v=b4xpgha7m7I.

14 He said this most recently in *Hugh Hefner: Playboy, Activist, and Rebel*, dir. Brigitte Berman (Metaphor Films, 2009).

Gregory's triumphant run at the Playboy Club earned him notice in *Time* magazine and an invitation to appear on *The Jack Paar Show* (the original *Tonight Show*), the most popular late-night program on television. An ardent fan of the show, Gregory was appalled when musician Billy Eckstine pointed out to him that black performers were never asked to sit next to Paar after they finished their acts. Crushed that he had failed to register such obvious instances of racial hypocrisy, he declined the invitation. When Paar himself called Gregory, he agreed to change the seating policy on the show. Gregory would appear on the show six times over the next eighteen months, always sitting down with the host after he performed to "talk with white America."

That it was Hefner who initiated the series of events that would break two hardened conventions of American entertainment was not surprising to those who were familiar with his career or his public pronouncements on race. With the profit generated by his immensely popular magazine, Hefner had been able to finance an independently produced television program that would promote the publication and showcase his artistic and political tastes. Beholden to no network or sponsor, *Playboy's Penthouse* debuted as a syndicated series in October 1959 on stations willing to invest in a racially integrated program featuring premiere jazz musicians, folk singers, and controversial comedians. No stations in the South made the investment.

Appearing on the first episode of *Playboy's Penthouse* were Lenny Bruce, Ella Fitzgerald, and Nat "King" Cole. Subsequent episodes featured Pete Seeger, Sammy Davis Jr., Tony Bennett, Count Basie, Dave Brubeck, Ray Charles, Josh White, Tony Curtis, and Dizzy Gillespie. More striking than the guest list of the series, however, was the visual form of each episode. Talk shows had become a popular TV genre by 1959, and variety shows had made the transition from stage to television as early as 1948, with *The Ed Sullivan Show*, but Hefner's creation was different. A hybrid of both genres to some extent, but with a verité inflection, it was a new, more contemporary way of talking, singing, and joking on television.

"What set it apart was the concept," Hefner claims. "It was a penthouse apartment in which the subjective camera came up the elevator and then into the apartment ... as if it was a guest there."[15] The premiere episode, for example, opened with shots of a sports car on its way to Hefner's penthouse (in reality, a Chicago TV studio), accompanied by Cy Coleman's jazzy "Playboy's Theme." After the car pulled up to a tall building, the introduction cut to a shot of an

15 Ibid.

elevator control panel, its buttons lighting as floors passed until the top button (identified only by the *Playboy* bunny icon) was lit. The door slid open, revealing the penthouse living room with Hefner in the center of the frame, his back to the camera. Like someone visiting the penthouse for the first time, the camera scanned the living room unobserved by the host, giving a first-person point of view shot of clusters of people in different parts of the large living room and balcony, all smoking, drinking cocktails, dancing, or affably talking.[16] After allowing time to take in the scene, Hefner, pipe in hand, finally turned to greet the viewer: "Hello there. Glad you could join us this evening." Subsequent episodes would find Hefner dancing or talking somewhere in the living room, always happily surprised to see "you" arrive.

The sophistication of the setting was mirrored in the sophistication of the talk between Hefner and his guests, but it was a casual sophistication — literate yet unpretentious, humorous and serious by turns, and, above all, confident, comfortable, and inclusive. Unlike the fly-on-the-wall verité viewer, Hefner's viewer wasn't spying or overhearing the guests; instead, "you" (in a style consistent with Hefner's opposition to prurience) were openly acknowledged by the host as a welcome member of the groups he chatted with, free to listen in as you chose.

Understanding an essential difference between film and television, Hefner presided over a mise-en-scène that, in spite of its luxury, was at heart deeply domestic and a soundtrack that often seemed remarkably like that of a middle-class neighborhood gathering (to the point of growing boring at times, as unscripted conversations are wont to do), but with one difference: the guest list was racially integrated. Had Hefner not been perceived by many Americans as a glorified pornographer, or had his magazine lacked centerfolds and sex jokes, his program might have been acceptable prime-time fare in many cities. In look and sound, *Playboy's Penthouse* was a production that easily accommodated itself to television's tacit role as a domestic medium by being, above all else, personal, and even intimate. Presenting de facto integration in such a context was unprecedented.

16 The unnamed (and some of the named) female guests on *Playboy's Penthouse* were clearly Playboy "Bunnies" or Playmates of the Month, and no middle-aged or older women made appearances on the show unless they were special guests.

The program lasted a year, and in 1961, eight months after Dick Gregory's groundbreaking performance at the Playboy Club, it began a second season, which ended later that year. In all, twenty-two episodes were aired. Hefner continued to alter the political landscape of entertainment, however, by installing the highly regarded "*Playboy* interview" as a monthly feature in his magazine in 1962 (the first interview being, notably, with Miles Davis) and in buying back the franchises of the New Orleans and Miami Playboy Clubs when their owners refused to honor the memberships of black patrons from clubs outside the South.

In June 1962, Hefner appeared on *The Jack Paar Show* to defend the "Playboy Philosophy," a loose collection of beliefs centered on personal and political freedom that he would soon publish in a book of the same name. "You have to understand the power of *The Jack Paar Show* in the sixties," Dick Gregory recalled in 2000 about the program whose race-based seating policy he had nullified in 1961.[17] "It was a hell of a thing to be on national television," he said, "on the biggest show in the country, and be allowed to make honest racial jokes right in everybody's living room."[18]

Thinking of television as "everybody's living room" was, as the directors, writers, and actors of live TV drama (and, yes, Hefner) had understood, the key that opened the medium to the greatest number of viewers. When Jack Paar had become the host of NBC's late-night show in 1957, he sensed that a television program could escort urbane, adult conversation into American homes if it recognized that "most people were watching it in bed or in their dens."[19] Although all-talk programs existed at the time, the "talk show" had yet to take shape as a recognizable genre. "There was no format," Paar insisted forty years later. "I did the only thing you could do: get a desk, and try and find witty people and start something called a conversation show."[20] At the same time, his late-night predecessor at NBC, Steve Allen, was also experimenting with the boundaries of broadcast talk on his weekly prime time show, which ran from 1956 to 1961. In 1959, Allen, a champion of free speech, had told his audience that "once a month, we will book a comedian who will offend everybody ... a man who will disturb a great many social groups watching right now." His first "offensive" guest was Lenny Bruce, who delivered a riff on the nature of offensiveness ("'Offend,' there's a funny thing .... There are words that offend me. Let's see, 'Governor Faubus,' 'segregation' offend me. Night-time television offends me — some night-time television. The shows that exploit homosexuality, narcotics, prostitution under the guise of helping the societal problem.")[21]

From 1957 to 1962, Paar brought eclectic groups of celebrities and eccentric artists together for almost two hours every weeknight simply to talk. Paar would be followed in 1962 by Johnny Carson, but by

17 Dick Gregory, *Callus on My Soul: A Memoir* (Lanham, MD, 2000), 274. Gregory's role is noted in a number of civil rights histories, though there is as yet no study dedicated to his activism. For his role in U.S. culture, see Monteith, *American Culture in the 1960s* (Edinburgh: Edinburgh University Press, 2008), esp. 5-6, 39-40, 47, 59-61, 121.

18 Dick Gregory, *Nigger: An Autobiography* (New York, 1965), 146.

19 *Jack Paar: 'As I Was Saying ...,'* dir. Michael Macari, Jr. American Masters, WNET New York, EagleVision, Inc. 1997.

20 Ibid.

21 David Skover and Ronald Collins, *The Trials of Lenny Bruce* (Napierville, IL, 2002), 16. *The Steve Allen Show,* April 5, 1959. Bruce's monologue is excerpted at https://www.youtube.com/watch?v=oCplnUga0hU.

then television talk — serious talk — was abundant, especially on Richard Heffner's *Open Mind*, David Susskind's *Open End*, and *The Irv Kupcinet Show*. Paar and Allen had made literate conversation not only glamorous for much of America but also, in some ways, normal. The ongoing presence of ironic, informed discussion in living rooms, dens, and bedrooms installed "talk" in the soundscape of domestic life during the height of Cold War tensions and resistance to civil rights. Having only three or sometimes four channels available, television viewers, whatever their politics, found urbane discourse about controversial subjects hard to avoid.

In a telling exchange on the afternoon of the March on Washington, Marlon Brando signaled an awareness that the influence of television had begun to eclipse that of the movies. Asked by a reporter from the Educational Radio Network whether "people like you could make an ever greater contribution if more of the products turned out by the movie makers in Hollywood concerned controversial social questions like the race question," Brando responded by deflecting the responsibility from movie makers to talk show hosts. "People like Johnny Carson, Jack Paar, Steve Allen, David Susskind," he said, "are interested in presenting this point of view fairly and using their good offices and programs for a revelation of little known facts about this issue to be brought before the court of American society." When pressed to disclose whether they would express "their personal values as well," Brando vouched for their politics: "Jack Paar has expressed himself to me about that. Johnny Carson has given support to this. Steve Allen certainly has great interest in this."[22]

By 1963, "the court of American society" could indeed be found in front of the television screen — a more advantageous position, from the perspective of the civil rights movement, than most jury boxes and judge's benches. After more than a decade of habituating viewers to the look and sound of American behavior, television found itself encouraged by the Kennedy administration and viewers themselves to move closer to its subjects. As live drama gave way to recorded performance, its emotional frankness was supplanted by the observational intimacy of verité-inspired documentaries, which, too, would fade from prime-time programming in several years. No genre, however, could offer greater cultural candor than the talk show, and its influence showed no sign of waning. From the early 1950s to the summer of 1963, television talk had been steadily attuning listeners to the unrehearsed rhythms of black and white discourse and acclimating

22 http://openvault.wgbh.org/catalog/march-bc109d-celebrity-participation-in-the-march-on-washington.

viewers to the shape of an informally desegregated society, its "good offices and programs" laying significant groundwork for the reception of the march as a broadcasting success.

In crucial ways, the unfolding of the March on Washington could not have been better suited to the constraints and liberties of live television. Both the procession from the Washington Monument to the Lincoln Memorial and the official program of events on the steps of the memorial were timed to the minute to ensure that marchers could leave Washington before nightfall. The possibility of any number of disasters shadowed the organizers until the end of the event: the embarrassment of a small turnout, the provocation of violence by segregationists, the inadequacy of the audio system, disorderly conduct by anyone, the failure of buses and cars to leave the city carrying all marchers. Going "off-script" could, in the eyes of the event's major directors, derail the production, hence the last-minute rewriting of John Lewis's "incendiary" speech behind the pillars of the Lincoln Memorial. On the other hand, improvisation could energize and redirect the narrative, as it did when Martin Luther King Jr., heeding Mahalia Jackson's promptings to "tell them about the dream," went off-script to chant what became the most famous words of August 28.

In the relief and exhilaration that evening of having helped to produce an almost flawless spectacle, the celebrity guests on *Hollywood Roundtable* showed how close the orchestration of the march might have come to upsetting the exquisite balance of tension and flexibility required of live television performances. With ninety seconds left in the program, host David Schoenbrun turned to James Baldwin to ask, "What's the most important thing to be done by each and every one of us?" When Baldwin hesitated, Schoenbrun indicated the direction he had in mind: "I happen to think, just to give you an idea of what I'm getting at, that the most important thing at the moment now is jobs." Not taking the prompt, Baldwin responded, "The American white republic has to ask itself why it was necessary for them to invent 'the nigger'," an idea he had articulated on talk shows earlier that year but hardly one that the U.S. government would have chosen as an internationally broadcast coda to the March on Washington.

Skillful orchestration of the march was not all that was needed to ensure its positive execution and reception on television, however. Three months earlier, Medgar Evers had delivered a 17-minute televised appeal in Jackson, Mississippi, for racial justice. Twelve days later, he was murdered in the driveway of his house, just hours after

23 Adam Nossiter, *Of Long Memory: Mississippi and the Murder of Medgar Evers* (Cambridge, MA, 1994), 30.

President Kennedy had delivered his own televised address on civil rights. "It seems probable," biographer Adam Nossiter claims, "that until his final month, Evers was an obscure figure to a majority of white Mississippians." By stepping in front of the WLBT camera, he "had entered a new, ultimately fatal zone of notoriety."[23] Three months after the march, U.S. networks were broadcasting live, continuous footage of the funeral of John F. Kennedy when NBC interrupted its coverage to show Lee Harvey Oswald's transfer from the Dallas jail. In the midst of a funeral, the network broadcast the first live murder in television history.

In 1963, the era of television's celebratory role in documenting debates, rocket launchings, and inaugurations was drawing to a close. Increasingly it would be drawn to immediacy of a different kind — in Birmingham, Newark, Selma, Watts, Vietnam. Poised midway between Evers's fateful television appearance in May 1963 and the doubly morbid broadcasts in November 1963, the March on Washington seems all the more remarkable for having navigated the straits of this "ultimately fatal zone of notoriety" to leave the most sustained record of the civil rights movement's fullest presence "in the moment."

Allison Graham is Professor of Media Studies at the University of Memphis and the author of *Framing the South: Hollywood, Television, and Race During the Civil Rights Struggle*. She was a producer and director of *At the River I Stand*, a documentary film about the 1968 Memphis sanitation workers' strike and the assassination of Martin Luther King Jr., and the co-editor of the "Media" volume of the *New Encyclopedia of Southern Culture*. She has published widely on American media's representation of race, region, and the civil rights movement.

AFTER THE DREAM DIED: NATIONAL MEMORIES OF THE KING ASSASSINATION AND HOW THEY PLAYED OUT IN SUBSEQUENT LEGISLATION

David L. Chappell

The main thing most people remember, or think they remember, about Martin Luther King Jr.'s death was the rioting that came in its wake.[1] Significant upheaval did follow the news of his death in April 1968 in some cities. *Newsweek* thought that King's murder had "touched off a black rampage that subjected the U.S. to the most widespread spasm of racial disorder in its violent history." *Time* said that the reaction to King's murder in city streets "seemed to threaten the onslaught of a race war."[2] Eldridge Cleaver, the Black Panther Minister of Information and a best-selling author, said that his contacts in the movement were now "unanimous" that the war had actually begun, and "holocaust" was imminent: "America will be painted red. Dead bodies will litter the streets." The ghettos would erupt in violence, Cleaver said, because the failure of nonviolence had just been proven. There had been hesitation and division before, he believed, "But now all black people in America have become Black Panthers in spirit." There would be no more nonviolent pleas for mercy: "Now there is the gun and the bomb, dynamite and the knife, and they will be used liberally in America. America will bleed. America will suffer."[3]

Another long hot summer of riots — like the first wave in 1964, or the massive, horrifying ones that followed in 1965, 1966, and 1967 — had been widely predicted even before King died. To this day, many textbooks and retrospective accounts of King's assassination in the media recall a national upheaval, a great orgy of violence and destruction.

This is misleading. Memory of the riots cuts the rest of national memory short. Americans actually began correcting their memory of the riots within a week of the assassination — very widely and publicly in the press, in white papers as well as black. Their experience of mass violence in the streets had swiftly failed to live up to the hype.

Large-scale violence, in the event, was confined to four cities: Chicago (11 dead), Washington, DC (10 dead), Baltimore (6 dead), and Kansas City (6 dead). (In 1968, as in previous years, there were great discrepancies in the reporting of deaths and other measures of destruction. Initial

1 Clay Risen faithfully reproduces this emphasis in his evocative recent book, *A Nation on Fire: America in the Wake of the King Assassination* (New York, 2009). It is almost entirely about the riots.

2 *Newsweek*, April 15, 1968, 31; *Time*, April 12, 1968, 17.

3 Eldridge Cleaver, "The Death of Martin Luther King: Requiem for Nonviolence," *Ramparts*, May 1968, 48-49. Violent words rarely matched deeds. See, for example, Nat Henttoff, interview of Cleaver in *Playboy*, October 1968, reprinted in *Eldridge Cleaver: Post-Prison Writings & Speeches*, ed. Robert Scheer (New York, 1969), 197-98. Cleaver struck some conciliatory notes about King a bit later in an October 1968 speech. The bullet that killed King, he said,"murdered nonviolence, and left the bullet and the echo of the bullet here in Babylon for us to deal with. And we might be wrong. Martin Luther King just might be right. Maybe everything we're doing is wrong, because we don't know about the universe." Stanford speech, Oct. 1, 1968, in *Eldridge Cleaver*, ed. Scheer, 137-38. See Harvey Swados, "Old Con, Black Panther, Brilliant Writer, and Quintessential American," *New York Times Magazine*, September 7, 1969; and Cleaver's own conversion narrative, *Soul on Fire* (Waco, 1978).

reports went as high as 46 dead nationwide. But that came down to a consensus figure of 43.)[4] The emphasis in the first few days after the assassination was on violence and pleas for calm. The other main theme in the headlines, long forgotten now, was the manhunt and the related question of the identity of the assassin, who turned out to be James Earl Ray. He was not caught for over two months, on June 8, and his capture was obscured by news of the assassination of Robert Kennedy two days earlier, on June 6. Within a few days after King's assassination, however, *Time* and other news outlets could not make up their minds which was more astonishing: the alarming violence in some cities, or the strange lack of it in so many others. How to account for the widespread failures to burn, kill, and maim was a big question at the time, though the question has since been forgotten.

In the event, *Time*'s tentative answer was the "[s]wift action by authorities" — with exceptions like Chicago's Mayor Daley — and that "restraint by police in direct confrontations kept the lid on most communities."[5] Most city governments apparently heeded the Kerner Commission's best-selling report on civil disorders, released about a month before King was killed, which argued that tough police tactics tended to provoke and to exacerbate rather than to deter or to quell riots. The *Baltimore Afro-American* took a similar view, the week after its copious riot coverage — even though its city was tied for third place in riot casualties, with six dead: "Police, National Guardsmen, and Federal troops don't deserve the abuse being heaped upon them," it editorialized, " ... [Commanders of these forces] did not panic. Baltimore owes them a tremendous debt of grat[i]tude."[6] The *Afro* even took the unusual view that "we did not have a riot" at all.[7] The *Afro* defined riot as mass violence directed against *persons*, a historically sound definition, though American riots after World War II deviated from the pattern by devoting more of their energy to destruction of *property*. Major black papers in the two other cities that witnessed great violence in 1968, namely, the *Chicago Defender* and the *Kansas City Call*, also adopted a calm, anti-alarmist editorial and reporting posture.

The *Baltimore Afro*'s neighboring white liberal paper, the *Washington Post*, was then beginning to integrate its news staff. The *Post* took a strange pride in interpreting its city, which ranked number two in

4   Sources for the death toll in the 1968 riots: Both the *New York Times*, April 14, 1968, and *Facts on File*, April 11-17, 1968, 147-49, stick with the figure of 43 dead nationwide after some initial overestimates. (*Facts on File* also reports the final totals used here for Baltimore, Chicago, Kansas City, and Washington, 147-49.) The Chicago and DC figures also appeared in, e.g., *Time*, April 19, 1968, 15-16. The Kansas City figure appeared in The *Chicago Tribune*, April 12, 1968, and the *New York Times*, April 12 and 13, 1968. The District of Columbia government later lowered the toll there from ten to nine: Associated Press in *New York Times*, May 2, 1968. For comparisons to previous years: AP, April 13, 1968; *New York Times*, April 13 and 21, 1968; and U.S. Sentate, Committee on the District of Columbia, *Hearings*, "Rehabilitation of District of Columbia Areas Damaged by Civil Disorders," 90th Cong., 2nd Sess., April 18, 30; May 20, 28, and 29, 1968.

5   *Time*, April 12, 1968.

6   "Reflections," lead editorial in the *Baltimore Afro-American*, April 20, 1968.

7   Ibid. The *Afro* apparently took the casualties in Baltimore — six dead — to be bystanders. It is possible that the *Afro* editors did not consider white vigilantes — a significant and possibly decisive feature of Baltimore's reaction to King's death — to be rioters. The *Afro* was widely respected by black and white journalists. Its editorial gloss on the riots was not widely shared.

total riot deaths with ten dead. The *Post* emphasized "the relative absence of personal violence, of open racial hostility in confrontations between whites and blacks, and of snarling defiance of police and soldiers."[8]

Black and white people on the streets of several cities had been quoted threatening violence in cities where, in fact, there was none. Generally, as in previous 1960s riots, the overwhelming majority of those who died were black. All eleven people killed in Chicago, for example, were Negroes, according to the Associated Press.

But when the riots ended that year (never to return on that scale), the press counted only 43 deaths nationwide — which was a smaller number than had been widely feared; exactly that number was reported in Detroit alone in the previous year's riots.[9] Several newspapers, black and white, ran long, speculative analyses and editorials about why certain places known for extreme violence had no riot at all in 1968: Watts, with 36 dead in 1965, did not even make the list of minor disturbances in 1968; Newark, with 23 dead in 1967, reported no deaths or major injuries in 1968; Detroit, with 43 dead in 1967, had no riot in 1968; and Harlem, which had pioneered the new phase of rioting in July 1964 (which left one person dead), had none of it in 1968.

One answer to the forgotten mystery of why there was comparatively little violence in the streets in 1968, and comparatively few deaths, was that, in many cases, militant figures like LeRoi Jones — soon to remake himself as Amiri Baraka — went into the streets to plead for calm, surprising many who expected him to deliver on his violent rhetoric. Charles 37X Kenyatta, Malcolm X's former bodyguard, then leader of the paramilitary Harlem Mau Mau, walked through Harlem arm-in-arm with Republican Governor Nelson Rockefeller, urging people to maintain the peace. Kenyatta also praised Republican Mayor John Lindsay for his brave efforts to calm people down.

Soul Singer James Brown was largely apolitical but a great symbol of black pride and defiant rejection of cultural assimilationism. He was in Boston (where a concert of his was almost canceled), sternly scolding obstreperous members of his audience for their disorderly and disruptive behavior, and calling on all to support their newly

9 *Time*, April 12, 1968. UPI also stated 43 dead: *Norfolk Journal & Guide*, April 13, 1968. For the previous year's death figure, 43 in Detroit alone, see the *Kerner Commission Report* (*New York Times* edition, 1967), 107. The AP initially reported a total of 39 deaths on April 13, 1968, all but 5 of them Negro (AP in *New York Times*, April 13, 1968). United Press International stated 46 deaths, e.g., in the *Kansas City Call*, May 3, 1968. Other outlets for a time stated 46, but 43 emerged as the consensus figure. Of the 43 dead, according to *Time*, 39 were men, 14 were under 21 years old. One tribute to restraint was that army and National Guard troops were apparently responsible for none of the deaths. Police were known to have killed 13. Ten died from fire or smoke inhalation. Nine were killed by private citizens. For 8, *Time* could not establish the killer's identity. Three others fell to various causes, including one black construction worker killed when the wall of a smoldering building he was walking by collapsed on him, another in a collision with a police car en route to the riots in Baltimore. According to *Time*, only 6 of the deaths were directly attributable to rioters' anger. *Time*, April 12, 1968. According to the Senate Permanent Investigations Subcommittee, about 10 percent of the deaths in the 1967 riots were public officials, mostly police and firemen. As the Kerner Commission emphasized, "The overwhelming majority of the civilians killed and injured were Negroes." House Committee in Kerner, and *Kerner Commission Report*, 116.

8 Editorial, *Washington Post*, April 16, 1968. It went on to say that instances of violence, hostility, and defiance "never reached the scale they did in Detroit and Newark last summer or even in Baltimore [this year]."

elected young, idealistic mayor (whom Brown called a "a real swingin' cat"). Brown was then called into Washington, DC, by Mayor-Commissioner Walter Washington to calm the crowds there. Despite Brown's attempted intervention in DC, the city still had a significant number of deaths (ranked second, with ten deaths).[10] Many thought the reason was that that Stokely Carmichael, former head of the Student Nonviolent Coordinating Committee, went into the streets either to rile people up or at least to preach a very different message from other militants' pleas for calm.[11]

The *Pittsburgh Courier*, often seen as the leading voice in black journalism, had a different answer: "No Riots Hit Race Mayors." There had been no riot in Gary, Indiana, where Gary Hatcher became the first black mayor elected in a major city, in November 1967, or in Cleveland, Ohio, where Carl Stokes had become the first black mayor elected to a major city with a white majority, the same day. The *Courier* managed to overlook Washington, DC, which had significant riot deaths but had also had a black "mayor-commissioner," Walter Washington, since 1967. (He perhaps did not count, since his office was still appointive, not elective, at that point, and DC still had no home rule.) Though its point was strictly correct, the *Courier*'s implied logic was misleading: the paper neglected to take into account the many other cities that also experienced no significant violence but had white mayors.

10 I thank Nancy Dillon and especially Keith Luf, who doggedly tracked down the video and audio recordings I sought of Brown's Boston concert. Before their efforts, all that was available were noisy, fragmented bootlegs. But the copy that Luf dug up — untouched since it went into storage in 1968 — is clear enough to allow researchers to see and hear nearly all that happened on or near the stage, including Mayor Kevin White's brief speech to the crowd, and Brown's scolding of audience members who jumped on stage. Much of the WGBH footage has since been made into a commercial film of the concert, *James Brown: Live at the Boston Garden, April 5, 1968* (Shout Factory, 2009). See Brown with Bruce Tucker, *Godfather of Soul* (New York, 1986), 187-88. The *Bay State Banner* also credited Boston councilman Tom Atkins and several community leaders for working hard to keep the peace in Boston streets. Jo Holley in *Bay State Banner*, April 11, 1968. On James Brown in DC, see *Pittsburgh Courier*, April 13, 1968; editorial in *Birmingham Post-Herald*, April 10, 1968; and *Human Events*, April 20, 1968.

11 There is much conflict over exactly what Carmichael said and did on the night of King's assassination when he appeared near the corner of 14th and U Streets and spoke to those who gathered there. There is agreement that he mentioned guns, but some testified that he was urging people not to use them lightly or impulsively that night. Others say he urged people to go home and get their guns, implying that they should bring them back into the streets and use them that night. The best work on that night in DC remains a collection of the *Washington Post*'s coverage: W. Gilbert, ed., *Ten Blocks from the White House: An Anatomy of the Washington Riots of 1968* (London, 1968). Some of the conflict over Carmichael's role stems from a tendency of some newspapers and magazines to conflate testimony about Carmichael on the night of April 4 with testimony about him on the following day, April 5. According to the available sources, Carmichael was much more firmly urging violence on April 5, when he attempted to speak to students at Howard University. On that occasion, however, his audience was clearly not inclined to follow his lead: Howard students did not resort to violence during or after Carmichael's appearance. According to DC police reports sent to the FBI, the police wanted to arrest Carmichael for inciting a riot (which would be a federal offense of interest to the FBI). But the officers and informants present stated that the students were walking away from Carmichael as he spoke: there was nobody to incite within hearing range. The only people listening to Carmichael, other than those who reported directly to the police, were newsmen. Police reports and other materials from Justice Department Case File 146-1-51-19654, released to the author under the Freedom of Information Act, in author's possession.

The best general answer, so far, to the forgotten question of why cities failed to riot came into public consciousness twelve years later, in the words of Andrew Young, when Miami broke out in a riot in 1980 — the first significant urban disorder since 1968 — and left 18 people dead.[12] The great lesson learned in the 1960s, Young said, was that "[n]o neighborhood riots twice." People in riot-torn areas learn, he explained, that whatever they may have wanted to achieve when they went out to burn and loot and rampage, they had ended up worse off. The painful memory stifled the impulse to riot the next time. Poverty and other "conditions" often worsened in poor neighborhoods in the 1970s and 1980s, but large-scale rioting became rare. There were no significant riots from 1968 to 1980, or from 1980 until the 1992 LA riot (53 dead).

Looking back, it appears that the most significant response to King's assassination was not the over-reported and over-remembered riots but the under-reported and under-remembered Civil Rights Act of 1968, also known as the Fair Housing Act. It was the third of the three great civil rights acts of the decade.

***

Supporters of the Civil Rights Act of 1968 said that they wished to pay homage to King and to show restive ghetto-dwellers that hope was not lost. King had strongly supported the bill for more than two years before his death. Since his strategic shift to northern cities in 1965–66, King had been losing hope of ever passing the bill or any other significant legislation. But the bill's prospects suddenly changed when King died. The resulting Civil Rights Act was not just a symbolic purge of emotion, or a mere show of respect: it was a substantive answer to some of the civil rights movement's most radical demands, and if King can be credited with any of the movement's victories, it was his last real victory. It was also the one victory for which King could most plausibly take the lion's share of the credit.[13]

Yet the Civil Rights Act of 1968 has been almost completely forgotten — unlike the previous two major civil rights acts of 1964 and 1965, which historians and the general public tend reflexively to attribute to King and the movement he has come to symbolize.

Before he died, King and other supporters of the housing bill highly doubted that any serious civil rights legislation could pass, given the widespread conservative reaction to the summers of rioting, in 1965, 1966, and 1967. People have forgotten how controversial King

12 Accounts differ on Miami's death toll. Early estimates ran from 14 dead (*Amsterdam News*, May 24, 1980) to 20 (*Los Angeles Sentinel*, May 22, 1980). The *Washington Post* (e.g., on July 8, 1982, and March 17, 1984) and the *Wall Street Journal* (e.g., on July 29, 1980), agreed on 18. The *New York Times*, after initially reporting 15 dead on May 20, 1980 (as did the *LA Times* that same day), later switched to "a dozen," and stuck with that (e.g., on September 12 and 13, 1984).

13 More information on the Housing Act can be found in David L. Chappell, *Waking from the Dream: The Struggle for Civil Rights in the Shadow of Martin Luther King* (New York, 2014), chapter 1.

was — that he was one of the most widely feared and hated men in American history. He was controversial within the black population as well as the white. Not only did Black Muslims and Black Panthers criticize him, rather viciously, along with the mainstays of the established old black civil rights organizations, who said he was a loose cannon with a messiah complex, but also many of his own best friends and associates on the staff and board of the Southern Christian Leadership Conference said that he had lost his way. Several urged him to abandon the Poor People's Campaign demonstrations he had planned to begin in April 1968. He himself worried he might have to call off the demonstrations, saying in March 1968 that the opening one, in Washington, DC, scheduled for April 22, was "doomed."[14]

Yet King had drawn some encouragement from a Harris Poll published in August 1967, at the end of what turned out to be the worst and last of the long, hot summers. The poll showed that a majority of white Americans were (as *Newsweek* glossed the poll) "ready and willing to pay the price for a massive, Federal onslaught on the root problems of the ghetto." Speaking to the DC Chamber of Commerce in early February 1968, King gave a hint as to why he was not following Bayard Rustin's advice to abandon protests in favor of working within the system. If violence broke out in the ghettos again that summer, he said, "I don't have any faith in the whites in power responding in the right way.... They'll throw us into concentration camps. The Wallaces and the Bircherites will take over. The sick people and the fascists will be strengthened." Launching the Poor People's Campaign in Washington had to succeed, King believed. The movement had to prove that people who had been left out in the cold of America's history of progress could still get a hearing by nonviolent means. "We're going to plague Congress," he said.[15]

Opponents of the pending civil rights bill — which had been languishing in Congress since 1966 — mercilessly flung King's name about as a symbol of all that had gone wrong in America. King was fomenting disorder, they said. He claimed to be "nonviolent," but in fact he preached and practiced disrespect for the law, they said. By choosing to obey the laws he liked and to violate those he disliked, King used his charisma — and the authority conferred on him by congressional attention, a Nobel Prize, and adoring masses — to turn lawlessness into a moral imperative. This is what his many critics charged, right up to his death, and in a few instances after

14 On King's fear of violence in planned April 22, 1968, protests in DC, see David Garrow, *Bearing the Cross* (New York, 1986), 594-618; King worried that the plan might have to be delayed or called off (597, 615).

15 Quotations from *Newsweek* and King in Garrow, *Bearing the Cross*, 596-97, 618; and Stewart Burns, *To the Mountaintop* (San Francisco, 2004), 395-96.

it.[16] But national grief, and the need to make at least some concessions to the grief following King's assassination, finally — if only temporarily — overwhelmed the growing backlash.

The bill was signed into law on April 11, two days after King's funeral, by President Lyndon Johnson — who had already fallen on his own sword, just days before King's assassination, resigning from politics by announcing he would not seek a second term, thereby cutting short one of the most impressive political careers in American history. This gave the news weeklies, including many of the major black papers in the country, trouble: they had to crowd the earth-shattering news of Johnson's surprise resignation onto the same front page as King's assassination a few days later. The act sweepingly outlawed housing discrimination on the basis of race, color, religion, or national origin, in about 80 percent of yearly housing transactions nationwide — including mortgage financing.[17] Some state laws raised the percentage higher, and a Supreme Court decision in June 1968 curtailed the exemptions nationwide, raising the coverage to nearly 100 percent.[18] (Strong enforcement provisions were not added until 1988, but the original formulation clearly put most housing discrimination outside the bounds of law.)[19]

16 See, e.g., *Congressional Record* [hereafter *CR*]-*House*, 89th Cong., 2nd sess., Aug. 28, 1966, 20724–25; *CR-House*, 90th Cong., 1st sess., Aug. 15, 1967, 22674–86, 22690–91, and 27815–27 (Ashbrook); *CR-Senate*, 90th Cong., 2nd sess., Feb. 2, 1968, p. 1968; *CR-Senate*, 90th Cong., 2nd sess., Feb. 7, 1968, 2495–96; *CR-House* 90th Cong., 2nd sess., March 28, 1968, 8247–48; *CR-Senate*, 90th Cong., 2nd sess., March 28, 1968, 8263–66, 8222, 8244, 8327–28; *CR-House*, 90th Cong., 2nd sess., April 1, 1968, 8380–81 (Kuykendal); 8509–10; *CR-House*, 90th Cong., 2nd sess., April 4, 1968 (Brock); *CR-Senate*, 90th Cong., 2nd sess., April 4, 1968, 8946, 8981; Rep. Jimmy Quillen (R-Tennessee), in House Rules Committee 90th Cong.,

2nd sess., *Hearings* on H.Res. 1100, April 4–9, 1968, 21–22. Augustus Hawkins defended King on April 4, 1968. John Conyers criticized the association of rioting with the housing legislation under consideration, without defending King: *CR-House*, Aug. 15, 1967, 22690. Robert Nix of Philadelphia also rejected the wave of condemnation of rioters, pointing to the conditions that caused them, but also criticized King for poor administrative work in Memphis, implying King might have been partially responsible. Nix in *CR-House*, April 4, 1968, 9092–9093.

17 Exceptions included (a.) those involving sale or rental of single-family dwellings without use of a broker or other professional help, or discriminatory advertising; (b.) rental of living space in an owner-occupied dwelling for four families or fewer; and (c.) rental of dwellings operated by religious societies or private clubs for the noncommercial benefit of their members. The act covered about 80 percent of the housing market, though state and local laws already covered exempted areas and court decisions soon raised coverage.

18 Even the exempted unassisted single-family-dwelling owner fell under the act's coverage if he or she used discriminatory advertising. The act went into effect in stages, expanding until it reached its final form, effective after Dec. 31, 1969. Herbert A. Danner, "The Civil Rights Act of 1968: Brief Summary of Basic Provisions," *Congressional Research Service*, April 22, 1968, 5. The estimate of the 80 percent left »

» after these exemptions (as of Jan. 1, 1970) is in the *Washington Post*, April 14, 1968, which also summarizes the 154 existing state laws. In June 1968, in *Jones v. Mayer Company,* however, the Supreme Court eroded these exemptions, on the basis of the 1866 Civil Rights Act, which affirmed that blacks had "the same right … as is enjoyed by white citizens" to buy and sell property, *New York Times,* June 22, 1968. Sex was added in 1974; physical handicap and family status were added in 1988.

19 The act banned discrimination not only in the sale and rental of housing but in the making of loans for purchase, renovation, and maintenance of housing, and for professional services of realtors and brokers. A buyer or renter who believed he was subject to discrimination could report it to the Department of Housing and Urban Development, whose secretary would have to investigate and respond within thirty days, though the secretary could defer to state or local fair housing laws where applicable. If the secretary or local agency failed to resolve the dispute, the complainant could file suit in federal court, which could award punitive damages as well as order an end to the discriminatory practice. PL-90-284, 82 Stat. 73, secs. 804 and 805; U.S. Code, *Congressional & Administrative News,* 90th, 2nd (St. Paul, 1968), 1:101–102. The best guide to the revisions of the act in 1988 and other changes in the law in the two decades after its passage is John Reiman, *Enforcing the Fair Housing Laws: A Practical Manual* (Washington, DC, 1990).

It was a toss-up whether Congress had honored King's memory directly or responded to the over-reported violence that followed his death. While some black militants insisted that white America had ignored or thwarted the pleas of nonviolent Negroes, Bayard Rustin would later complain that America's rich and powerful went in the other direction and actually rewarded violence. American authorities had failed to respond to responsible political action — to the peaceful efforts of black Americans to take responsibility for their blighted communities and reconstruct them — Rustin said. He was referring to all the attention given to rioters and all the programs directed at riot-torn areas. There may thus be some perverse justice in America's amnesia over its last great civil rights act. For the act's passage did not unambiguously honor the constructive politics of nonviolence. King wanted and fought for the housing law. But in the event, its passage was ambiguous. Those who wanted King to win could interpret the act as a tribute to his methods, an endorsement of his plans to empower the poor to liberate themselves. But to other observers — aided by the national habit of exaggerating the extent and severity of the 1968 riots, which so many scholars reinforce — looked too much like a reward for the rioting that King and his supporters opposed.

White conservatives emphasized their view that the act was a capitulation to the rioters. The *Pittsburgh Courier* argued, however, that that conservative line was, at best, illogical and shortsighted. The *Courier*'s editor believed that violence actually increased congressional resistance to civil rights. Referring to passage of the housing bill as "A King Dream," the *Courier* pointed out that before King's death, "a riots-aftermath-angry 1967 Congress and a rock-willed 1968 Congress were almost solidly against passing" it. Yet its passage "miraculously" came, according to the editorial — and its passage was "directly due to Dr. King's assassination, subsequent riotings in 110 cities and more than 150,000 persons of all walks of American life who attended his [memorial march on April 8 in] Memphis."[20]

Segregationists and other conservatives generally took the narrower line that Congress had responded to the rioting. The segregationist standard-bearer, the *Charleston News & Courier*, scolded Congress for surrendering to "emotional pressure" to create new buyers' rights that sacrificed sellers' "more precious" rights, and for raising expectations that "the law cannot fulfill." The law thus presaged "greater disappointment and more violence." Rep. William Colmer of

20 *Pittsburgh Courier*, April 20, 1968. The *Courier* added that it was nonetheless only a minor step toward the goal of eradicating poverty in America — the goal that King had founded the PPC to accomplish.

Mississippi, who had held the bill hostage in his Rules Committee for some time, said his committee caved in "under the gun." Only King's murder and the reaction to it made it possible to muster the votes to move the bill to the floor. "Needless to say," he added, "it was a great disappointment to me." When the bill passed the House, Republican Rep. H. R. Gross of Iowa suggested flying the flag at half-staff in mourning for "this once great House" that had now surrendered to intimidation by rioters.[21]

The best measure of the depth of the memory hole into which the 1968 Civil Rights Act has fallen is the failure of King's opponents to recall it when they were debating legislation to establish the Martin Luther King Jr. national holiday, eleven to fifteen years later, in 1979-1983. Holiday opponents failed to make what could have been the best argument against passage of the holiday. Congress had already paid tribute to King, they could have said. Indeed, Congress had paid him a far more meaningful and substantive tribute than a ceremonial day off in his name. Congress had, that is, done something real to advance his cause, in April 1968, by passing a major law that he himself had supported — as opposed to a merely symbolic gesture of a holiday, which King would in all likelihood have opposed. He was on record, after all, opposing grandiose tributes that smacked of a cult of personality. Indeed, he always minimized his own significance, insisting he was just a poor, ordinary sinner.[22]

As it was, the holiday opponents' arguments in 1979-1983 were weak and unmemorable. Almost all opponents confined their objections to two. The first was to the cost of paying federal employees for another day off ($195 million in salaries and wages paid out for a day when no work would be done, according to the Civil Service Commission), during an unprecedented economic crisis.[23] The second was a concern that other great heroes — conservatives emphasized Abraham Lincoln and Booker T. Washington — who didn't have federal holidays were being passed over and that King's death was too recent: more time was needed to determine King's true historical significance, relative to other past heroes, and to gain a nationwide consensus on it. Only two members of the House — Democrat Larry McDonald of suburban Atlanta and Republican John Ashbrook of rural Ohio — publicly opposed a national holiday devoted to King on ideological grounds. By resorting to ugly, unseemly tactics of character assassination and guilt by association, they helped supporters of the holiday in the same way that arch-segregationists Bull Connor and Sheriff

21 William Colmer and H.R. Gross, in *CR-House,* April 10, 1968, 9528, 9540.

22 For a discussion of the King holiday, also see Chappell, *Waking from the Dream,* chapter 4.

23 For Civil Service Commission figures, see U.S. Congress, House Committee on Post Office and the Civil Service, and Senate Judiciary Committee, *Joint Hearings,* 96th Cong., 1st sess., "Martin Luther King, Jr., National Holiday, S. 25," March 27, 1979, and June 21, 1979, pp. 93-94.

Jim Clark had inadvertently helped the movement back in King's day, when their unpopular brutality was caught on camera.[24] At any rate, Ashbrook died on April 24, 1982, and McDonald died (dramatically, in a civilian Korean airliner, Flight 007, shot down by the Soviet air force when it strayed into Russian airspace) on September 1, 1983. Both were dead before final congressional action on the bill in October 1983.

Just one member of the Senate took an openly ideological stance against King, and he did so only at the last minute. Jesse Helms had generally stayed out of the congressional debates and hearings on the King holiday, only jumping in to repeat what Ashbrook and McDonald had said so counterproductively in the House. Helms's party leaders, and the Reagan White House (which had initially opposed the bill, though it had also issued some respectful and laudatory statements about King) began to support the holiday on October 4. It was widely rumored that Helms took his eleventh-hour stand for the cynical reason that he wanted a tobacco subsidy, which he would indeed get, by agreeing to give up his threat of a filibuster, along with a lot of publicity that energized his right-wing supporters. By such means, Helms generated sufficient turnout among his right-wing base in North Carolina — barely enough — to keep getting re-elected in close elections.

It is tempting to see the holiday as a sop — a consolation prize, at best, for the dismal string of disappointments and failures the movement had endured since 1968 — especially in light of the failure of the last legislative campaign of the old social-democratic/labor-liberal-civil rights coalition, the campaign for the Humphrey-Hawkins full employment law, which absorbed the legislative attention of Coretta King and labor-movement allies, and much of the Congressional Black Caucus (along with figures ranging from Hubert Humphrey and Jesse Jackson to Stevie Wonder) from 1973 to 1978.[25] Thus, the King holiday may appear, in retrospect, as a bone thrown to the tattered remnants of the civil rights movement and its liberal-labor allies in Congress.

The holiday, however, helped to touch off a remarkable — though still unheralded — run of successful civil rights legislation in the 1980s, beginning with the extension and strengthening of the Voting Rights Act in 1982, and, after the holiday, comprehensive sanctions on South Africa, passed in October 1986, overriding President Reagan's veto; the Civil Rights Restoration Act, which reversed major conservative Supreme Court decisions on civil rights, passed in 1988, also over President Reagan's veto; the final fulfillment of Congress's original

24 On the efforts of extreme anti-communists to discredit King during debate over the King holiday legislation in the 1970s, see Chappell, *Waking from the Dream*, Chapter 4.

25 On the Humphrey-Hawkins crusade, see Chappell, *Waking from the Dream*, Chapter 3.

tribute to King, strengthening amendments to the Fair Housing Act, also in 1988; and what became (after a false start in 1990) the Civil Rights Act of 1991, which also reversed major Supreme Court decisions.

These remarkable achievements — more significant civil rights victories than in any decade other than the 1860s and 1960s — were all the more striking in light of the Republicans' control of the Senate from January 1981 to January 1987, and the opposition of the Reagan administration to many of the initiatives.

The conjunction of those substantive victories with the holiday is the strongest evidence against suspicions that the holiday was just designed to pacify black voters and distract them from the lack of real progress. To be sure, during the Reagan-Bush years, civil rights, and many other programs supported by black voters and their remaining liberal allies, were incrementally and gradually cut back, in quiet ways, which established a general and demoralizing pattern of backlash against the gains black protesters and voters had made in the decades since A. Phillip Randolph threatened to mobilize them and forced Franklin Roosevelt to desegregate military industry in 1941.[26] When seen from the perspective of major, national legislation, however — the sort of legislation that got sustained public attention — the holiday victory marked a new mood, a new disposition, and a new resolve among those carrying on King's unfinished business. That new mood, partly because of its lowered expectations, led to greater achievement and perhaps to greater resilience in an inconclusive, uphill struggle.

This new democratic realism — in contrast to the bureaucratic and judicial leverage, often funded by corporations that purchased a separate peace from Jesse Jackson's Operation PUSH (People United to Save Humanity) and the NAACP — led the Congressional Black Caucus and its allies in Congress to work towards more achievable goals than they had pursued in the 1970s. Many of the goals they achieved warrant far more of our attention than they have gotten. Those new civil rights laws of the 1980s and early 1990s are among the most significant, yet most underappreciated, parts of King's legacy.

26 The most comprehensive sources on all that incremental backlash activity are the yearly reports of the National Urban League and the various reports from the Leadership Council on Civil Rights from the years 1982-1992.

David L. Chappell is the Rothbaum Professor of Modern American History at the University of Oklahoma. His research focuses on the civil rights movement, and his books on this topic include *A Stone of Hope: Prophetic Religion and the Death of Jim Crow* (2005), *Inside Agitators: White Southerners in the Civil Rights Movement* (1996), and, most recently, *Waking from the Dream: The Struggle for Civil Rights in the Shadow of Martin Luther King, Jr.* (2014).